MAKING COLLEGE WORK

Making College Work

Pathways to Success beyond High School

Harry J. Holzer
Sandy Baum

BROOKINGS INSTITUTION PRESS
Washington, D.C.

The Brookings Institution is a private nonprofit organization devoted to research, education, and publication on important issues of domestic and foreign policy. Its principal purpose is to bring the highest quality independent research and analysis to bear on current and emerging policy problems. Interpretations or conclusions in Brookings publications should be understood to be solely those of the authors.

Library of Congress Cataloging-in-Publication data
Names: Holzer, Harry J., 1957– author. | Baum, Sandy (Sandra R.), author.
Title: Making college work : pathways to success for disadvantaged students / Harry J. Holzer, Sandy Baum.
Description: Washington, D.C. : Brookings Institution Press, 2017. | Includes bibliographical references and index.
Identifiers: LCCN 2017000424 (print) | LCCN 2017020168 (ebook) | ISBN 9780815730224 (ebook) | ISBN 9780815730217 (paperback)
Subjects: LCSH: People with social disabilities—Education (Higher)—United States. | Poor—Education (Higher)—United States. | Students with social Disabilities—United States. | Education, Higher—United States—Costs. | Universities and colleges—United States—Admission. | BISAC: BUSINESS & ECONOMICS / Education. | EDUCATION / Educational Policy & Reform / General. | SOCIAL SCIENCE / Social Classes. | EDUCATION / Secondary.
Classification: LCC LC4069.6 (ebook) | LCC LC4069.6 .H65 2017 (print) | DDC 378.0087—dc23
LC record available at https://lccn.loc.gov/2017000424

9 8 7 6 5 4 3 2 1

Typeset in Sabon

Composition by Westchester Publishing Services

Contents

Acknowledgments

We are grateful to the Smith Richardson Foundation for providing funding that made it possible for us to write this book. Senior Program Officer Mark Steinmeyer provided very helpful guidance as we developed our ideas. The Bill and Melinda Gates Foundation also offered support.

We would also like to thank the many other people who made the writing and publication of this book possible.

First, several individuals read the manuscript and provided helpful comments. They include Tom Bailey, Charles Clotfelter, Lauren Eyster, Katherine Hughes, Lou Jacobson, Mike McPherson, David Baime, and an anonymous reviewer.

Second, we had extremely helpful conversations with leaders of community colleges who informed our thinking a great deal. These leaders include Jim Jacobson (president of Macomb Community College in Michigan), Ken Ender (president of Harper College in Illinois), Gail Mellow (president of LaGuardia Community College in New York), and Rolando Montoya (provost of Miami Dade College in Florida).

Third, we thank Kennan Cepa, Yessica Yang Choi, and Chenxi Lu for excellent research assistance. Kennan helped us generate the statistical estimates of postsecondary effects on earnings for the state of Florida that we used in chapter 3, Yessica managed our references, and Chenxi assisted with analysis of data from the National Center for Education Statistics.

Finally, we thank Bill Finan and Valentina Kalk of the Brookings Institution Press, who guided us through the production process and helped market the book.

1

Introduction

As a nation, we are making progress in increasing the number of people from disadvantaged backgrounds who manage to enroll in some form of postsecondary education. But the results are discouraging. Many students leave school without any certificate or degree. They have lost valuable time and frequently have student debt to repay, but they have not managed to measurably improve their prospects. Most of the students from low socioeconomic status backgrounds who do succeed in completing their programs of study earn occupational certificates or associate degrees, not bachelor's degrees. Some of these credentials yield significant returns in the labor market, but others do not.

The evidence points clearly to the need for significant change. Changes in federal and state policies and in postsecondary practices, particularly at the institutions that serve large numbers of low-income and older students, are central to improving these outcomes. There are unlikely to be any easy answers, and solutions will involve both using existing resources more effectively and devoting more resources to the effort. But there is strong evidence that some of the innovations that have been implemented on a small scale could make a real difference for many more students.

Reforming the postsecondary experience is necessary but not sufficient. Over the long run, reductions in the economic and educational inequality throughout society should reduce the gaps in preparation for college. But given the current realities of socioeconomic inequality and inadequate elementary and secondary education for disadvantaged students, many recent high school graduates and older adults have such large gaps in their academic preparation, and so many other challenges to successful degree completion, that other routes to remunerative careers may hold more promise for them. Strengthening career and technical education in high schools, apprenticeship opportunities, and other routes to occupational success outside of postsecondary institutions is a necessary part of the solution.

This book explores this reality, seeking explanations for our failure to provide pathways to success for such a large segment of the population and evaluating potential policy reforms that could improve the lives of many Americans.

The Importance of Postsecondary Education

As is well known, it has become difficult for workers to succeed in the American job market without some type of college credential—whether it is a bachelor's degree, an associate degree, or an occupational certificate. In an era when the earnings of most American workers have been stagnant or declining, less-educated workers have fared worst. A high school education no longer provides a reasonable chance for earnings that can support a family. Improving educational attainment is widely seen as a mechanism for improving living standards and moving more people into the middle class, where they can expect some level of economic security.

Political leaders from both major parties have embraced the goal of increasing participation in postsecondary education. For instance, expressing dismay over disappointing college attainment rates in the United States, which have fallen behind those of many other countries around the world, President Obama set a goal that by 2020 America will once again have the highest proportion of college graduates in the world. This is an objective shared by many members of Congress, as well as state and local officials. The president also called for community college to be tuition-free, in an effort to make the first two years of postsecondary education as universally available to young

Americans in the twenty-first century as high school became in the twentieth century. In 2014 the state of Tennessee implemented a policy of tuition-free community college for qualifying recent high school graduates; Oregon followed suit in 2015; other states are in the process of implementing similar policies. That Republicans dominate the Tennessee state house and legislature makes it clear that the interest in expanding access to college and reducing its price is bipartisan.

Indeed, many scholars and policymakers share a strong belief that improving educational attainment and skill acquisition for all Americans, particularly those from low-income backgrounds, is essential for a healthy economy. In other words, in addition to promoting equity through economic opportunity for all and upward social mobility for the poor, economic efficiency is at stake. Higher education can improve people's lives in many ways, and getting a good job is only one of the numerous good reasons to go to college. But for many, and particularly for those from disadvantaged backgrounds, stable and well-paying employment afterward is often a primary motivation for attending college.

Many low-income youth and adults are following the advice they hear to "go to college." As shown in figure 1-1, the percentage of recent high school graduates from the lowest family income quartile enrolling within a year in a two- or four-year college increased from 36 percent in 1984 to 42 percent in 1994, to 51 percent in 2004, and to a peak of 56 percent in 2008. Indeed, the increases in their rate of enrollment were greater than the increases among students from middle- or higher-income families. By 2014, 67 percent of all recent high school graduates—and 52 percent of those from the lowest income group—went straight to college.[1]

A small fraction of disadvantaged students manages to enroll in selective four-year institutions, while a larger number attend broadly accessible public four-year colleges and universities. But a majority of them, including many who have weak academic backgrounds, attend community colleges and for-profit institutions. The for-profit sector focuses on specific occupational programs, while community colleges

---

1. NCES (2016, table 302.30).

Figure 1-1. Percentage of High School Graduates Enrolling Immediately in College, 1984–2014

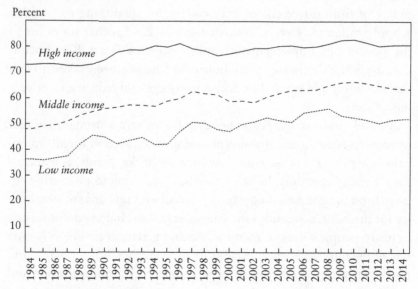

Percent

Source: NCES (2015b, table 302.30).

provide similar programs in addition to more traditional academic courses designed to facilitate transfer to four-year colleges.

The paths followed by disadvantaged students, who are often first-generation college attenders, too often do not lead to college *attainment*—which requires both *enrollment* in a program and its *completion*—and to labor market success. Although our economy rewards people—including those from disadvantaged backgrounds—who *finish* a college degree or certificate at a two-year or four-year institution, too many disadvantaged college students fail to achieve this outcome.

Figure 1-2 presents data on trends over time in educational attainment. Since 1980, the percentage of Americans ages twenty-five and older who have completed four years of college or more has risen from 17 percent to 33 percent. The percentage with some college, but less than four years, increased from 15 percent to 26 percent between 1980 and 2015. The earlier data are based on questions about years of college, so it is not possible to determine how many people actually completed a degree.

Figure 1-2. Educational Attainment of People Ages 25 and Over, 1980–2015

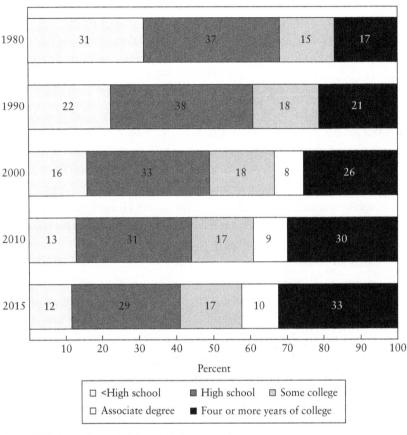

Source: U.S. Census Bureau (2016, table A-4).

But data reported in figure 1-2 also reveal that between 2000 and 2015 the percentage with an associate degree rose from 8 percent to just 10 percent. The percentage with some college but no degree was 18 percent in 2000 and 17 percent in 2015. While some of these individuals were still enrolled and will eventually earn a degree, a significant number of adults had started college but had not completed their programs; and we see little improvement in these outcomes since 2000.

Moreover, even among those who complete credentials, too many either concentrate in fields with low economic returns or for other reasons find themselves poorly prepared for the labor market. As a result, many who attend college have relatively low earnings afterward, making it difficult to sustain a satisfactory standard of living and to meet student debt repayment obligations.

These weak educational and employment outcomes for some students generate challenges to the goal of increasing postsecondary attainment among low-income youth and adults. Some strong voices argue that too many people are already going to college. The contention is that pushing individuals who are unprepared, uninterested, or incapable of doing college-level work to spend more time in school is a waste of resources and leaves too many people with nothing other than student debt to show for their time.[2] But given the currently available paths to financial security, avoiding postsecondary education is rarely the solution. We must find constructive ways to strengthen the completion rates and workforce outcomes of all individuals seeking to improve their lives through postsecondary education and training, at the same time that we develop more reliable and effective alternative paths to promising career opportunities.

Lowering the price of community college is not enough. Already, the majority of students who get through the door do not graduate. For some, the obstacles are primarily financial, but for others, weak academic preparation, family responsibilities, or other issues create insurmountable challenges. Among those who do graduate, too many never experience the payoff in which they thought they were investing. Improving these outcomes should be at the top of the agenda.

Funding Postsecondary Education

Total undergraduate enrollment (in two- and four-year institutions combined) grew by nearly 70 percent between 1985 and 2015.[3] Although per-student funding has not kept up with enrollment, enormous public and private resources are invested in higher education in the United States. Indeed, federal, state, and local governments invest about $250 billion each year in appropriations for higher education and student aid.[4] Total spending, including funds from students,

2. Vedder, Denhar, and Robe (2013); Murray (2013).
3. NCES (2016, table 303.70).
4. State Higher Education Executive Officers (2016); Ma and others (2016).

families, and other private sources, is two to three times that amount.[5]

A good deal of this money is spent on the poor. The Pell Grant program, the federal government's foundational grant program for low- and moderate-income students, doubled in inflation-adjusted dollars between 2008–09 and 2010–11. In 2015–16, 7.6 million students received $28 billion in Pell Grant funds.[6] In 2014–15, the state and local governments spent $91 billion to subsidize higher education and reduce tuition costs for in-state students, with lower tuition benefiting students from both disadvantaged and more affluent backgrounds.[7]

More resources could almost certainly improve postsecondary outcomes for disadvantaged students. But we must also ask if the resources now available are being used effectively. This book probes the question of why educational and employment outcomes of disadvantaged students are often disappointing and examines the evidence about the potential policy solutions most likely to improve those outcomes.

The Purpose of This Book

We begin from the premise that, as a society, we can and must narrow the gaps in postsecondary success associated with family background. The labor market requires a wide variety of skills, but most jobs that pay a living wage require some form of education or training beyond high school. Our fundamental question is how—while we work to strengthen secondary school outcomes—to ensure that individuals who leave high school unprepared for the challenges ahead get the opportunities they need to lead successful and rewarding lives. As we encourage more people, particularly those from disadvantaged backgrounds, to go to college, we must be sure that we are directing them onto constructive pathways.

5. NCES (2015a).
6. Baum and others (2016).
7. Illinois State University (2016).

A relatively large research literature exists on many of these topics, including a body of policy evaluation evidence; but there are also significant gaps in this literature, and neither the causes of nor the solutions to the problems are entirely clear.

This book does not fill the gaps in the literature by developing new research estimates of the impacts of various policies or programs. Instead, it draws on existing knowledge, in addition to insights from newly available data, to develop promising, evidence-based policy proposals. In the long run, we certainly need more research. But we believe that we know enough now to make useful improvements. Our goal is to bridge the gap between the academics pursuing definitive answers and the policymakers who must make immediate progress on solving these critical problems.

The structure of the book reflects these goals. The first part lays out what we know about the problematic outcomes of disadvantaged students in higher education. We focus on low completion rates, concentrations in fields of study with low labor market returns, and debt accumulation among those not completing a degree and/or not finding well-compensated employment afterward. The second part of the book discusses potential policy solutions to each of these problems, with an additional chapter on potential additional pathways to gaining credentials or skills, starting with career and technical education (CTE) in high school.

Some Background

The chapters that follow analyze the enrollment patterns, completion rates, student debt, and labor market outcomes of disadvantaged students. To provide context for that discussion, we first provide an overview of the importance of postsecondary education for financial security and social mobility, and outline differences in enrollment patterns and outcomes across demographic groups.

Enrollment and Completion Patterns

Low-income and under-represented students are relatively concentrated at community colleges, less prestigious four-year colleges, and for-profit institutions.[8] For example, in 2011–12, half of all first-year undergraduates who were recent high school graduates from the lowest family income quartile were enrolled in community colleges, and another 14 percent were in the for-profit sector. Among older adult students, these figures were 54 percent and 28 percent, respectively. In contrast, 40 percent of students from the highest family income quartile enrolled in one of these two sectors; this affluent group was disproportionately represented in public and private nonprofit four-year colleges and universities.[9] Chapter 2 provides more detailed evidence on this issue.

In addition to enrolling in different types of institutions, students from different backgrounds have systematically different educational outcomes. Completion rates are very low for disadvantaged students. They lag far behind other students in completing four-year college degrees, and they are also less likely than other students to complete two-year programs, where overall completion rates are very low. Using data from the National Education Longitudinal Study (NELS) on students who were eighth graders in 1988, Harry Holzer and Erin Dunlop found that completion rates at four-year colleges, roughly eight years after high school graduation, were over 60 percent for all students, but just over 30 percent for those in the bottom quartile of socioeconomic status (SES).[10] In the associate degree programs where so many low-income or minority students are concentrated, comparable completion rates both for all and for disadvantaged youth were 30 to 40 percent, but under 30 percent for black students.

The Job Market: Returns to Higher Education

It is by now well known that the average labor market return to the attainment of a higher education credential is quite high for all students, including those from low-income backgrounds.[11] This result

---

8. NCES (2012); Baum and Kurose (2013); Deming and others (2012); Holzer and Dunlop (2013).

9. NCES (2012).

10. Holzer and Dunlop (2013).

11. Card (1999); Goldin and Katz (2008); Baum, Ma, and Payea (2013). Most studies find even higher job market rewards for higher education among the poor

includes those who finish an associate degree and even an occupational certificate at a community college,[12] although the average returns to these credentials are lower and have risen less over time than those to bachelor's and particularly higher degrees.[13]

Earnings differences among individuals with different levels of education do not provide a precise measure of the returns to education, since there may be systematic differences in people's cognitive or noncognitive skills (motivation or self-discipline, for example) that would cause people who earned college degrees to earn more than those who did not even if they had not gone to college. However, careful statistical analyses suggest that earnings comparisons do not significantly overestimate the actual earnings premium for education.[14]

Median incomes have declined in real terms since the late 1990s for men with all levels of education and since the early 2000s for women with all levels of education. However, the declines have consistently been smaller for those with a bachelor's degree than for those with lower levels of education. Median earnings for men whose highest degree was a bachelor's degree were 67 percent higher than earnings for male high school graduates in 1995, 72 percent higher in 2005, and 93 percent higher in 2015. For women, the margins were 100 percent, 96 percent, and 102 percent, respectively.[15]

These averages hide considerable variation within levels of educational attainment. People with similar degrees have very different earnings patterns in different industries, in different parts of the country, and with different personal circumstances. Moreover, there

---

than among other groups. (See, for example, Zimmerman 2014; Oreopoulos and Petronijevic 2013). Hershbein (2016) has recently added to the more mixed evidence (Carneiro, Heckman, and Vytacil 2011), arguing that the rewards are lower for those who grew up in poverty. However, even his estimates show substantial rewards for low-income students who earn a college credential.

12. Kane and Rouse (1995); Bailey and Belfield (2013).

13. Autor (2010).

14. Card (1999); Rouse (2007); Oreopoulos and Petronijevic (2013).

15. U.S. Census Bureau (2016b, table P-16).

is growing evidence both that completion rates vary considerably across programs, institutions, and sectors, and that earnings are higher for individuals with technical certificates and associate degrees than for those with general sub-baccalaureate degrees.[16]

What postsecondary programs of study do students from low-income families pursue? Some go to college with specific occupational goals and enroll in short-term training programs—sometimes credit bearing, sometimes not—geared toward acquiring a necessary skill. Others seek associate degrees in health-related fields, technology, communications, or other areas. But many community college students follow a general education path, taking courses that might qualify for credit toward a bachelor's degree if they manage to transfer to a four-year institution. About two-thirds of community college students and half of those at for-profit institutions who are in associate degree programs are enrolled in general studies and transfer-oriented programs, as opposed to occupational and technical programs.[17]

In 2015, when median earnings for associate degree holders age twenty-five and older were $39,000, 25 percent of these individuals earned more than $60,000, while another 25 percent earned less than $23,000.[18]

As we document in later chapters, data show relatively fewer disadvantaged or minority students in high-compensation fields of study, such as STEM (science, technology, engineering, and math), and relatively more in less well compensated fields, including "general studies" associate degree programs. This is true even though the likely primary interest of most disadvantaged students (unlike many middle- and upper-income students in liberal arts programs who plan to attend graduate school) is to attain a credential that will lead directly to stronger earnings upon graduation.[19]

16. Backes, Holzer, and Velez (2015).

17. NCES (2012, PowerStats calculations).

18. U.S. Census Bureau (2016b, PINC-03).

19. Jacobson and Mokher (2009); Backes, Holzer, and Velez (2015).

Financing College

A related issue is that students increasingly rely on loans to finance postsecondary education.[20] There is considerable variation in debt levels as well as in postcollege earnings. The percentage of associate degree recipients who borrowed $20,000 or more increased from 3 percent in 2003–04 to 17 percent in 2011–12, when 55 percent of those from the for-profit sector had this much debt. The percentage of certificate recipients who borrowed $20,000 or more increased from 1 percent to 10 percent, including 13 percent of those from the for-profit sector.[21]

The debt problems are particularly acute for those who fail to complete a degree, in addition to those who complete one in a low-compensation field, and those who have lower than expected earnings after completion, as was not uncommon in the weak job market for youth generated by the Great Recession of the early 2000s. Not completing a credential is the strongest predictor of defaulting on student loans;[22] and among borrowers who began repayment in 2011–12, 24 percent of those who had not earned a credential defaulted within two years, in comparison with 9 percent of those who had completed a degree or certificate.[23]

The issues we address are complex and deeply rooted in the unequal circumstances facing Americans. We do not pretend to have solutions that will eliminate the barriers confronting people growing up in disadvantaged circumstances and seeking to improve their lives through postsecondary education and training. But we are confident that a more thoughtful approach to developing evidence-based public policies can improve the lives of many Americans.

20. Baum and others (2016).
21. Baum and others (2016).
22. Gross and others (2010).
23. Looney and Yannelis (2015).

The Questions We Address

This book addresses six key questions:

- Why are completion rates for disadvantaged students so low?

- What causes the uneven employment and earnings outcomes of those students who do complete their course of study?

- How does the issue of financing postsecondary education relate to the unsatisfactory outcomes we observe?

- What kinds of interventions targeting students have the greatest potential to be cost-effective strategies for increasing completion rates and improving labor market outcomes?

- What kinds of interventions targeting higher education institutions—especially community colleges—have the greatest potential to be cost-effective strategies for improving post-college outcomes?

- Are there alternatives to enrollment in postsecondary institutions that can give individuals the skills and capacities they need to succeed in the labor market?

Each of the next six chapters addresses one of these questions. We address the first three questions in part I of the book, which includes chapters 2, 3, and 4. Chapters 5 through 7, in part II, address the next three questions. Chapter 8 then summarizes what we have learned and includes our policy recommendations.

Young people from disadvantaged backgrounds, as well as adults returning to school to improve their labor market opportunities, need more than a chance to enroll in college. They need much better chances of completing a degree or certificate program that will serve them well in an evolving labor market.

PART I

Postsecondary and Labor Market Outcomes

What Are the Problems and What Causes Them?

2

Who Completes College and Why?

Americans attend a wide range of colleges and universities, including two-year public colleges, four-year public and private nonprofit colleges and universities, and for-profit institutions. But too many students who start college, especially minorities and students from lower-income families, never complete credentials, particularly in the public two-year, nonselective public four-year, and for-profit sectors.

In this chapter we explore in detail the question of who completes college and why. We begin by looking at some national data, comparing completion rates across types of institutions and examining the associations between college completion and race, gender, socioeconomic status, and high school achievement.

After considering data on the completion problem, we explore what the research literature tells us about the causes of leaving college without a credential. We are particularly interested in why dropout rates are highest among minorities and low-income students. In this discussion, we distinguish between effects associated with *students*, particularly their personal and family backgrounds and characteristics, and those reflecting the quality and characteristics of the *institutions* they have chosen (or were able) to attend.

Poor academic preparation in the K–12 years, particularly among disadvantaged students, plays a significant role in the completion problem. But the high price of college, combined with very limited student and family resources and resistance to borrowing, also contributes. A lack of familiarity with the academic world and what social scientists refer to as "social capital" add to these difficulties, as does the inability of many students to attend college full time, frequently because of responsibilities for caring for and supporting families.

But institutions also matter. Some colleges are better than others at enabling students to complete their chosen programs of study. For any given student, the quality of the institution attended, as well as the characteristics and preparation of the student body, helps determine the probability of completing a credential. The level of institutional resources affects the quality of academic programs and support services offered, especially to disadvantaged and academically weaker students, thereby influencing completion rates. But there is also considerable variation in student completion rates among institutions with similar levels of resources and similar student bodies, so other characteristics and practices also affect outcomes.

Institutional Variation in Higher Education

The effects of institutions on higher education outcomes of students are important at least partly because the range of institutional types, quality, and prices is so wide in the United States; access of different demographic groups to different types of institutions varies considerably. There are over 2,000 private nonprofit and public baccalaureate colleges and universities today, and about 1,000 community colleges. (Because the latter are starting to provide bachelor's degrees in some states, drawing the line between sectors is not always simple.) For-profit colleges grew dramatically from the mid-1990s through 2010. The approximately 1,300 institutions in this sector now include traditional proprietary colleges for particular occupations such as cosmetology or culinary arts as well as newer, broader, and larger institutions such as Phoenix, Strayer, and DeVry. (Two of the largest proprietary schools, Corinthian Colleges and ITT Tech, closed in 2015 and 2016, respectively.) Most of these larger institutions offer the full range of undergraduate and graduate credentials to their students, and many are publicly held.

The number, structure, and governance of public two-year and four-year colleges vary greatly. Some states have much more centralized governance by state higher education officials than others. Community colleges traditionally saw themselves as primarily academic institutions and as stepping stones to four-year colleges. Even today, a quarter of all students from the sector transfer to four-year colleges, and more intend to do so when they first enroll.[1]

But today community colleges are also expected to function as workforce development institutions, where workers—especially those who are disadvantaged or displaced from a recent job—attend to receive job training in a new occupation or industry. These dual missions of the community colleges are handled quite differently by individual institutions, even within the same states, with some focusing much more of their attention and resources on one or the other goal. The history of a college or even its proximity to a four-year college can have persistent effects on how it balances these roles.[2]

As already noted, both older and disadvantaged students are concentrated at community and for-profit colleges, often seeking to meet specific occupational training goals rather than earn a bachelor's degree. Within any community college, degree programs are sometimes quite distinct from "workforce" programs, where the former include any associate (or bachelor's) degree offered, while the latter include only certificate programs that may or may not carry academic credit.

Young people enrolling immediately after high school are more likely to be enrolled in degree programs, while older adults are more likely to be enrolled in certificate programs. In addition, younger students are much more likely than older students, who juggle school with supporting their families, to enroll full time.[3] Still, the distinctions between degree programs for young students and workforce programs for adults can be overstated. Older students sometimes pursue an

1. Shapiro and others (2015, p. 15).
2. Bailey, Jaggars, and Jenkins (2015).
3. In 2011–12, 6 percent of undergraduates age twenty-three and younger were enrolled in certificate programs, as were 11 percent of older students. Fifty-nine percent of the younger group were enrolled full time, compared with 39 percent of the older group (NCES 2012).

associate degree, such as a technician or licensed practical nursing degree that directly prepares students for work. And young people can enroll in a certificate program right after high school, either full time or part time.

Many, though not all, community colleges and for-profit institutions have relatively open access, with minimal admission requirements. Having a high school diploma or GED (high school equivalency certificate) might be the only requirement for admission, and even this is not always necessary.

Because access to and enrollment in such institutions is so broad, students often enter unprepared for college-level academic work and are placed in developmental or remedial classes until they can pass either these courses or proficiency tests in math and reading. About 68 percent of students entering public two-year and 40 percent of those entering public four-year colleges in 2003–04 took at least one remedial class by 2009.[4] Indeed, students are often not allowed to take any for-credit classes until they pass these required courses.

Public and private four-year colleges also vary widely in quality even within states, reflecting very different student bodies, resources, and missions. Their resources reflect different levels of funding from state legislators, local governments, tuition payments, and endowments. The students' socioeconomic backgrounds and academic preparation vary dramatically. Commentators often distinguish "elite" or very selective colleges and universities from the rest; the former include the flagship public and top-ranked private universities. Many of the flagships attract large numbers of out-of-state applicants who are willing to pay tuition rates that can be as high as those charged by selective private colleges.

In contrast, minority and low-income students more frequently enroll in much less selective public colleges, which have lower prices and lower admission requirements—although generally higher than community colleges. Aggressive and often successful marketing campaigns by the for-profit colleges have attracted many low-income students to that sector, despite the relatively high tuition prices.

4. Chen (2016).

This enormous variation in higher education institutions and in their student bodies must be kept in mind as we consider the data on students' differing completion rates and different explanations about why they vary.

What Do the Data Tell Us?

To get a handle on the difference in completion rates between disadvantaged students and others we examine data from the Beginning Postsecondary Students Longitudinal Study (BPS) of American college students.[5] The survey was first administered to a representative sample of 15,000 new college students in 2003–04. These students were reinterviewed in 2006 and 2009, providing a six-year window within which to observe students and their completion rates, together with their other experiences and characteristics.[6]

Of course, the characteristics and choices of students entering postsecondary institutions since 2003 may have changed. But comparing data on the institutional choices of students beginning college in 2003 with a more recent cohort of students represented in the National Postsecondary Student Aid Study (NPSAS) reveals similar overall enrollment patterns in 2003–04 and 2011–12, despite a few notable trends such as an increase over time in the share of students attending for-profit institutions. Given the mostly consistent patterns over time, we continue to focus on the cohort who first entered college in 2003–04, for whom enough time has elapsed to observe academic performance and completion rates.

5. The BPS data are available online at the website of the National Center on Education Statistics (NCES), though access to the transcripts of individual students is restricted.

6. As with any longitudinal survey, there is some attrition over time from the BPS sample, causing those in later years to be a less representative sample than those who began in 2003.

Where Are Students Enrolled?

Figure 2-1 shows the distribution of students by the first and last sectors in which they enrolled. It includes public four-year colleges, private nonprofit four-year colleges, public two-year colleges (which are mostly community colleges but also include technical schools in a few states), and private for-profit colleges, but excludes the 2 percent of students enrolled in other types of institutions. The graph shows the distribution for all students, then separately for students who are dependent on their parents for purposes of financial aid allocation and for independent students, who are either age twenty-four or older or independent of their parents for other reasons. The graph also breaks dependent students down by family income.

We focus on the last institution in which students enroll for most of our analysis, since we are particularly concerned with the labor market outcomes of students based on the credentials they earn. However, figure 2-1 reveals that while 36 percent of students *last* attended a two-year public college, 43 percent began in this sector. The increase from 27 percent of students first enrolling in public four-year institutions to 33 percent ending up there reflects transfers among students seeking a bachelor's degree. Notably, this shift appears primarily among dependent students from higher-income families, not among independent students and lower-income dependent students.

Among students who first enrolled in college in 2003–04, 14 percent last enrolled in a for-profit institution, including 26 percent of independent students and just 9 percent of dependent students. Among dependent students, 16 percent of those from the lowest family income quartile were in the for-profit sector, compared with just 4 percent of those from the highest-income families. The patterns are similar, but not quite so stark, for the much larger public two-year sector. As discussed below, much of this difference in enrollment patterns reflects differences in earlier student achievement, as opposed to other disadvantages of those from low-income families.

As table 2-1 shows, demographic characteristics other than family income are also closely associated with the distribution of students across postsecondary sectors. For instance, older students are much less likely to attend a four-year college or university than younger students, with just 16 percent of those first enrolling at age twenty-

Figure 2-1. Enrollment by Sector: First and Last Institution by Dependency Status and Dependent Students' Family Income

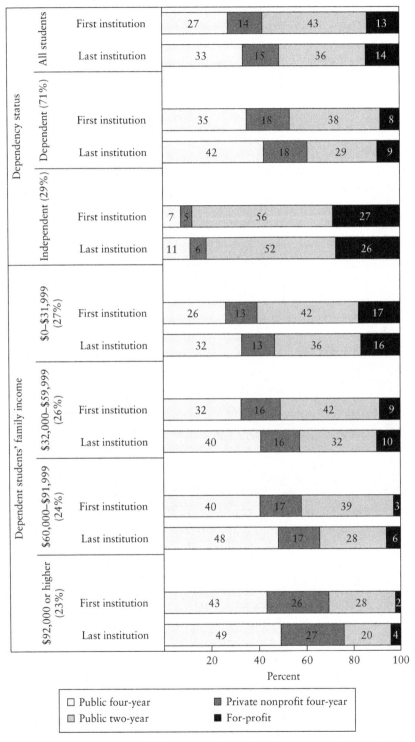

Source: NCES (2009, PowerStats calculations).
Note: Excludes the 2 percent of students enrolled in other types of institutions.

Table 2-1. *Distribution of Last Sector of Enrollment by Age, Gender, and Race/Ethnicity*

Percent

	Public four-year	Private nonprofit four-year	Public two-year	For-profit	Other
All students	33	15	36	14	2
Age at first enrollment					
19 or younger	43	19	28	9	1
20–23	17	8	48	25	3
24–29	10	6	48	31	5
30 or older	9	7	58	21	6
Gender					
Male	35	14	36	12	2
Female	32	15	35	15	2
Race/ethnicity					
White	37	17	35	10	2
Black / African American	24	11	38	25	2
Hispanic / Latino	23	10	41	22	4
Asian	47	18	26	7	1
Other	31	12	38	16	4

Source: NCES (2009, Power Stats calculations).

four or older ending their studies in these institutions, but 62 percent of those age nineteen or younger following this path. More than half of the older students first enrolling in 2003–04 last attended community colleges, compared with only 28 percent of those enrolling by age nineteen. Younger students are also much less likely to attend a for-profit school.

The enrollment patterns of minorities differ from those of whites. About 40 percent of black or Hispanic postsecondary students last attended two-year colleges, and another 25 percent attended for-profit or other programs; in contrast, just 35 and 10 percent of whites last attended these institutions, respectively. Over half of white undergraduates last attended a four-year college, while only about a third of minorities did so. Nearly two-thirds of Asian students last enrolled in a four-year college, with much smaller fractions in the other sectors.

Who Completes College and Where?

Attainment of a college degree or credential requires both *enrollment* in a postsecondary program and *completion* of that program. Overall attainment rates refer to the percentage of the population holding different types of degrees. In contrast, completion rates reflect the percentage of those who begin at particular types of institutions who succeeded in earning degrees—either at their first institution or after transferring elsewhere. The data below focus on outcomes for students with different characteristics who enrolled in different types of institutions. In other words, we ask about the highest level of education students who enrolled in postsecondary institutions have attained six years after beginning college. When these data are presented separately by type of institution, they illustrate completion rates, as well as overall educational attainment.

Figures 2-2a and 2-2b, as well as table 2-2, show the highest level of education attained by students who first enrolled in postsecondary institutions in 2003–04. Figure 2-2a shows higher educational attainment six years after students began college by dependency status and for dependent students, by family income. Six percent of independent students and 41 percent of dependent students earned a bachelor's degree. Thirty-four percent of independent students and 56 percent of dependent students earned any degree or certificate. Among dependent students, bachelor's degree attainment among enrolled students is highly correlated with family income, ranging from 26 percent for the lowest quartile to 59 percent for the highest quartile. Forty-five percent of the lowest-income students and 68 percent of the highest-income group earned some type of credential.

Figure 2-2b reports attainment rates for both the first and last type of institution in which students were enrolled. We include information by first institution to show that, although students whose last institution was a two-year public college did not earn a bachelor's degree, 12 percent of those who *began* at a community college did transfer to four-year institutions and earn a bachelor's degree. Among those whose last institution was a four-year college or university, over 60 percent completed a bachelor's degree (with completion somewhat higher at the private nonprofit than the public institutions); but, of

Figure 2-2a. Highest Level of Education Attained Six Years after Enrolling, by Dependency Status and Dependent Students' Family Income

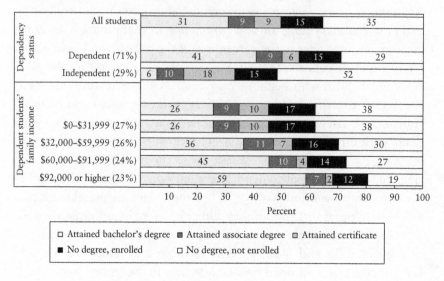

Figure 2-2b. Level of Education Attained Six Years after First Enrollment, by First and Last Sector

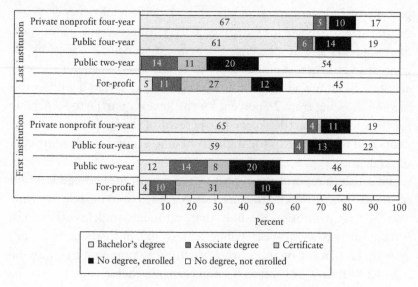

Source: NCES (2009, PowerStats calculations).

Table 2-2. *Students Who First Enrolled in 2003–04, Distribution of Attainment after Six Years by Sector of Last Enrollment and Age, Race/Ethnicity, and Gender*

Percent of students in each category

	Bachelor's degree	Associate degree	Certificate	No degree, enrolled	No degree, not enrolled	Any credential
All students	31	9	9	15	35	50
Public four-year						
All students	61	6	1	14	19	68
Age first enrolled						
19 or younger (88%)	65	5	1	13	17	71
20–23 (6%)	37	11	2	18	32	50
24–29 (2%)	27	6	2	25	41	34
30 or older (3%)	19	15	7	21	38	41
Race/ethnicity						
White (68%)	64	5	1	11	18	70
Black / African American (10%)	44	9	2	21	24	55
Hispanic / Latino (10%)	49	8	2	19	22	59
Asian (7%)	68	5	0	17	11	72
Other (5%)	57	6	1	15	21	64
Gender						
Male (45%)	57	5	1	17	20	63
Female (55%)	63	7	1	11	18	71

	Bachelor's degree	Associate degree	Certificate	No degree, enrolled	No degree, not enrolled	Any credential
Public two-year						
All students	0	14	11	20	54	26
Age first enrolled						
19 or younger (52%)	1	16	10	23	51	26
20–23 (17%)	0	12	10	21	56	23
24–29 (10%)	0	11	16	16	57	27
30 or older (21%)	0	11	14	14	61	25
Race/ethnicity						
White (60%)	1	17	12	18	53	29
Black / African American (14%)	0	9	11	24	56	20
Hispanic / Latino (17%)	0	10	11	21	58	21
Asian (3%)	0	17	10	26	47	27
Other (5%)	0	9	9	28	54	18
Gender						
Male (43%)	0	13	10	20	56	24
Female (57%)	1	14	12	20	53	27
Private nonprofit four-year						
All students	67	5	1	10	17	73
Age first enrolled						
19 or younger (85%)	73	4	1	8	14	78
20–23 (7%)	35	5	4	32	25	43
24–29 (3%)	38	17	2	3	40	57
30 or older (6%)	29	8	7	13	43	44

Race/ethnicity						
White (70%)	71	5	1	7	15	78
Black / African American (10%)	53	4	2	14	27	59
Hispanic / Latino (10%)	47	5	3	22	23	55
Asian (6%)	71	1	0	15	13	72
Other (4%)	66	5	0	12	17	71
Gender						
Male (42%)	65	4	1	11	20	69
Female (58%)	68	6	1	10	15	75
For-profit						
All students	5	11	27	12	45	43
Age first enrolled						
19 or younger (42%)	6	16	26	14	39	48
20–23 (22%)	5	8	28	12	47	41
24–29 (17%)	2	9	29	12	47	41
30 or older (19%)	5	5	27	8	55	37
Race/ethnicity						
White (43%)	6	16	22	11	45	44
Black / African American (25%)	2	6	26	15	50	34
Hispanic / Latino (24%)	4	7	40	6	43	51
Asian (2%)	12	16	21	24	27	49
Other (6%)	11	11	17	21	40	39
Gender						
Male (37%)	7	16	18	13	47	41
Female (63%)	4	8	32	11	44	0

Source: NCES (2009, Power Stats calculations).

those who ended up at a public two-year college, only 14 percent and 11 percent earned an associate degree and a certificate, respectively.

Table 2-2 shows dramatic differences in attainment, and therefore in completion rates, by sector. Sixty-eight percent of students who last enrolled at a public four-year college or university and 73 percent of those whose last institution was in the private nonprofit sector completed a credential within six years.

But completion rates are much lower at the two-year and for-profit institutions where low-income and adult students are concentrated. Only about 25 percent of all 2003–04 beginning students whose final institution of enrollment was a community college completed a credential, with 14 percent earning an associate degree and 11 percent earning a certificate. Because more successful students are more likely to transfer out of this sector, the completion rate for those who began at a two-year public college is considerably higher. One-third of these students completed a credential, including 12 percent who ultimately earned a bachelor's degree by transferring to four-year colleges and universities.[7] Many more students (43 percent) in the for-profit sector received a certificate. A much smaller percentage of students who began in for-profit institutions than of those who began in community colleges earned a bachelor's degree, and associate degrees were also less common in the for-profit sector.

Table 2-2 breaks down the degree attainment data by the institution type in which students were last enrolled before the final survey in 2009 (six years after initial enrollment), and within sectors, by personal characteristics such as dependency status, family income among dependent students, age, race/ethnicity, and gender.[8]

Some of the 35 percent of students who were still enrolled in 2009 but had not yet earned a credential might have transferred to a

---

7. A variety of data sources indicate that nearly one-quarter of students who enter community colleges ultimately transfer to four-year institutions, and about half of them obtain a bachelor's degree.

8. Since the BPS does not separately measure enrollments for associate degrees and certificates in community colleges, or for these and bachelor's degrees in the for-profit sector, our completion rates can only be obtained by summing across these credentials for each category of school.

different type of institution after the final survey and earned a credential. Many students stop in and out of school. For example, among 2011–12 undergraduates, 28 percent had first enrolled in college more than six years earlier.[9]

How do these results differ across income, age, race, and gender groups within sectors? Table 2-2 shows that completion rates at each type of institution are lower among independent than dependent students and are higher for students from higher-income families. Among the different age groups, 65 percent of students first enrolled in college at age nineteen or younger who ended up at a four-year public institution completed a bachelor's degree. Only about 30 percent of those who enrolled at older ages (37 percent among twenty- to twenty-three-year-olds and 19 percent among those age thirty and older) earned a bachelor's degree from a public four-year university.

Attainment of associate degrees is also higher among younger students at public two-year and for-profit colleges, though the differences across age groups are much smaller. Older students, in contrast, are a bit more likely to complete certificate programs. It is likely that both academic and nonacademic factors—such as the pressure to provide incomes for their families—make it harder for older students to persevere and finish their programs of study. Moreover, within each type of institution, younger and higher-income students are more likely to attend more selective institutions, which also affects their chances of completing.[10]

Other patterns are evident as well. In general, females have higher completion rates than males, especially at four-year institutions; whites and Asians have higher completion rates than blacks and Hispanics.

Does Earlier Achievement Drive Higher Education Disparities?

We know that achievement gaps between whites and minorities and between nonpoor and poor students start early in life and then widen when students enter school, before stabilizing. Over time, achievement gaps between whites and minorities have narrowed somewhat

---

9. NCES (2012).
10. Bound, Lovenheim, and Turner (2010).

but remain large, while those between the poor and others have been stable or have grown slightly. These achievement disparities are captured, at least to some extent, by grades and test scores measured throughout the K–12 years.[11]

The BPS data include some information on high school grade-point averages (GPAs). We divide the 73 percent of students for whom this information is available into three categories: GPA 3.5 or above, 3.0 to 3.4, and lower than 3.0.[12] Figure 2-3 shows higher education attainment rates within each of the three GPA categories. The data report the highest credential attained at any institution within six years of first enrollment.

The results indicate, not surprisingly, that educational attainment is highly correlated with high school achievement—especially at the bachelor's degree level. The differences in overall completion rates partly reflect the fact that higher achievers attend better-resourced colleges with higher-achieving student bodies. They are more likely to attend private rather than public four-year colleges, PhD-granting public universities rather than those not granting PhDs, and four-year institutions rather than two-year colleges. However, they also have higher average completion rates and perform better within similar institutions than do students with lower levels of high school achievement.[13]

But the disparities across dependency and family income groups *within* each high school performance category are also substantial. Very few high-achieving independent students earn bachelor's degrees, and bachelor's degree attainment among the highest-achieving students is nearly 25 percentage points lower for the lowest-income students than for the highest-income students. Among those in the

11. Achievement is sometimes measured by standardized test scores and sometimes by grade-point average (GPA), where the latter may be defined differently across schools. But GPA has stronger predictive power for postsecondary performance or completion, while test scores sometimes have larger effects on earnings (Backes, Holzer, and Velez 2015).

12. The restricted-use BPS data contain individual student transcripts with much more detailed data on student performance, but these are not publicly available online.

13. Bound, Lovenheim, and Turner (2010); Backes, Holzer, and Velez (2015).

Figure 2-3. Attainment Rates after Six Years by Dependency Status, and Family Income within GPA Categories

GPA Category	Income group	Bachelor's degree	Associate degree	Certificate	No degree, enrolled	No degree, not enrolled
3.5 or higher	$92,000 or higher (30%)	79	4	6		10
	$60,000–$91,999 (28%)	66	8	1	7	10
	$32,000–$59,999 (23%)	62	8	3	10	18
	Less than $32,000 (19%)	55	3	6	12	17
	Independent	17	11	5	18	49
3.0–3.4	$92,000 or higher (21%)	56	6	3	14	21
	$60,000–$91,999 (25%)	44	10	4	15	27
	$32,000–$59,999 (28%)	35	12	6	19	27
	Less than $32,000 (26%)	19	7	10	17	48
	Independent	6	8	18	22	46
Less than 3.0	$92,000 or higher (18%)	29	14	4	19	34
	$60,000–$91,999 (22%)	20	12	8	21	39
	$32,000–$59,999 (29%)	17	12	10	19	42
	Less than $32,000 (32%)	13	11	14	20	42
	Independent	6	8	18	20	47

Percent (10 20 30 40 50 60 70 80 90 100)

Legend: □ Bachelor's degree   ▨ Associate degree   ▨ Certificate   ■ No degree, enrolled   □ No degree, not enrolled

Source: NCES (2009, PowerStats calculations).

3.0 to 3.4 GPA category, the gap in bachelor's degree attainment between the highest- and lowest-income dependent students is a stunning 37 percentage points (56 and 19 percent, respectively). The disappointing attainment rates for all lower-income students suggest that the limitations of their academic achievement in high school explain only a fraction of the barriers to strong performance these students face.

Table 2-3 reports similar measures of higher education attainment within each high school achievement category broken down by race and gender. These data document clearly that, even within fairly narrow ranges of high school academic achievement, minority students who enroll are less likely to complete college than others. The gaps are most notable when considering bachelor's degree attainment, and especially within the top-performing achievement group. Females have higher rates of bachelor's degree attainment among the highest

Table 2-3. Students Who First Enrolled in 2003–04, Distribution of Attainment Rates after Six Years by Race and Gender within GPA Categories

Percent of students in each category

	Bachelor's degree	Associate degree	Certificate	No degree, enrolled	No degree, not enrolled
GPA less than 3.0					
Race/ethnicity					
White (57%)	20	14	9	19	39
Black / African American (19%)	12	9	11	19	49
Hispanic / Latino (17%)	13	9	17	21	40
Asian (3%)	25	15	9	25	25
Other (5%)	12	8	7	30	42
Gender					
Male (50%)	17	11	8	21	43
Female (50%)	17	12	14	18	39
GPA 3.0–3.4					
Race/ethnicity					
White (61%)	43	9	5	13	30
Black / African American (12%)	26	7	11	24	33
Hispanic / Latino (18%)	21	11	11	18	39
Asian (5%)	40	9	1	31	19
Other (5%)	28	10	10	26	26

Gender					
Male (44%)	37	9	5	17	32
Female (56%)	36	10	8	17	30
3.5 or higher					
Race/ethnicity					
White (75%)	67	7	2	8	17
Black / African American (6%)	48	7	8	14	23
Hispanic / Latino (8%)	70	3	1	11	15
Asian (6%)	58	6	1	10	25
Other (5%)					
Gender					
Male (38%)	60	7	2	10	21
Female (62%)	66	6	3	9	17

Source: NCES (2009, Power Stats calculations).

achievers, though other differences in higher education outcomes by gender are fairly small.

Similar results emerge from other data sources, including the state longitudinal administrative data we discuss in chapter 3. Lower enrollment rates at four-year colleges among the best students from low-income families illustrate the "undermatching" of high-achieving low-income students, who often do not enroll in the selective colleges and universities for which they would likely be eligible. But the lower completion rates of low-income students at any of these schools, even among equally able students, suggest that disadvantaged students face other barriers wherever they go.

Gaps in attainment rates across family income groups within the same achievement categories are often larger than those by race within the same categories. In other words, precollege achievement levels appear to explain differences in postsecondary outcomes by race and ethnicity better than they explain differences across income groups.[14]

The bottom line: while high school achievement is an important predictor of college enrollment and completion, family income, race, gender, and age as reflected in independent student status matter a great deal as well—even among those with equal earlier achievement levels.

Summary

Overall, the data in this chapter clearly indicate that college completion rates are lower at public two-year and for-profit colleges than at four-year colleges and universities. College enrollment, completion, and degree attainment patterns also differ considerably across students by dependency status, family income, and race. Disadvantaged students are more heavily concentrated in two-year and for-profit colleges, as are those with low high school achievement levels. Completion rates are lower within each type of institution for disadvantaged students, even after controlling for high school GPA. There are large disparities in educational attainment, especially by family in-

14. This finding also appears in Backes, Holzer, and Velez (2015).

come and by dependency status, even among high-achieving students, with disadvantaged students who do complete a credential least likely to earn a four-year degree.

Why Are College Completion Rates Low among Disadvantaged Students?

Following John Bound and coauthors, we distinguish the *personal* effects of individual students, including their family backgrounds, from the *institutional* effects of the colleges they attend. The individual effects reflect a range of factors, including a lack of effective academic preparation before college, the financial constraints on low-income families, too little information or "social capital" about how to be successful in college, and frequently, attending college part time because of work and family responsibilities. Moreover, many students enroll in college with no clear idea of where they are headed and what they hope to accomplish.

The institutional effects reflect the lower quality of the colleges attended by low-income students because of their weaker academic backgrounds, financial constraints, or lack of information about selective schools. These institutions, in turn, graduate a smaller percentage of their students because of resource constraints, peer effects, and inadequate incentives to allocate resources in ways that raise graduation rates. As overall enrollment rates have risen over time, the concentration of low-income students at minimally selective, under-resourced institutions has also risen, apparently contributing to the longer time to degree and lower bachelor's degree completion rates among these at-risk students.[15]

Personal and Family Characteristics

The clearest way in which the personal characteristics of students affect their college enrollment and completion rates is through their weaker academic preparation for college. The data clearly indicate that students with lower high school achievement levels have lower

---

15. Bound, Lovenheim, and Turner (2010).

college completion rates; and minority and economically disadvantaged students have lower levels of achievement than their white and more advantaged counterparts.

The achievement gap across racial and ethnic groups, while still substantial, has declined somewhat over time. But the gap between lower- and higher-income students has grown.[16] Although institutional resource constraints appear to be the driving force,[17] as college enrollment rates have risen over time, with a large majority of high school graduates now enrolling soon after high school, weak academic preparation no doubt contributes more than before to low college completion rates.

Academic Preparation

The strongest academic proponent of the view that weak academic preparation limits college enrollment and completion has been economist and Nobel laureate James Heckman. In a series of papers with various coauthors, Heckman argues that low test scores and relatively low high school graduation rates are far more important determinants of low college attainment than other factors, such as financial constraints.[18] In addition, he argues that the achievement gaps that limit minority and lower-income students begin to appear very early in life and grow over time. This widening impact of low achievement occurs because, in Heckman's view, "skill begets skill." In other words, weaker skills early in life limit a student's ability to build further skills,

16. See Magnuson and Waldfogel (2008) for evidence of modest declines in the achievement gap by race over time and Reardon (2011) for evidence of widening gaps by family income. But Reardon and Portilla (2016) also find some modest improvements for very young poor children relative to the nonpoor since 2000.

17. Bound, Lovenheim, and Turner (2010).

18. Despite some controversy over exactly how to measure high school graduation rates (Swanson 2004; Mishel and Roy 2006), Murnane (2013) shows clear evidence that graduation rates have risen substantially since the 1990s. By his measure the dropout rate is about 16 percent nationally but over 20 percent for minorities.

in what he and others refer to as the "dynamic complementarity" of education over time.[19]

In recent years, Heckman and others have emphasized the importance of various noncognitive skills. Heckman refers to the role of "character" as opposed to "cognition" in building achievement over time. The character traits that improve educational attainment and achievement include motivation, ability to delay gratification, and "stick-to-it-ness," sometimes called "grit."[20] In Heckman's view, early childhood experiences have considerable influence on both cognition and character development. These factors, which begin to develop very early in life, have a major impact on both high school completion and success in college.

A considerable research literature has developed in recent years on academic achievement gaps and their determinants. Unlike Heckman, other researchers have emphasized school characteristics, especially segregation by race and/or income, and its deleterious effects on student learning. Segregated public schools are most often found within segregated neighborhoods, and social scientists are still trying to sort out the effects of both on student achievement.[21] Within schools, high-quality teachers make a big difference, and their effects can last well into the college years.[22] The effects of family background on student achievement reflect not only parental characteristics, but

19. See Heckman (2008).

20. See Heckman and Kautz (2013), as well as the books by Paul Tough (2013) and Angela Duckworth (2016).

21. Fryer and Katz (2013) try to disentangle the effects of school and neighborhood poverty on youth outcomes. Black and others (2014) show evidence of several high school characteristics on student outcomes, while Hanushek and Rivkin (2009) show negative effects of racial segregation, specifically on black student achievement.

22. See Chetty, Friedman, and Rockoff (2014) for evidence that the effects of high-quality elementary school teachers on student outcomes can last well into college and beyond. While the estimates of teacher "value added" have been somewhat controversial in the research literature, the most recent evidence suggests that these estimates closely correlate with more trustworthy measures of teacher impacts based on randomized experiments. See Chetty, Friedman, and Rockoff (2013).

also their income levels and the many stresses on children associated with growing up in poverty, which researchers are increasingly labeling "toxic" in their effects on children's learning.[23]

Another possibility is that what students do once they get to college exacerbates the problems. A provocative and controversial recent book argues that a large fraction of U.S. college students are academically "adrift," achieving little growth in their critical thinking and problem-solving skills in college.[24] A number of scholars have questioned the methodology and conclusions of this work. But a lack of rigor in college classes and a secular decline in time spent studying by students, to which the authors attribute some of their findings,[25] could contribute at least somewhat to the overall decline in completion rates. For our purposes, it would also be important to know whether the trends in these outcomes and in studying habits differ by income and race/ethnicity in ways that might help explain the differential completion rates. In fact, in the data this book reports, disadvantaged students have worse academic outcomes on some dimensions and spend less time studying or in more rigorous courses than do other students.[26]

Financial Constraints

Weak academic preparation alone cannot fully explain the lower college completion rates of economically disadvantaged students. The financial constraints faced by low-income students and their families—on which we focus in chapter 4—are also an issue. About three-quarters of dependent undergraduate students get financial assistance from

23. See, for example, Shonkoff (2012).

24. Arum and Roksa (2011).

25. Arum and Roksa (2011) argue that the lack of rigorous assignments in college classes is driven at least partly by professors who want high student ratings on evaluations, but we have little evidence that this factor is the most important or that it is growing.

26. Arum and Roksa (2014) find evidence that the levels of critical thinking skills are lower for minorities and those with less-educated parents. Improvement in these skills during the college years is fairly comparable across parental education categories, but still lower for blacks and Hispanics.

their parents to cover expenses. About 60 percent of parents from the lowest income quartile manage to help, but their average contribution was about $1,400 in 2011–12, whereas almost 90 percent of parents in the top quartile contributed an average of about $12,000.[27]

This is not surprising, given the inequality of income and assets across families in the United States. Lacking family resources, low-income students have little option other than to supplement any financial aid they receive with work and borrowing. While banks and other private lenders are likely to limit credit availability for low-income students and families who lack both collateral and strong credit ratings, federal loans are available to all students.

Although there is some evidence of resistance to borrowing among low-income and minority populations,[28] the share of low-income dependent students who borrow for college (43 percent in 2011–12) is now similar to the overall share (40 percent), which is brought down by a lower borrowing rate among the most affluent students.[29]

Despite the availability of federal loans, enrollment decisions of low-income students are particularly price-sensitive. The availability and accessibility of grant aid strongly influence whether and where these students enroll. The evidence is clear that financial aid that lowers the prices students pay increases educational attainment, particularly for low-income students.[30]

Research indicates that the housing bubble before 2006 helped improve both college attendance and completion rates among middle-class students, as well as the poor. Many people took advantage of the long period of relatively low interest rates to repeatedly refinance their homes, turning their rising home values into cash, making it easier for them to pay for their children's (and perhaps their own) higher education. This process was even more important for poor or minority homeowners than for others.[31] The subsequent crash of the housing market beginning in 2006 eliminated this mechanism and

27. NCES (2012, PowerStats calculations).
28. Caliber Associates (2003).
29. NCES (2012, PowerStats calculations).
30. Scott-Clayton (2015).
31. Lovenheim (2011).

was particularly devastating for the households whose wealth in those years was almost exclusively concentrated in their homes.

Social Capital

Social capital refers to the networks and relationships that help people to navigate society and its institutions. In addition to weaker academic preparation and limited wealth and liquidity, economically disadvantaged and minority students have fewer social capital resources. In particular, their lack of information and connections, as well as the pressure they often feel to work full time and therefore enroll only part time in college, weakens educational attainment.

Low-income students have little information about the world of higher education. This is particularly true for first-generation college enrollees and those who attend public schools in minority or low-income neighborhoods.[32] Since individuals derive a great deal of information and assistance from their social networks, a lack of effective or knowledgeable social networks related to higher education will deprive them of both.[33] The trend among students from affluent public and private high schools of applying to numerous selective colleges gets quite a bit of attention, but many disadvantaged students never consider more than one college option.[34] Among 2004 high school seniors from the highest socioeconomic quartile who applied to college, 27 percent applied to only one institution, but 36 percent submitted four or more applications. Among those from the lowest socioeconomic quartile, 44 percent applied to only one institution and only 16 percent applied to four or more colleges.[35] This pattern surely contributes to enrollment in inappropriate institutions and programs.

32. See Hoxby and Avery (2013) and Hoxby and Turner (2013), among others.

33. See Putnam (2000) and Putnam, Feldstein, and Cohen (2003) for a fuller discussion of how a lack of social capital among disadvantaged or first-generation students can impede their educational success.

34. Rosenbaum, Deil-Amen, and Person (2006).

35. NCES (2002, PowerStats calculations).

It is difficult for students to develop clear goals when they lack information and guidance. Community college leaders with whom we have spoken about their efforts to improve outcomes are unanimous in pointing to the lack of direction as a central cause of low completion rates. Students who enroll with at least a broad idea of the career to which they aspire are more likely to be on a path to success than those who have only a vague idea that they need some sort of credential.

Poor information creates significant problems for relatively high academic achievers in low-income families and neighborhoods, who frequently choose to attend the colleges closest to home rather than the best ones to which they could be admitted.[36] Once they enroll in college, a lack of information can limit their progress in many other ways.

First-generation students might not know which majors they are best suited for, given their academic skills and interest; or how to study most efficiently and allocate their time effectively; or where to receive support services, such as tutoring or counseling.

A lack of social capital at college, especially for those who are socially isolated, sometimes because they live at home with their parents, may deprive students not only of key information, but also of informal assistance and supports such as study groups or "learning communities" that can be helpful for navigating college.[37] Even if they manage to complete a particular course of study, these students may have difficulty making a transition from a two-year to a four-year college, or to a new major and program of study, or from college to the job market or graduate school.[38]

Finally, many low-income students, especially young single parents, may have to support their families, working part time—or even full time—while in school. This makes it difficult or impossible to attend college full time; and part-time enrollment is a very strong

36. Hoxby and Avery (2013).

37. See the books on the difficulties faced by low-income college students by Bowen, Chingos, and McPherson (2009); Bowen, Kurzweil, and Tobin (2005); and Goldrick-Rab (2010).

38. See Jenkins and Cho (2012).

predictor of failure to graduate.[39] These students will, for instance, have difficulty completing required courses that are offered only irregularly, or finding enough time to study and complete assignments.

These difficulties are compounded by the fact that "stuff happens," especially when you are poor. In the early 2000s, David Shipler described the often tumultuous nature of the lives of the working poor and how quickly stable arrangements can unravel when one thing goes wrong—like a relative becoming sick or a car breaking down.[40] It makes sense that, in the face of emergencies, the school performance of working parents or older offspring in such families would suffer—though at this point we have anecdotes but little hard data to back this up. In addition, we have evidence that, in stressful circumstances, individuals focus too much on the present or make mistakes in haste, in ways that might hurt their academic or labor market performance.[41]

In sum, a wide range of personal circumstances—such as poor skills; lack of family resources and financial assistance; lack of information or social capital; and pressure to enroll only part time while taking care of family—all contribute to low completion rates for low-income students.

Institutional Characteristics

In addition to the personal circumstances of low-income students that contribute to their low rates of college completion, many of the colleges they attend diminish their chances for success. For instance, low-income students tend to be concentrated in colleges with low completion rates. These institutions and their qualities reduce the probability that individual students will succeed, even when control-

39. For evidence that part-time enrollment, especially among older students, impedes college completion see Baum and Scott-Clayton (2013) and Complete College America (2011).

40. See Shipler's (2004) book on the working poor, and evidence on fairly short but frequent poverty spells among some of the poor in Blank (1997).

41. See Mullainathan and Shafir (2013) and work on behavioral effects on educational outcomes by Lavecchia, Liu, and Oreopoulos (2014).

ling for students' own personal characteristics.[42] Why do some institutions generate low completion rates? And why are low-income students concentrated at these schools?

The correlations between socioeconomic background and academic preparation, and between the academic preparation of the student body and institutional completion rates, make it almost inevitable that low-income students will be disproportionately represented at nonselective institutions with low graduation rates. Colleges that admit many low-income students have lower average SAT scores; in these schools, *peer effects* are weak. In addition, *financial resources* are stretched at these schools, and measures of resources such as students per faculty member and total expenditures per student affect completion rates, given student characteristics. The flagship state universities usually receive more generous state funding per student than do the less selective universities and community colleges. As a result, states tend to spend less per low-income college student than per affluent student.[43] Colleges where resources are more constrained have greater difficulty hiring highly qualified faculty, providing needed supports such as high-quality developmental classes and tutoring, and even offering multiple sections of courses that are required for students to complete their programs of study.

The most obvious reason for the concentration of low-income and minority students at underresourced public colleges and universities is academic: many of these students are simply not prepared for the more rigorous classes at more selective institutions and do not qualify for admission. Lower achievement during high school—as measured by standardized test scores or grade-point average—strongly

42. See Bound, Lovenheim, and Turner (2010) and Goldrick-Rab (2010) for discussions of institutional characteristics of schools attended by low-income students that might impede completion. Completion rates at community colleges overall are much lower than at four-year colleges and universities, though it is not clear that community colleges vary much from one another in these characteristics, once we control for the attributes of the students who attend (Clotfelter and others 2013).

43. The fact that state funding of higher education is regressive, because subsidies tilt so heavily to the flagship institutions, was first noted by Hansen and Weisbrod (1969).

predicts who enrolls in a community college rather than a four-year institution. The greater concentration of needier and less academically prepared students in community colleges exacerbates the resource gap that exists purely because of the distribution of funding.

But even allowing for academic achievement, poor students enroll in lower-quality programs much more frequently than nonpoor students. Low-income students in the top achievement quartile are significantly less likely to enroll in a four-year college than their peers from other families and less likely to complete degrees wherever they enroll. This greater tendency of low-income students to enroll in less selective colleges is often called *undermatching*.[44]

The evidence suggests that inadequate information contributes significantly to undermatching, at least among the small group of students qualified for the most selective institutions in the country, many of which promise their low-income students a free or close-to-free education.[45] Providing small amounts of information customized to individual situations can have fairly large effects on enrollment decisions.[46] A wide range of other interventions, such as requiring all students to take the ACT exam or providing them intensive counseling about college choice, appear to have similarly sizable effects on where low-income students apply and enroll.[47]

A few other factors no doubt also contribute to the concentration of disadvantaged students, including those with strong academic preparation, in nonselective, underresourced institutions. While some students appear not to be fully aware of available financial aid, even the net prices at many colleges are out of their reach. The maximum Pell Grant is currently under $6,000 per year, which is well below

44. See Bowen, Chingos, and McPherson (2009).

45. Roderick and others (2008); Bowen, Chingos, and McPherson (2009); Hoxby and Avery (2013).

46. Hoxby and Turner (2013).

47. See the study by Hoxby and Turner (2013). Castleman and Goodman (2014) and Goodman (2012) find that simple rules, such as requiring all students in a state to take the ACT test, significantly raise college attendance, improve the average quality of the colleges they choose, and increase completion rates by providing more information to students about their own potential to do well in good colleges and universities.

typical four-year in-state tuition. Many students are also eligible for state grant aid, which varies dramatically from state to state. The generosity of institutional grant aid at many of the better-resourced public flagship and selective private colleges and universities sometimes makes it cheaper for low-income students who can get into these selective colleges to attend them than to enroll even in community colleges. But for the majority of low-income students, any college choice involves a significant amount of unmet need, particularly when living expenses are added to the costs of tuition, fees, and books.

At least partly for financial reasons, some lower- and even middle-income students choose to attend a community college for two years and plan to transfer to a four-year college. But a relatively small percentage of these students successfully manage the transition, especially in the face of insufficient academic or career counseling. Judith Scott-Clayton has compared many community colleges to "shapeless rivers" in which students flow along with very little structure or guidance, with academic outcomes suffering accordingly.[48] We return to this issue, and its effects on labor market outcomes, in chapter 3.

Some analysts find that many community college students fail to successfully make major transitions at key points in their schooling, or to gain the academic momentum that is important for finishing degree programs.[49] Considerable evidence suggests that the likelihood of completing a bachelor's degree is lower among those who begin at a community college than among similar students who begin at a four-year college or university.[50] Many students who transfer still enroll at nonselective four-year colleges, particularly those located near their community college.[51] Nonetheless, bachelor's degree

48. See Scott-Clayton (2011b).

49. See Jenkins and Cho (2012) for a discussion of difficulties with transitions, and also the importance of getting into a specific program of study, for many students. Tinto (2013) writes about the importance of students gaining "momentum" toward completion in their studies.

50. For evidence on this issue see Andrews, Li, and Lovenheim (2012); Leigh and Gill (2003); and Light and Strayer (2000).

51. See Backes and Velez (2014) for evidence from Florida that most community college students who transfer to four-year colleges go to the college located nearest to their community college (and to their home).

completion rates of community college students who do manage to transfer compare favorably with those of similar students who begin their studies at those institutions.[52]

On the other hand, it is possible that some students might be overmatched (or *mismatched*) to more selective institutions than they can academically handle. This allegation has been leveled against affirmative action programs for African American and Hispanic students in college admissions. But the evidence on this point is mixed, at best. Only colleges and universities in the top quintile of schools, as measured by average SAT scores, practice significant affirmative action in admissions. These schools have very high graduation rates, probably due to their superior resources as well as their selectivity, and tend to have higher graduation rates for minority students than do lower-ranked institutions.[53] The evidence in more specific contexts, such as selective law schools, continues to be debated.[54]

What about For-Profit Colleges?

Proprietary or for-profit colleges, which accounted for only about 2 percent of undergraduate enrollment as recently as 1997, grew rapidly and enrolled 1.7 million undergraduates—10 percent of the total—in 2010.[55] In the past several years, the sector's enrollment has

52. Bowen, Chingos, and McPherson (2009).

53. Kane (1998).

54. Antonovics and Backes (2012) and Hinrichs (2010) also analyze what happens to minority student quality and graduation rates when states ban affirmative action. They find either constant or rising quality among these students and slightly higher graduation rates at the flagship colleges among those who still attend, but overall minority attainment rates are lower than before because of the drop in minority enrollment. Evidence of "mismatch" in law and other specific graduate programs or more difficult college majors such as STEM fields can still be found, though the former is controversial (Sanders and Taylor 2012; Arcidiacono and Lovenheim 2016).

55. NCES (2016, table 303.70).

declined as labor market opportunities have improved and problems at some of these institutions have garnered attention.[56]

About half of all undergraduate students are independent—either age twenty-four or older or with other circumstances that cause their eligibility for federal student aid to be based only on their own resources. At community colleges, 60 percent of the students are independent, but in the for-profit sector the proportion is 80 percent. As table 2-4 indicates, almost half of the dependent students enrolled in for-profit institutions are from the lowest family income quartile of undergraduates, and only 11 percent are from the top quartile. Looked at another way, 10 percent of students from the lowest family income quartile and 20 percent of independent students—and much smaller shares of dependent students from more affluent families—were enrolled in the for-profit sector in 2011–12.

For-profit institutions market to and recruit students aggressively, especially low-income students with Pell Grants, and since the implementation of the post-9/11 GI bill, veterans. The sector now accounts for 18 percent of the country's Pell Grant recipients, a decline from 25 percent in 2009–10 and 2010–11.[57] Low-income students at for-profit colleges borrow much more than those at community colleges because of the higher tuition rates they charge, because they are more likely to complete applications for federal financial aid, and because many community colleges do not participate in the federal student loan program.[58]

For-profit colleges sometimes do a better job than other institutions of preparing students for occupations in sectors with strong labor market demand.[59] For example, 53 percent of students who enroll in certificate programs in for-profit colleges complete these

56. National Student Clearinghouse (2014).

57. U.S. Department of Education (2015, table 5).

58. Institute for College Access and Success (2014).

59. James Rosenbaum (2002) has argued that the proprietary occupational colleges, by providing structure and assistance to students to finish their programs and obtain jobs using their skills, have a much better track record than community colleges on completion rates and earnings. But Deming, Goldin, and

Table 2-4. *Distribution of Students by Dependency Status and
Family Income at For-Profit and Community Colleges, 2011–12*

Percent

	For-profit	Community college	All undergraduates	Enrolled in for-profit sector
Independent	80	60	51	20
Dependent	20	40	49	5
Family income among dependents				
Lowest quartile	46	31	25	10
Second quartile	26	28	24	6
Third quartile	17	25	25	4
Highest quartile	11	17	25	2

Source: NCES (2012).

Note: The percentages of dependent and independent students within each institutional category add up to 100 percent, as do the percentages across family income groups among the dependent students.

programs, while only 42 percent do so at community colleges. Completion rates in associate degree programs are more comparable at the two kinds of institutions—28 percent at for-profit colleges and 21 percent at public two-year colleges after six years.

On the other hand, completion rates in bachelor's degree programs at for-profit colleges are much lower than in public and private nonprofit institutions; students leave with much higher levels of debt and are more likely to default on their loans. The earnings of for-profit degree recipients are similar to or a bit lower than those of public college graduates, despite the higher costs of attending, so the return to the investments made by students is clearly lower. It is little wonder that for-profit institutions are sometimes considered "nimble critters" but also "agile predators."[60] We discuss these issues more fully in chapters 3 and 4.

Katz (2013) describe a much more mixed track record of the large for-profit colleges.

60. See Deming, Goldin, and Katz (2011); Deming and others (2015).

The controversial nature of for-profit colleges, along with the weaker outcomes among their students, who receive considerable public student aid money, has led to calls for more regulation. Lobbyists for the sector successfully challenged in court attempts by the Obama administration to implement regulations before weakened standards for continued participation in federal financial aid programs were finally implemented in 2015. The sector lobbies Congress very effectively, as we discuss in chapter 6.

One More Issue: What Do Students Study in College?

After students have chosen to enroll in an institution, what they choose to study affects not only what they will earn later but also their college completion rates. Students with different levels of achievement will likely choose different major fields. For instance, we expect the STEM fields to attract higher-achieving students at the bachelor's degree level, especially in math and science. Gender is also a factor, with some fields heavily dominated by either males or females. Similarly, students with different preferences—for math/science, the liberal arts and other academic subjects, or fields that are more directly occupational in nature—will pursue different paths.

Figure 2-4 reports the distribution of students at each of four types of postsecondary institutions—public four-year, private non-profit four-year, for-profit, and public two-year—across five broad categories of majors: undeclared, STEM, social sciences and humanities, occupational, and other. The major reported is the latest one declared. Table 2-5 presents data on these chosen fields by dependency status of students, family income among dependent students, and high school GPA. Students in the "undeclared" category in table 2-5 did not declare a major when they enrolled and left school without choosing a specific area of study.

A number of patterns are clear in these data. The distribution of majors at public and private nonprofit four-year colleges and universities is similar, although social science and humanities majors are somewhat more prevalent in the private sector and occupational fields are more common in public colleges.

Figure 2-4. Last Declared Major, by Type of Institution

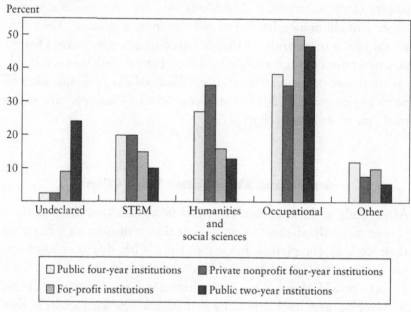

Percent

Source: NCES (2009, PowerStats calculations).

But students at public two-year and particularly for-profit institutions are less likely to concentrate in the humanities and social sciences and more likely to be in occupational areas than students at four-year colleges and universities. Looking at more detailed occupational categories (within these data) than those presented in the figure and table reveals that for-profit institutions have more business and STEM majors, but fewer in health care, than two-year public colleges.

Perhaps most striking is the fact that nearly one-quarter of students at public two-year colleges never declare a major. Many students leave school without a degree before declaring a major. But other tabulations of these data (not presented here) on the breakdowns of majors for those who have completed degrees tell a similar story: while virtually all bachelor's degree recipients have reported majors, 7 percent of associate degree recipients—and 10 percent of those who earned associate degrees at public two-year colleges—have no major reported. These students are probably intending to transfer

Table 2-5. *Distribution of Last Declared Major among Students Who First Enrolled in 2003–04*

Percent

	Major when last enrolled 2009 (condensed)				
	Undeclared	STEM[a]	Humanities and social sciences	Occupational[b]	Other
Total	7	17	25	41	10
Dependency status 2003–04					
Dependent	6	19	27	39	10
Independent	16	9	14	52	8
Dependent Students' family income 2003–04					
Less than $32,000	9	18	23	41	9
$32,000–59,999	7	17	26	40	10
$60,000–91,999	5	20	28	37	11
$92,000 or more	3	19	30	37	11
High school grade point average (GPA)					
Less than 3.0	10	13	23	42	11
3.0–3.4	7	14	27	41	10
3.5 or higher	3	23	28	36	9
Missing	15	14	16	46	8

Source: NCES (2009, Power Stats calculations).

a. STEM = science, technology, engineering, mathematics.

b. Occupational major consists of education, business, health, and vocational-technical enrollments.

to a four-year college and expect to declare a major there. But for too many of them, this never happens.

When combined with social science and humanities, nearly 40 percent of community college students—and one-quarter of those who earn associate degrees in this sector—do not have a major they can expect to generate any substantial labor market payoff, an issue we pursue further in chapter 3. This is particularly disturbing since labor market rewards are a large part of the motivation of many students enrolling in community colleges.

It is important to remember that these reported majors are at the last institution in which these students enrolled, and are measured up to six years after initial enrollment. At that point, it is unlikely that many two-year college students will transfer to a four-year institution and earn a bachelor's degree. These data suggest that many community college students are adrift, gaining little information or guidance and making little progress while they are enrolled for lengthy periods of time.

From table 2-5, we see that the tendency to not declare a major is higher for lower-income, independent (older), and lower-achieving students than for others. These students usually receive less guidance in choosing a postsecondary path than recent high school graduates and those from more affluent backgrounds. They know that college is supposed to provide a path to economic security, but they do not know how to choose among the dizzying array of choices, and they may not understand that all college degrees do not carry the same weight in the job market. While the lack of direction partly reflects the greater concentrations of older and low-income students at community colleges, these differences also appear within the population of those enrolled at community colleges.

High school achievement and dependency status are highly correlated with choice of major, as is family income to a lesser extent. High achievers are much more likely to choose the STEM fields and less likely to choose occupational fields. Independent students have high concentrations in specific occupations, especially health fields, perhaps reflecting the immediate job payoffs they seek. Dependent students from higher-income families also choose the STEM fields, as well as social sciences, more frequently than others and the occupational fields somewhat less frequently, at least partly reflecting their greater concentration in four-year colleges and universities.

Overall, students choose very different fields of study at different kinds of institutions, depending on both their high school achievement levels and their dependency status (which reflects age). The high percentage of students who leave community college without a declared major—either with or without a degree—bodes poorly for their labor market outcomes. Too many older and disadvantaged students enroll without a clear purpose and leave without a credential.

We explore the implications of these chosen fields of study for subsequent earnings in chapter 3.

Conclusion

This chapter focuses on the relatively low postsecondary completion and attainment rates of students with weak academic preparation, older students, those from low-income backgrounds, and black and Hispanic students relative to white and Asian students. It also highlights differences in majors across types of institutions and groups of students, and the problem that 40 percent of community college students leave with no declared major or one in the humanities or social sciences.

Disadvantaged students have lower completion rates partially because they are more concentrated in community and for-profit colleges with low graduation rates and in other poorly resourced institutions, but the completion gaps exist within all sectors of postsecondary education. Weaker academic preparation among disadvantaged students is clearly a major explanation of these differences. But other factors contribute to their lower completion rates as well, including a lack of clear goals and direction, financial barriers, poor information and social capital, and pressure to work full time or deal with crises while supporting families.

We discuss the effects of low completion on labor market outcomes in chapter 3, and its relationship to the financial costs of higher education and student debt in chapter 4, before turning to potential policy solutions in part II.

3

Which College Credentials Does the Labor Market Reward?

For many students who attend college, especially those from disadvantaged backgrounds, a primary motivation is the hope of higher earnings afterward. And, on average, those who earn a college degree in the United States find themselves handsomely rewarded in the job market. But as the previous chapter discusses, Americans attend a wide range of postsecondary institutions, choose many different fields of study, have very mixed success in completing their courses of study, and when they do succeed, earn a wide variety of credentials.

How does the job market reward these highly varied opportunities, choices, and outcomes? How well does the labor market reward associate degrees and other credentials below the level of a bachelor's degree, such as occupational certificates? Do returns to a two-year degree or a vocational credential vary by field, as they do for a bachelor's degree? And, for the many students who earn some college credits but do not complete their degree programs, are there labor market rewards as well?

To answer these questions we use administrative data on students from the state of Florida, during the period 2000–12. The national data discussed in chapter 2 do not follow students into the labor market for a long enough time to provide insight into the returns to different educational paths. In contrast, for certain high school cohorts, the Florida data contain academic records for every student who attended a public postsecondary institution there, including every course taken, grades earned, credits received, major chosen, and credentials attained. We can also link these to data on work experience and labor market earnings during and after college. Since we also have data on these students during their K–12 years, we can control statistically for earlier achievement and cognitive skills to estimate the effects of college outcomes on subsequent earnings.

Are the education and earnings outcomes of Florida students and workers representative of the nation as a whole? For various reasons, patterns in Florida are likely to be quite similar, although not identical, to those in other states. Earnings in Florida are somewhat lower than the national average, but the gaps in earnings by level of education are similar.[1] Studies relying on data from other states similar to the Florida data on which we report yield conclusions consistent with ours.[2]

We begin with a broad overview from the economics literature on the theoretical role of expected earnings in how individuals choose their levels of education and fields of study, and on the statistical evidence about the returns to higher education in the U.S. job market over the past three decades. Then we briefly describe the Florida data and present results on how well the labor market rewards various college outcomes and experiences. We focus on the issue of differential returns across credentials and fields of study to better understand why certain gaps in earnings persist over time.

This discussion lays the groundwork for a review of policy options to improve labor market rewards, especially for disadvantaged students, in the second half of the book.

---

1. Lower earnings levels in Florida than elsewhere in the United States on average, seem largely accounted for by the larger Hispanic population in Florida and its lower levels of educational attainment. But the earnings gaps that we present below across educational categories in Florida are roughly similar to those observed broadly for the United States in Autor (2014).

2. Jepsen, Troske, and Coomes (2014); Stevens, Kurlaender, and Grosz (2015); and Bahr and others (2015) use data from Kentucky, California, and Michigan, respectively. See also Center for Analysis of Postsecondary Education and Employment (CAPSEE) for data on California, Michigan, North Carolina, Ohio, and Virginia.

Enrollment in Higher Education: What Do Economic Models Suggest?

Many economic models begin with the idea that schooling is an investment that individuals make in their "human capital" to maximize their future earnings, much as they would invest in financial capital like stocks and bonds, or other assets such as real estate, to maximize unearned income.[3] Of course, these models make many assumptions to simplify the analysis; in reality, people have motivations besides just higher earnings for entering higher education, and their knowledge of how their education choices will affect their future earnings is limited at best. Moreover, this approach underemphasizes the different constraints individuals face and the ways in which limited information and opportunities shape lives. Although the vision of potential students as fully informed actors weighing the long-term costs and benefits of their choices is far from realistic, the model offers a way to think about how rational actors would behave and what the implications are for actual decisionmaking processes.

Figure 3-1 illustrates how labor market factors might affect the investment decisions of individuals, and vice versa. A typical individual faces a decision about whether or not to attend college and obtain a new degree. A completed degree would open up a future of higher earnings, the additional value of which must be discounted to present value and compared with the immediate costs of obtaining the degree, including tuition, fees, books, additional expenses, and lost earnings while in college. If the expected additional return from schooling exceeds the cost of attending—including both financial and nonfinancial costs and benefits—the student will, according to this model, choose to enroll.

This decision is heavily influenced by the earnings of typical high school graduates and college graduates with similar degrees, as shown in panel B, which compares forgone earnings (the lower shaded box) to the college earnings premium (the higher shaded box). But the relative earnings of the two categories of workers in the market are, in turn, affected by the sum of all individual decisions on whether or

3. See Schultz (1961) and especially Becker (1967) for the original versions of this model.

Figure 3-1. Investment Decisions and Labor Outcomes

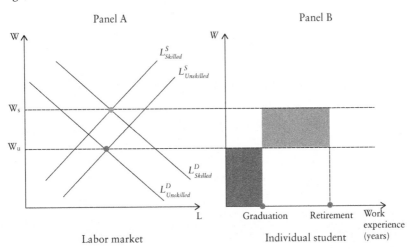

Note: W and L represent wages and employment levels respectively in the diagram. "SK" and "UK" refer to skilled and unskilled workers respectively, such as those with and without college degrees.

not to enroll. The greater the number of individuals who earn a college degree, all else equal, the greater the supply of college-educated workers relative to the supply of those with only a high school diploma. Over time, as more people complete college credentials in response to the higher expected earnings, the greater supply will drive down the relative earnings of those workers, discouraging more students from enrolling, until we arrive at the long-run equilibrium point in the market at which, in theory, the optimal number of students enroll in college.

Of course, at any point in time, the optimal level of education will differ across individuals. Enrollment in college will make sense for some but not others—perhaps because some students have a greater taste for or ability in the classroom, and because the costs of attending college are more easily borne by some students than by others. As we noted in chapter 2, those from higher-income families with greater liquid assets will face lower costs (or will bear the same costs more easily), as will those who have better access to credit in financial markets. And for students who feel pressure to earn income to support their families, the costs of forgoing work to attend college will be—or will feel—greater; they will be less likely to succeed in college if they continue to work full time.[4] Those with stronger academic tastes or abilities and those facing lower costs will attain more undergraduate and graduate degrees, increasing their lifetime earnings.

The market equilibrium can change over time owing to shifts in the demand for workers with different skills and levels of education. If, for example, economic forces like new technology and globalization shift demand from high school graduates to college graduates, market wages will rise for the latter relative to the former. The higher wage premium for college-educated workers, in turn, should encourage more students to enroll. Eventually, the outward shift in the supply of college graduates could offset the initial shift in demand, causing the relative wage of college graduates to return to its earlier level.

Economists Claudia Goldin and Lawrence Katz have argued that this process occurred in the first half of the twentieth century, when demand for high school graduates rose during the second Industrial Revolution.[5] The higher earnings of those who had these diplomas initially led to higher earnings inequality. But this, in turn, encouraged an increase in the supply of high school students and graduates in the next few decades, which tended to reduce the earnings premium enjoyed by high school graduates and lower overall inequality in the labor market.[6]

---

4. If low-income people apply a higher discount rate to future earnings because they have relatively greater income needs today, this would reduce the expected benefits of their investments in higher education today relative to its costs.

5. Goldin and Katz (2008).

6. The "second Industrial Revolution" refers to changes in production associated with the widespread adoption of electricity and its use in producing automobiles and a range of other appliances early in the twentieth century. The large increase in high school enrollments in the subsequent decades represented both private investment decisions and the public high school movement, in which free access to K–12 education became regarded as a right. Schooling to at least age sixteen is compulsory in every state in the United States. The large increase in the supply of high school graduates, along with other policies that were implemented after the Great Depression (such as the Wagner Act of 1935, which protected the rights of workers to unionize) and World War II, all generated a "Great Compression" of earnings inequality. The lower level of earnings inequality was fairly

A similar process has at least partly occurred in recent decades as well, with a rising college wage premium leading to rising college enrollment. But the enrollment response to the higher college wage premium since 1980 has been more limited—and college *attainment* increases have lagged behind rising *enrollments,* as completion rates have remained low. The inequality between higher-wage college graduates and lower-wage high school graduates has risen over time.

Why might college enrollment and attainment increases lag behind, despite the allure of higher relative wages for college-educated workers? Students who do not like school or are not attracted to the kinds of jobs that college graduates get are unlikely to enroll in college. Those who know that their academic skills are weak, which could make their college experiences unsuccessful and unpleasant, are also unlikely to enroll. Limited ability to pay, either real or perceived, might also interfere.

The labor market rewards to college might be an incentive for students to enroll, but several market failures could limit their ability to earn a credential. For instance, students with inadequate information about the labor market rewards of a college degree might be unaware that they could be accepted into and pay for a college where success rates are high. Some students might overestimate their ability to complete certain programs and then have disappointing results. Both circumstances seem to exist, with many low-income but high-achieving students enrolling in nonselective institutions, while lower-achieving students enter programs at a community or for-profit college, only to end up leaving without a credential or with a credential that does not lead to the hoped-for labor-market opportunities.

The fact that jobs in some fields, frequently including STEM and skilled technology occupations, are better compensated and easier to find than those in other fields will likely affect student choices to some extent. But students' poor preparation, lack of confidence, and sometimes distaste for math and science likely limit the extent to which STEM enrollments rise along with relative earnings in these fields.

---

stable in the postwar years, and even diminished in the 1970s, before rising dramatically after 1980.

Specific field of study is most important for sub-baccalaureate degrees and certificates designed to lead directly to the labor market. Students earning bachelor's degrees and considering graduate school can better afford to indulge their purely academic tastes in college. And it is important to note that a strong liberal arts education—with the broad intellectual development and skill creation that such education entails—does generate labor market rewards right after college; in addition, the skills and habits of mind fostered are critical to performance in a wide range of occupations.[7]

The fact that students have imperfect information about the requirements for success in different fields limits their ability to make optimal choices. Young students without good sources of information might lock themselves out of certain technical fields by taking fewer math and science courses than they later wish they had.[8] Students in schools with low-quality teachers or limited capacity to offer the necessary classes, during either their K–12 or their college years, will also suffer.

Finally, there are important lags between the time when students *choose* a field of study, based on *current* labor market circumstances, and when they ultimately join the labor force. These time lags, plus the failure of students to anticipate the effects of higher enrollments on relative earnings in a field, could cause enrollment in some fields to overshoot what the market can handle, driving down earnings. Wage declines, in turn, will cause fewer students to enroll and lead to earnings increases in the future. These forces can thus lead to oscillations

7. To the extent that a liberal arts education generates "twenty-first-century skills" such as critical thinking and communication skills that employers value, it should raise earnings substantially, and perhaps for a longer period of time than more specific occupational skills, the value of which diminishes over time as workers change jobs. But whether or not employers believe that liberal arts graduates have these skills, especially when they graduate from less-selective institutions, is also questionable. See the report by the National Research Council (2012), as well as more popular treatments of these issues by Bruni (2015) and Zakaria (2015). Reich (2015) offers a more critical view of the traditional liberal arts model and the costs it imposes on students and families.

8. See Altonji, Blom, and Meghir (2012).

over time in wages and salaries, even when demand in a field or profession is stable.[9]

Fluctuation in demand in a given field over time—as seen in the rising demand for energy workers resulting from the shale oil and gas boom during the years 2011–14, followed by declining demand as energy prices dropped—exacerbates the difficulty of choosing fields that will have high labor market returns. Wages will rise in response to short-term shortages or fall in response to short-term surpluses, affecting the choices students make. This adjustment process can go on for years, depending on how quickly workers gain new skills or migrate to other fields of study or geographic regions where demand is stronger. Longer-term trends in the job market, such as a declining demand for lawyers, could also generate job market imbalances that persist over time.[10]

College Degrees and the Labor Market since 1980

During the 1970s, the average earnings differential between high school graduates and college graduates was relatively small. Many young baby boomers had attended college during the previous decade—in many cases, for men, to avoid being drafted for combat duty in Vietnam. Richard Freeman of Harvard University wrote, at

---

9. One such model of labor markets that requires extensive higher education generates a "cobweb" in supply to these occupations, along with oscillating wages. See Freeman (1971).

10. There are differences of opinion about whether a weaker market for lawyers is primarily cyclical or represents a long-term structural shift. Stevens (2012) documents the declining labor market fortunes of new law school graduates in the past decade. Henderson and Zahorsky (2011) and Tamanaha (2012) argue that globalization, technological change, and other factors have generated a long-term decline in the demand for lawyers and in the relative salaries they will command. In contrast, McIntyre and Simkovic (2016) contend that, as of 2013, there was no evidence of a structural shift reducing the relative value of the law degree to below its historical average. The absolute decline in earnings and employment opportunities for lawyers, along with the increase in loan default rates, was typical of the economy as a whole.

the time, about the "overeducated American"; newspapers were filled with stories of unemployed college graduates, and even of those with graduate degrees who were driving taxicabs or waiting on tables in restaurants.

But after 1980 this pattern started to change. The gap between the earnings of high school graduates and college graduates began to rise and had roughly doubled in magnitude by the year 2000. During the early years of the twenty-first century, the earnings premium stabilized at a high level. Figure 3-2 illustrates the widening earnings gap between workers with different levels of education since the 1970s. On average, women's gains (adjusted for inflation) have exceeded those of men, and the earnings of less-educated men have actually declined over this period. The steepest gains have occurred for those with the most education: those with degrees beyond the bachelor's degree have experienced the greatest gains in earnings over time, while those with some college but no bachelor's degree—and particularly those with some college but no degree at all—have experienced barely any gains.[11]

Because of a weak overall labor market, most workers, including those with bachelor's degrees, have seen flat or declining wages since 2000; real earnings have risen only for those with graduate degrees.[12]

What explains the growing labor market returns to those with a college credential? Most economists agree that these changes result from the interaction of labor market forces and institutional structures, though disagreement remains on the relative importance of these two sets of factors in explaining changes over time.

Those who stress labor market forces point to *skill-based technical change* (SBTC) and *globalization* as two forces that have caused shifts in the demand for labor away from less-educated workers toward

11. It is important to note that most workers with "some college" have not completed any college credential, so the earnings of workers in this category lag behind those earned by workers with an associate degree.

12. The patterns of change in relative earnings over time likely understate differences by education, since the focus is on earnings rather than compensation, where the latter includes the value of health benefits that more-educated workers are more likely than less-educated workers to have.

Figure 3-2. Changes in Real Wage Levels of Full-Time U.S. Workers by Sex and Education, 1963–2012

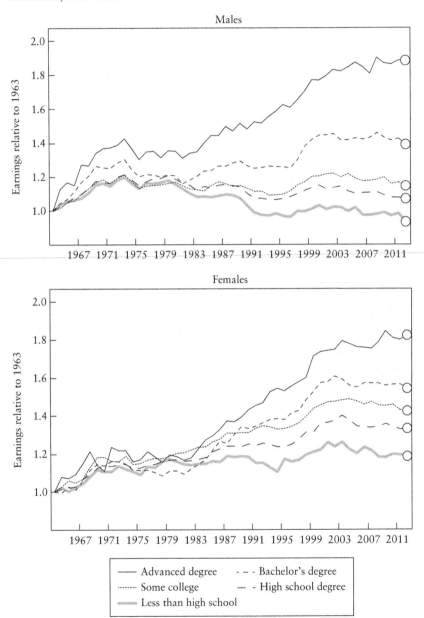

Source: Reprinted with permission from Autor (2014).

more-educated ones.[13] SBTC theory suggests that the growing role of computers in the 1980s and advances in digitization and the Internet in the 1990s and beyond have reduced the demand for less-educated labor, for which computers can *substitute* in production; these forces raise the demand for certain skilled workers, like engineers or technicians, to which they are *complements*. Those facing the greatest displacements are less-educated workers who perform fairly routine tasks, such as those on assembly lines and clerical workers.

Globalization can take a variety of forms: greater imports of goods, immigration of workers, and offshoring of specific tasks or services. While not all of these forces individually have had large effects on workers, they all tend to reinforce the effects of SBTC. All have tended to raise demand for skilled relative to unskilled workers. For instance, less-educated immigrants to the United States are seen as partial substitutes for less-educated native-born workers but as complements to the highly educated.[14] And, while globalization was seen in the 1990s as having weaker effects than SBTC on labor demand, many observers view its effects as stronger since 2000, especially given the rise in imports of manufactured goods from China and the increasing ability of firms to outsource or offshore work.[15]

Interestingly, there is some question about whether the pace of shifting demand in favor of more-educated workers really accelerated after 1980. What is more certain is that the growth in the *supply* of such workers slowed in that period, and that the demand for skilled workers relative to their supply is what really drove the growing gap between workers with and without higher education. Claudia Goldin and Lawrence Katz, in particular, note the contrast between the strong growth in the supply of high school graduates in the United States after the 1920s and its tendency to equalize or compress wages during the

13. Autor, Donohue, and Schwab (2006).

14. See Borjas (2003) for an analysis that suggests stronger substitution between less-educated native-born workers and immigrants; in contrast, Ottaviano and Peri (2006) finds weaker substitution between them, and therefore weaker competition and negative effects of immigration on the earnings of the native born.

15. See Autor, Dorn, and Hanson (2014).

1930s and 1940s, and the lagging growth of college graduates in the 1980s and 1990s, when labor market inequality grew dramatically.

In recent years the wage premium has not declined, but it has leveled off, at least temporarily, at a historically high level. There is some evidence that demand for workers with a bachelor's degree has stopped increasing, or even declined a bit, while the supply of these workers has risen over time.[16] Some labor economists now argue that the flattening of the college wage premium since 2000 (and of real wages for college graduates in general) reflects the fact that the relative supply of graduates has finally caught up with demand.[17] If this is true, it raises questions about whether policies to continue increasing the supply of college graduates over time will diminish the payoff to higher education. The closing of the gap between demand and supply could cause some college graduates to have difficulty finding employment in the short term. The gaps in earnings across workers with different levels of education could narrow, potentially diminishing income inequality, but making the investment in education less valuable for some graduates.

Other labor economists have argued that supply and demand cannot explain labor market changes without incorporating institutional forces. Explaining why inequality grew rapidly in the 1980s, and why it has increased more in the United States than in other countries, requires understanding the role of weakening institutions like collective bargaining and the minimum wage.[18] Indeed, private sector unionization has fallen from about 35 percent to just above 6 percent. While public sector unions grew rapidly in the 1970s, the pattern of growth was highly unequal across states, and since that time union membership has been flat or declining.[19]

In addition, the statutory level of the federal minimum wage, relative to the median wage of workers in the economy, has declined over

16. Beaudry, Green, and Sand (2013); Autor (2014).

17. See Autor (2014) and also Beaudry, Green, and Sand (2013).

18. Card and DiNardo (2002).

19. See Farber (2005) for a comparison of the very different forces driving trends in public and private union membership in recent decades; Hirsch (2008) attributes at least part of the declining private sector rate to growing labor and product market competition over time.

time, likely contributing to growing inequality. An increasing tendency of firms to outsource their human resources might also contribute to rising inequality.[20]

Regardless of the exact magnitude of each factor, this mix of market and institutional forces has clearly raised the gaps in earnings between workers with only a high school education and those with some type of college credential. But a few additional complications are also important. First, the average reward to a particular level of education masks a great deal of variation across fields. In particular, some workers with STEM credentials—ranging from engineers, doctors, and math/science PhDs to technicians at the sub-baccalaureate level—are paid well above average for their degree levels, while those in the arts and humanities, teachers, and social service workers are paid considerably less.[21]

Furthermore, the *average* return to a credential for a worker today might be higher or lower than the *marginal* returns for new workers, for a variety of reasons.[22] Ongoing labor market weakness in the wake of the Great Recession might exacerbate the difficulties of new college graduates, especially in lower-demand fields, leading the benefits for the newer graduates to fall short of those observed in the fairly recent past.[23]

Finally, the rising skill premiums in the labor market have not been evenly distributed. Instead, employment and earnings growth

---

20. David Weil (2014) calls this the "fissuring" of the workplace and discusses the potential effects on wage levels. See Dube (2014) for evidence on the declining relative value of the federal minimum wage over time, though Neumark, Salas, and Wascher (2014) believe any minimum wage has stronger negative effects on employment than Dube does.

21. See Carnevale, Strohl, and Melton (2011) or Owen and Sawhill (2013).

22. On the one hand, the marginal students might face better returns, if they are well qualified for postsecondary work and had not enrolled before because of financial or informational problems. On the other hand, if they are less qualified for such work and have more difficulty completing their credential programs, their returns might be lower. Card (1999) reviews evidence showing that, on average, lower-income students benefit more from college credentials than middle- or higher-income students, though this might not be the case for those on the margin now of completing or not completing a credential.

23. See Kahn (2010).

have been more negative since the 1990s in the middle of the wage distribution—in the third through eighth deciles—than at either the top or the bottom.[24] And the Great Recession, by hitting industries like construction and manufacturing so hard, and perhaps permanently, has likely also contributed to ongoing wage inequality.[25]

Why have wages fallen more in the middle than at the bottom of the wage distribution? The often routine tasks performed by middle-wage workers, especially in the 1980s and 1990s, made it easier for digital technologies to replace them than many low-wage service sector workers, whose personal interactions with customers and clients are harder to digitize. It is easier to replace an assembly line worker or a typist than a childcare provider or elder caregiver.[26]

This story does not necessarily imply that helping workers to improve their middle-level skills—perhaps with an associate degree or other postsecondary credential—is not warranted; if anything, it strengthens the case for helping them. For one thing, the decline in earnings of those with middle-level wages, while other workers' wages have grown, has been most concentrated among production and clerical workers who often earned middle-level wages despite having low levels of education (usually a high school diploma or less). Unionism and other specific institutional factors (including minimum wage laws) may have elevated their earnings in earlier periods but do so less frequently now.

But there is another set of "middle-skill" or "middle-wage" workers for whom employment and earnings have actually risen in recent years, and those trends are likely to continue.[27] These include technicians and other skilled workers in health care, advanced manufacturing, information technology (IT), and transportation and logistics; they also include sales reps and managers at the higher end of retail, hospitality, and many other service industries.[28]

24. Autor (2010).
25. See Jaimovich and Siu (2012).
26. Autor (2010).
27. Holzer (2015b).
28. Holzer and Lerman (2009).

Furthermore, baby-boomer retirements will likely exacerbate middle-skill shortfalls over the next decade or two, perhaps generating a corrective force to the polarization observed recently. And workers with a middle-skill postsecondary *credential* (as opposed to some college but no degree) will likely continue to earn more than those with high school only, especially in STEM and other high-demand fields, such as health care and elder care.[29]

How all of this will play out in the future is hard to say. According to some observers, new digital technologies will grow so dramatically in the coming years that their labor market displacement effects will reach much higher into the education spectrum, with many workers, even among those with a bachelor's degree or higher, increasingly at risk.[30] The future pace and distribution of such changes in the labor market remain highly uncertain. Some occupations requiring at least a bachelor's degree might see more displacement than others requiring less education, depending on the exact skills involved. On the other hand, those without postsecondary education, who are most limited in their ability to shift to areas with new demand, will remain particularly vulnerable.

What Do the Data Tell Us about Returns to College in the Job Market?

Our results on labor market rewards for different kinds of postsecondary credentials are based on administrative records of students in Florida.[31] We study administrative data here, as opposed to longitudinal survey data, because they contain great detail on student experiences and outcomes in public high schools and colleges for the entire

---

29. See Holzer (2010); Holzer (2015b).

30. See Brynjolffson and McAfee (2014) for an analysis that predicts very large displacements in the labor market associated with new applications of digital technologies; Levy and Murnane (2013) predict milder effects. The notion that the impacts of digital technologies on the production process have been overstated also appears in Gordon (2014).

31. The data presented in this section are drawn heavily from Backes, Holzer, and Velez (2015).

population, including all courses taken, grades and credits received, and credentials earned. The data also include extensive information about postschool labor market earnings.

The confidential individual-level data that we use have been made available to a limited number of researchers, both in Florida and elsewhere.[32] They reflect a growing tendency of states, with support from the federal government, to use these data to provide information to the public about student outcomes at different colleges, so that students might make better choices about where to enroll. Some states have also begun using these data to hold colleges more accountable for the student outcomes they generate, basing at least some funding provided to public colleges on these outcomes.[33]

The findings presented here cover two cohorts of Florida students: those who were attending either eighth or tenth grade in Florida in 1997–98 and any who joined those classes later. The data on postsecondary and earnings histories run through 2012. If these students graduated from high school on time (in 2000 or 2002) and immediately enrolled in college, they would be finishing college and graduating as early as 2002 from two-year programs or 2004 from four-year colleges. Of course, many students take a break from school rather than enrolling immediately after high school or take much longer than two or four years to finish, if they do so at all. The data include information on later enrollments as well. This relatively wide window of time enables us to explore labor market outcomes and experiences, whether before, during, or after college, when we merge the education data with labor market data.

---

32. Early papers by Jacobson and Mokher (2009) and Furchtgott-Roth, Jacobson, and Mokher (2009) also use the Florida data; more recent work by Jepsen, Troske, and Coomes (2014), Stevens, Kurlaender, and Grosz (2015), and Bahr and others (2015) use data from Kentucky, California, and Michigan, respectively.

33. See College Measures (2015) as an example of how these data could help students make more-informed choices about which institutions to attend. Making these data available at the state level has been strongly encouraged by the federal government through its grant programs for School Longitudinal Data Systems (SLDS) and the Workforce Data Quality Initiative (WDQI) of the National Skills Coalition (Zinn and Van Kleunen 2014).

In the discussion that follows, we examine higher education outcomes for students who enrolled in three types of programs in Florida public colleges and universities—those leading to an occupational certificate, an associate degree (associate of arts: AA; associate of science: AS; or associate of applied science: AAS), or a bachelor's (BA) degree. The first two of these credentials are available at twenty-eight community colleges in Florida, the largest of which is Miami Dade College.[34] Students can pursue a BA and more advanced degrees at Florida's twelve universities, and the community colleges have also recently started to offer some bachelor's degrees.[35]

The certificate programs include several categories: most are associate in science certificates (ASCs) and vocational certificates. All are credit bearing, enabling students to be eligible for federal Pell Grants and other financial aid, though only the ASC credits count toward AA and BA degrees. The other categories, such as applied technology diploma (ATD) and advanced technical certificate (ATC), as well as apprenticeship certificate, are much smaller in number and generate career and technical credits that can be used only toward attainment of these certificates.

The data follow students who pursued graduate studies in a Florida public university after college and students who began their college studies at a community college and then transferred to a four-year school. We have data on each course in which postsecondary students enrolled and every grade they received. We can measure the credits they earned in each class completed and the total number they accumulated by the end of each semester. We can identify the field of study they have chosen and whether or not they have the relevant degree in each semester for which we have data.

34. Miami Dade Community College is now known as Miami Dade College, since it offers bachelor's as well as associate degrees.

35. By some definitions, Florida's community colleges that offer some bachelor's degrees are now four-year colleges. We continue to call them community colleges and differentiate between colleges offering predominantly bachelor's degrees or higher and those where the balance is tilted toward shorter-term credentials.

The data include the gender and race of each student, as well as whether they are U.S.- or foreign-born. Although family income is not available, we know whether a student was eligible for free or reduced-price lunch (FRL), which we use as an indicator of whether the student comes from a low-income family.

The postsecondary educational data for each student have been merged with quarterly earnings data from the unemployment insurance (UI) records, which every employer must file with the state for all workers covered by the UI system—about 96 percent of all private nonfarm workers nationally.[36] The data cover wage and salary earnings but not tips or the value of fringe benefits such as health insurance, paid vacations, or employer contributions to pensions. We have these data for up to five years after workers completed their schooling.

Finally, our data have an advantage not shared by most administrative postsecondary data for other states: we also have access to the K–12 data for each Florida student. That means we can measure their grade-point averages in high school and their scores on the Florida Comprehensive Aptitude Test (FCAT). We can also identify the courses they took in high school, so we can measure the extent of their math and science backgrounds, as well as their academic performance in each class. Thus we are able not only to measure the effects of K–12 achievement on postsecondary enrollment and program completion, but also to test other hypotheses controlling for achievement, and to compare college outcomes and their determinants within and across high school achievement categories. Controlling for earlier achievement brings us closer to estimates of the true *causal* (rather than only correlational) effects of credentials on earnings, though we still cannot control for all factors that we would like to—especially noncognitive traits like motivation, self-control, and "grit."[37]

For all of the strengths of these very rich data, they also have some weaknesses that need to be acknowledged. We do not have data for

36. See Andersson, Holzer, and Lane (2005). The UI data do not include the self-employed or employees who are illegally paid cash with no official reporting.

37. Duckworth (2016).

those individuals who went to school out of the state or to a private college in Florida—including the for-profit schools that many low-income individuals now attend. We also lack employment data on those who left the state for work, the self-employed, and those who did not participate in the formal labor market. From other data, we know that only about 10 percent of Florida college students attend a college or university out of state, and only 5 percent attend a private institution within the state.[38] Thus our data are reasonably representative of the Florida traditional-age college population, but not quite the entire student population, and not of older adults returning to school.

In addition, our administrative data tell us less about the personal and family characteristics of students than do many other well-known survey data sets.[39] And, as noted earlier, our data are limited to the state of Florida, where demographic and higher education profiles differ to some extent from those in other states. A slightly lower percentage of students earn BAs in Florida than in other states, although sub-BA attainment is more comparable. Finally, we have no data on credentials earned at for-profit institutions, including industry-generated credentials such as Microsoft certifications, or on licenses that affect worker earnings.[40]

We can anticipate some problems that might bias our results in one direction or another and account for them when interpreting our findings. On one hand, students who attend a private nonprofit college in Florida or an out-of-state institution come disproportionately from higher-income families and tend to have higher-than-average high school achievement levels. Therefore any gaps we find between lower and higher achievers in our data might understate actual gaps. On the other hand, the students attending private for-profit institutions are likely to be from the lower portion of the income and academic achievement distributions.

38. See Backes, Holzer, and Velez (2015).

39. Data sets with more demographic details include the National Longitudinal Survey of Youth (NLSY), the National Educational Longitudinal Survey (NELS), and the Beginning Postsecondary Students Longitudinal Study (BPS), on which much of the information in chapter 2 is based.

40. Kleiner (2015).

Our Results: Average Returns to Credentials

The results we present here are drawn from our analysis of the determinants of the quarterly earnings of individuals in these Florida data. We focus on the oldest two cohorts of students—those who were in the eighth and tenth grades in 2000—to allow as many years as possible for students to complete their postsecondary education and get labor market experience. The samples on which our estimates are based are limited to individuals age eighteen and older from 2002 through 2012 and include only those quarters when they were not enrolled in school, since earnings among students are not representative of what they will earn when they have finished their schooling.

We analyze the percentage differences in earnings associated with different levels of postsecondary attainment relative to those of high school graduates with no postsecondary education. Our results come from regression equations, where we estimate the effect of educational attainment on individuals' quarterly earnings. We control statistically for differences in race, gender, low-income family background (as indicated by eligibility for free/reduced price lunch), math scores on the Florida Comprehensive Assessment Test (FCAT), years of labor market experience, and tenure with the current employer. We also control for additional degree programs in which students enrolled but did not complete.[41]

Figure 3-3 shows the effects on labor market earnings of obtaining career and technical certificates and associate, bachelor's, and graduate degrees. Each bar measures the effect of the credential on mean quarterly earnings, relative to having a high school diploma

41. In our estimated equations, quarterly earnings are the dependent variable, in natural log form. Because of this fact, we can interpret the estimated coefficients on education variables as approximately the percentage effects on earnings of a unit change in that variable. The equations include dummy variables for year, quarter, and which of the two cohorts each person is part of. Each observation is a person-quarter in which the person had labor market earnings after finishing their schooling. Experience and tenure appear in quadratic form, while FCAT scores are measured by a set of dummies for deciles of the achievement distribution. We control for year effects, since the years we include are a mix of pre– and post–Great Recession.

Figure 3-3a. Effects of Higher Education Credentials on Earnings of Young Workers

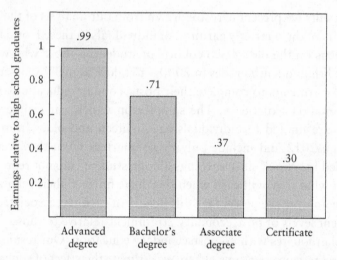

Note: Based on regressions using administrative data on postsecondary education and earnings from Florida. Controls are described in the text. The bars in this and subsequent figures represent the percentage increase in earnings associated with each credential, relative to those with high school diplomas only.

Figure 3-3b. Effects of Higher Education on Earnings: Earnings Premium Relative to High School Graduates

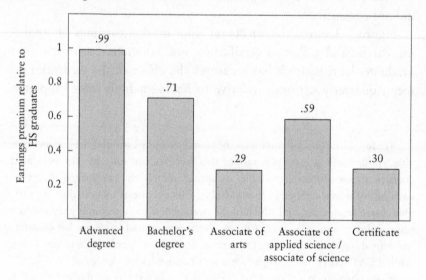

only. For example, an estimate of .2 would indicate that the particular credential raises earnings by 20 percent relative to a high school diploma. In Figure 3-3a we lump together all associate degrees at the community college level, while in Figure 3-3b we separate out the AS and AAS degrees from AAs. For students who earned multiple degrees—particularly those who earned an associate degree and then transferred to a college or university where they earned a BA—we consider only their highest level of attainment. For those with AA/AS degrees who transferred but failed to complete the BA, only the credentials they completed are recorded here.[42]

Both figures clearly indicate that earnings rise after students complete postsecondary credentials. Figure 3-3a indicates that career and technical certificates generate an increase of about 30 percent in earnings over a high school diploma. Since these credentials can often be earned in a year or less, this differential constitutes quite a strong average return in the labor market. Figure 3-3a indicates that the average earnings premium for an associate degree is nearly 40 percent, but figure 3-3b shows that individuals with the more technical AAS and AS degrees do better than those with other associate degrees. In fact, the almost 60 percent earnings premium for a technical associate degree is nearly as large as that for the average BA. The other associate degrees generate an earnings boost of under 30 percent—somewhat less than what a shorter-term occupational certificate generates.

Bachelor's and higher degrees generate even larger earnings increases over high school only—about 70 percent and nearly 100 percent, respectively. If anything, these earnings gaps will likely rise as young people with college degrees get more experience, since earnings growth over the life cycle is generally stronger among more-educated workers than among the less-educated.[43] The broad pattern of results here, especially for more technical sub-BA credentials, is consistent

42. Because quarterly earnings are measured in logarithmic form, we can interpret the estimated coefficients on education variables as approximately the percentage effects on earnings of a unit change in that variable.

43. A partial explanation is that in the United States on-the-job training is highly correlated with education level, leading to greater earnings growth over time for those with more education than less (Mincer 1974).

with what others observe in administrative data from states such as California, Kentucky, and Michigan.[44] In other words, these results are not unique to Florida.

These are the average returns earned by young workers in the labor market. But do some groups benefit more from postsecondary education than others? What are the returns to more disadvantaged workers, including minorities and those from low-income families?

Table 3-1 reports results from regression equations estimated separately for race and gender groups, and also for family background and gender groups. Each table entry measures the percentage effect of having the particular credential on an individual's quarterly earnings, relative to those of a high school graduate; thus each is comparable to a bar in figure 3-3. The control variables are those described above, including accumulated labor market experience and FCAT score.

The results indicate a strong earnings premium associated with a completed credential among all groups. In general, men get a somewhat larger earnings boost for career and technical certificates, as well as bachelor's and graduate degrees, while women's earnings premium is higher for an associate degree. Black graduates see a somewhat larger premium than white graduates at all levels, while the earnings gaps for Hispanics are similar to those of whites, though somewhat smaller among Hispanic women. In contrast to recent findings based on other data,[45] in the Florida data labor market rewards for all credentials are a bit larger among disadvantaged students than among the nondisadvantaged.[46]

Earning a bachelor's degree increases earnings for black men by 82 percent and for white men by 73 percent relative to high school

---

44. Jepsen, Troske, and Coomes (2014); Stevens, Kurlaender, and Grosz (2015); and Bahr and others (2015).

45. Hershbein (2016).

46. Hershbein reports higher observed returns to college over the entire lifetime among those who are not from disadvantaged backgrounds. It might be true that the longer-term returns are lower for the poor, whose college degrees are likely from much less selective institutions and who are unlikely to obtain graduate degrees, and that the market returns to these factors develop slowly. It is also possible that there are omitted variables, like family networks, for which Hershbein does not control and which bias his estimates in favor of advantaged students.

Table 3-1. *Effects of Higher Education on Earnings in Florida: Separate Estimates by Race/Gender and Family Income, 2000–12*

Highest completed degree	Female			Male			Female		Male	
	White	Black	Hispanic	White	Black	Hispanic	FRL[a]	No FRL	FRL	No FRL
	(1)	(2)	(3)	(4)	(5)	(6)	(7)	(8)	(9)	(10)
Complete master's degree or PhD	0.90	1.09	0.74	1.10	1.35	1.11	1.02	0.84	1.27	1.07
Complete bachelor's degree	0.69	0.73	0.57	0.73	0.82	0.73	0.75	0.61	0.78	0.69
Complete associate degree	0.41	0.45	0.30	0.31	0.35	0.28	0.45	0.34	0.37	0.27
Complete Vocational certificate	0.18	0.36	0.12	0.33	0.46	0.32	0.27	0.16	0.39	0.31

Note: These effects are measured the same way as those portrayed in figure 3-3. The regression equations from which they are drawn are explained in the text.

a. FRL = free or reduced-price lunch.

graduates. The earnings premium is 45 percent for low-income women with an associate degree, and 34 percent for those not receiving free and reduced-price lunches.

But we should also remember that fewer minority and disadvantaged students earn the credentials with these strong payoffs. For instance, 17 percent of the white men in the sample earned a bachelor's degree, but only 8 percent of the black men did; among women, 22 percent of "other" women but only 15 percent of low-income women earned an associate degree.

Disadvantaged students thus have a strong incentive to complete their programs. Yet many fail to do so. The reality that black and low-income men experience such large benefits from all credentials, including career and technical certificates, suggests that it is particularly important to strengthen their postsecondary outcomes. A range of job-related credentials, including those short of an associate degree, can significantly improve their prospects.

Credits Earned Among Noncompleters

The results of figure 3-3 and table 3-1 indicate strong labor market returns to completing a postsecondary credential. However, as chapter 2 reveals, many students begin college but fail to complete any program. How does the labor market reward the attainment of postsecondary credits for those who fall short of earning a credential?

Results are from regression equations that are identical to those that produced the results in figure 3-3 and table 3-1, except they now include credits attained at either the community or four-year college level for those who did not complete a program.[47] Figure 3-4 displays mean market returns per credit earned (part a) and the mean number of credits earned by noncompleters (part b) in occupational/AA/AS programs within four years or in BA programs within six years of first enrolling. Multiplying the average hours completed

47. Including some measures of credits earned by those who enrolled but did not complete college tends to raise estimated returns to those who completed their credentials, since the latter are now compared only with those who graduated from high school but did not enroll in any college afterward.

by the estimated return per credit hour allows us to calculate the typical earnings returns to the schooling efforts of noncompleters.

Figure 3-4a shows small labor market returns to each credit earned. Indeed, if someone earned 100 credits in a community college program (though only sixty credits are generally required for an associate degree), his or her earnings would rise by 18 percent. Similarly, if a student earned 100 credits in a BA program (out of 120 required), his or her earnings would rise by 27 percent.

As figure 3-4b indicates, the average noncompleter in a community college earns fewer than twenty-five credits within four years after enrolling—less than half of what would be needed to attain an associate degree. Incorporating the return per credit earned, our calculations suggest that average community college noncompleters earn just a 4 percent return over what they would earn with a high school diploma.[48]

The typical noncompleter in a BA program completes just under fifty credits in six years, which again is fewer than half the number needed to earn a degree. Combining that figure with the estimated return per credit, we find that BA noncompleters earn just 12 percent more because of their efforts in college. Of course, for those who complete a degree or certificate in a community college and then transfer to a four-year college but fail to earn the BA, the return to additional credits would be on top of the return to their credential shown in figure 3-3.

These results enable us to calculate how much of the earnings premium for a higher education credential is a return to credits earned along the way as opposed to a "sheepskin" effect for completing the credential. The typical associate degree program in Florida requires sixty credits for completion, while BA programs require 120 credits.[49] Our calculations indicate that the credits actually earned in an

48. This and the following calculation are simply the product of number of credits earned and percentage return per credit.

49. Our estimate of the sheepskin effect is the difference between the estimated return to any credential and the part of that return based only on credit completion, calculated as the return to credits multiplied by the numbers of credits needed to earn that credential.

Figure 3-4a. Effect of Credit Attainment on Earnings of College Noncompleters

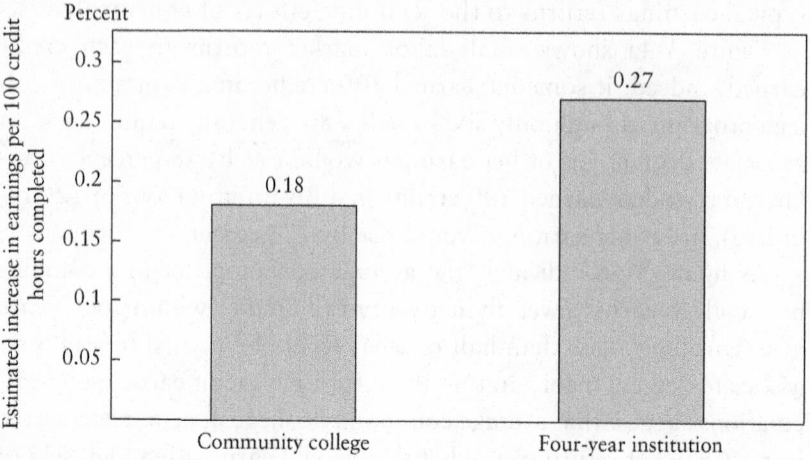

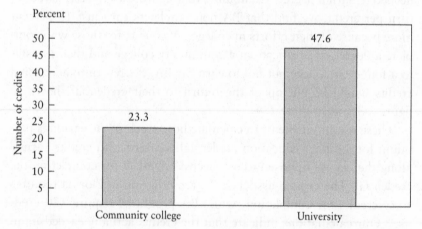

Note: Results are based on regressions using administrative data from Florida. Effects are for the attainment of 100 credits.

Figure 3-4b. Average Number of Credits Earned by College Noncompleters

Note: Credits attained are measured after four years for community colleges and six years for other colleges and universities.

associate or certificate program generate an earnings premium of 11 percent, or less than one-third of the return to the completed associate degree (figure 3-3a). The comparable return to the credits earned for a BA is 31 percent, which is under one-half of the return to the completed credential.

In other words, those who enroll in but fail to complete their programs lose both the premium for the credits they never complete and the significant return to the degree itself. Of particular significance for students with low levels of high school achievement and those who enroll in college as older adults, completion of a short-term certificate has more labor market value than a similar number of credits earned toward an incomplete bachelor's degree.

One final point concerns the question of the specific courses in which credits are earned. Courses in math and science have a stronger effect on earnings than others.[50] Sometimes, a course that updates a student's skills by teaching a new programming language, for example, might be enough to improve his or her earnings. We must therefore continue to pay attention to what students study, among program completers and noncompleters alike.

Returns to Fields of Study

The average earnings among young adults who have completed a credential illustrated in figure 3-3 mask a good deal of variation across fields of study. In this section we explore how labor market returns to BA, AA/AS, and occupational certificates vary with these chosen fields of study.

The Florida data use the detailed Classification of Instructional Programs (CIP) from the U.S. Department of Education to classify fields of study. These are not identical to those used in the BPS data, but we can aggregate them into broader categories similar to those we used when analyzing completion rates in chapter 2. However, the results presented here separate the fields of health, education, and business, which we had earlier combined into the "occupational" category.[51]

50. Jacobson and Mokher (2009); Backes, Holzer, and Velez (2015).
51. The appendix in this volume shows how we have mapped fields of study from the BPS in chapter 2 with the Classification of Instructional Programs (CIP) categories used here. The remaining occupations for those with BAs include accountant and providers of other professional services that require the BA or higher, and categories such as construction, culinary work, precision production, security, and transportation/moving/logistics at the sub-BA level.

The distribution of students across these fields of study in Florida is similar to that reported in chapter 2, with one major exception. Many fewer students in Florida than in the BPS data declare no major, but more Florida community college students—about 40 percent—earn their associate degrees in "general studies" or "liberal studies" (which here are listed as humanities), and an even higher percentage of non-completers have these majors. Our discussions with administrators in Florida suggest that these majors are the residual categories to which students are assigned when they do not otherwise know what they want to do. In other words, this category seems comparable to the undeclared and humanities majors discussed in chapter 2.

Figure 3-5 shows the results from a single regression estimating the effects of different fields of study on earnings for workers who have earned a certificate, an associate degree, or a bachelor's degree, controlling for all of the other factors mentioned above. Figure 3-5 compares earnings generated by all other degrees and fields to those of associate degrees in humanities. Categories with very few cases are combined into the "other" category.[52]

A number of findings emerge from figure 3-5. First, bachelor's degrees in all fields generate higher pay than AAs in the humanities, though how much varies by field. Not surprisingly, STEM and health workers with a BA or higher are the best compensated, while those with a BA in the humanities earn the least. Second, an AA or AS degree in health or an occupational category is compensated significantly better than an AA in the humanities; only individuals with an AA in education are paid less. Third, some career and technical

---

52. The estimated regression model now includes dummy variables for fields of study interacted with the level of credential or degree attained. Separate dummies are also included but not reported for the very small number of credential completers with missing field of study or CIP categories; and small cells with very few individuals were combined into the "other" category when they did not fit into the table. For example, the number of certificate holders in social sciences and humanities is 5 and 104 respectively, while the number of AA holders with social science degrees is just thirty-nine in our data. Those finishing high school but no postsecondary credential are included with their own dummy but no interactions with field. Those with graduate degrees above BA also have their own dummy variable in the model.

Figure 3-5. Earnings by Field of Study

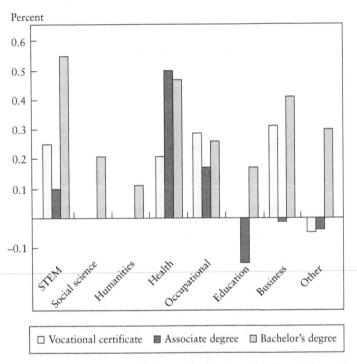

Percent

□ Vocational certificate ■ Associate degree □ Bachelor's degree

Note: All effects on earnings are measured relative to having an associate degree in humanities.

certificates, such as those in the occupational categories and business, and to a lesser extent STEM certificates, lead to better pay than AAs in humanities. The occupational categories that pay relatively well among certificate holders include construction, manufacturing, and transportation.

Of course, there are likely systematic differences among students who enroll in different programs. While our analysis cannot totally isolate these factors from the credentials earned as causing the earnings differentials, the fact that we are able to control for so many background characteristics suggests that many students could increase their earnings if they chose different fields of study.

Our data cover earnings for just the first five years after graduates earn their credentials. Over time, many of those with BAs in the humanities will complete graduate degrees and increase their earnings, while others will find occupations that better reward their writing or analytical skills.

Unfortunately, the same cannot be said of the 40 percent of associate degree holders in Florida who concentrated in the humanities.[53] Most of them may have intended to transfer to a four-year institution, aspiring to earn a bachelor's degree. But not having succeeded in reaching that goal, *many of those who completed an AA did so in categories that generate very small labor market returns.* Since our analysis included controls for earlier achievement and experience and tenure in the job market, differences across workers in these characteristics do not explain these findings.[54]

Why Do These Differences Persist over Time?

Evidence from other studies indicates that the large differences observed here in labor market rewards for different fields of study persist over the life cycle and across time periods. Why don't more students choose to enter the high-return fields—which, in turn, would expand the labor supply in these markets and likely reduce these earnings differentials over time? Why do so many students who manage to complete their programs end up with general humanities associate degrees or other credentials associated with weak labor market outcomes?

We noted at the beginning of this chapter that students often choose fields of study based on their personal preferences and their achievement levels. Many students in the United States simply do not like math and science—perhaps because of poor teaching or because they have performed poorly in these areas—and therefore do not choose fields of study that require math and science proficiency. The same low achievement that keeps many students from completing a postsecondary credential in general might also deter them from more demanding fields of study such as STEM. Even those whose overall

53. This group includes only those whose highest degree is the associate degree (though some might have transferred to a four-year college or university and not completed the BA program).

54. An interesting comparison would be between students who complete two years at a four-year college but never earn a degree and those who earn a general associate degree.

achievement is strong might be too weak in math and science to obtain a STEM or technician credential. Students may fail to develop the necessary skills in their K–12 years, especially if they do not know that they will need them in college and in the labor force.

But even some stronger students face two obstacles to making the choices in college that will lead to the best financial outcomes. They do not know which associate degrees and certificates the labor market rewards, or whether they would enjoy and succeed in employment in those fields. In other words, these students lack sufficient *information* about relative rates of compensation, as well as about the nature of the work in different fields, to make fully informed decisions.

Many students need more academic and career guidance and advising to facilitate their decisionmaking. One strength of some for-profit institutions is their focus on and guidance toward specific occupational credentials and jobs.[55] In contrast, most community colleges tend to have relatively unstructured environments in which students are able to make a very wide range of choices with very little guidance. Students receive too little advising about both academics and the labor market to make well-informed decisions. The lack of structure likely generates low labor market earnings among many of those who complete degree programs, as well as low completion rates.[56]

Better information about the range of earnings associated with degrees and certificates should be readily available. But information is not enough, and is unlikely to override students' lack of confidence, skills, and affinity. Moreover, many simply believe that their hard work and persistence will pay off, even when the odds are stacked against them.

The lack of guidance and structure so common at community colleges is at least partially attributable to a lack of institutional resources. The two-year and less-selective public institutions tend to charge lower tuition and to receive less public funding than more selective public universities. In addition, institutions frequently face too few incentives to respond to the labor market. In many states, funding is based on enrollment, regardless of whether the students successfully complete courses or programs and regardless of field of study. Since it is

---

55. See Rosenbaum (2002); Rosenbaum, Deil-Amen, and Person (2006).
56. Scott-Clayton (2015); Bailey, Jaggars, and Jenkins (2015).

more expensive to educate students in technical fields, institutions may have insufficient motivation—and limited capacity—to direct students into the fields likely to be most remunerative. As a result, student choices are not always the determining factor.

Programs in fields with high labor market returns often fill a limited number of places through selective admissions and/or waiting lists. Not only do the colleges face few incentives to encourage stronger student performance in the job market, they also face higher costs and greater obstacles in staffing their technician and STEM classes, especially at the sub-BA level. Technician classes require a college to have up-to-date, and sometimes expensive, equipment in the classroom. In addition, instructors in well-paying and growing fields such as nursing are often in high demand in the job market and therefore have relatively high salaries, which may be difficult for these institutions to match. In the STEM fields, long-time faculty members with tenure might not have kept up with the latest technical developments in specific fields. Thus, to train students as machinists or in other rapidly changing fields requiring up-to-date skills, a community college might have to hire adjunct engineers from local industry. These instructors might be expensive on a per-course basis and require much time and effort to recruit.[57]

Given how many functions we now expect community colleges to perform—preparing students both for four-year colleges and for the workforce—and the limited resources we provide them, it is understandable that the institutions sometimes provide too little teaching capacity in certain fields. Financial constraints can prevent community colleges and other nonflagship institutions from offering enough classes to meet the demand in popular fields of study such as health care and health technician work. Working students may be unable to find classes that fit into their schedules, and there may be too few classroom seats to accommodate all the students who want them.

The limited capacity generates competition for spaces in some high-demand programs and sends some students to the for-profit

57. We thank Jim Jacobs, president of Macomb Community College in Macomb County, Michigan, for this insight. He discussed his need to hire engineers from Ford Motor Company to teach these classes as adjunct faculty.

sector and others to second-choice majors. It also contributes to a shortage of trained workers in nursing and other fields.

Conclusion

The data on labor market rewards to postsecondary credentials tell a mixed story. On the one hand, the labor market offers strong rewards, on average, to those who complete a degree or even a career or technical certificate. This is particularly true for minority and low-income students. On the other hand, students who enroll in but fail to complete programs tend to earn very modest rewards for the credits they accumulate. And many students who graduate with associate degrees or certificates do not earn their credentials in well-compensated areas such as STEM, health technician, and some other occupational fields, but instead major in general studies, liberal studies, or other fields with relatively low labor market value for those without bachelor's degrees.

The labor market outcomes among these students at least partly reflect their weak academic preparation in the K–12 years, but our statistical results indicate that students with similar backgrounds fare quite differently depending on their fields of study. Students receive little information or guidance about the labor market and the academic steps required to reach their goals.

Because the public institutions many disadvantaged students attend have multiple missions, many face unrealistic demands on their resources. More resources would help them meet the needs of their students. Moreover, because they receive subsidies from their states based on the number of enrolled students, they have little incentive to use their limited resources to generate success, especially in fields of study where labor demand is strong but where the costs of instructors and equipment are high.

We address the need for appropriate policy responses in the second half of this book. In the meantime, a closer look at the financial issues in higher education faced by both students and institutions is in order.

4

Financial Barriers to College Success

Rising tuition prices have captured considerable public attention in recent years. The perception that college has become unaffordable to all but the wealthy is widespread.[1] But the evidence about the role of financial barriers to college enrollment, and particularly to success once students get in the door, is not so clear. As chapter 2 pointed out, the postsecondary students with the most limited financial resources are the same students who graduate from high school academically unprepared for college—if they graduate at all. Many enroll in underresourced institutions with poor records of success and without a peer culture of high academic achievement. It is certain, however, that in an era of stagnant wages, growing income inequality, and widespread insecurity in the labor market, many students are struggling to manage the financial demands of postsecondary education.

In this chapter we review the components of the cost of going to college—tuition and fees, books and supplies, and forgone wages—as well as the other living expenses students must cover while they are in school. We focus both on changes over time and on the prices of different types of higher education. Published tuition and fees paint an inaccurate picture because of the important role of grant aid

1. Harris (2013); Lewin (2008); Kingkade (2014).

in lowering the net price students actually pay. But because some financial aid is in the form of loans, it is important to ask how both the prospect of debt and the actual debt students accrue affect postsecondary outcomes. In order to better understand rising tuition levels, we summarize trends in state funding of public higher education. Finally, we review the evidence about the impact of financial constraints on college enrollment and completion among low-income students.

The Price of College

In discussions about the expenses associated with college, the terms "cost" and "price" can be confusing. It is common to talk about the cost of college as the amount students and families must pay to enroll. But the reality is that the cost of educating students is frequently quite a bit higher than the tuition and fees they are charged. The difference comes primarily from state funds at public institutions and from private donations at private nonprofit colleges and universities. In other words, expensive as college is, many students outside the for-profit sector are actually being subsidized—even before they get any financial aid to help them pay the published prices. So it is clearest to use "cost" to refer to how much institutions spend to produce education and "price" to refer to the amount they charge students.

Every college and university has a website, and somewhere on that website is information about the published or "sticker" price. Tuition and fees may be set regardless of how many credits a student enrolls for within a specified range, or charges may be on a per-credit basis. In addition, there is a price for room and board for students who live on campus. But whether or not a student lives on campus there is a "cost of attendance." Cost of attendance (COA) adds together tuition and fees, room and board (or housing and food for off-campus students), books and supplies, transportation expenses, and other miscellaneous expenses. (COA is really a price, not a cost.) When colleges tell students how much financial aid they are eligible to receive, they put that amount in the context of the full COA, with the difference being the students' out-of-pocket expenses.

In fact, however, the largest component of the true cost of going to college for most students is forgone wages. Although some students do work full time while they are in school, there are only twenty-four hours in a day and it is very difficult to find the time both to work full time and to study full time.

On the other hand, housing and food are not true costs of education. People have these expenses whether or not they are in school, although sometimes enrollment causes one's expenses to rise. Nonetheless, from a student's perspective, expenses are more visible than forgone earnings. And since their earnings if they did not go to college would probably be quite comparable to their living expenses, it is a reasonable approximation to look at the expenses people incur while they are in college—including living expenses—as a proxy for what it really costs them to be in school.

Tuition and Fees

As table 4-1 shows, sticker prices vary considerably across types of institutions. In 2016–17, the average tuition and fee price for in-state students at public four-year colleges and universities across the nation was $9,650. This sector includes doctoral institutions, with an average price of $10,510; master's institutions, with an average price of $8,340; and a small number of colleges offering only bachelor's degrees, with lower prices.

Tuition and fees at community colleges are quite a bit lower, averaging $3,520 in 2016–17. Private colleges have higher prices, with the nonprofit four-year average $33,480 and, of particular importance for our focus on low-income students, average tuition and fees of $16,000 at for-profit institutions.[2]

These prices for public colleges reflect charges to students who are state residents. Twenty-one percent of first-time degree-seeking undergraduate students are enrolled in institutions outside of their home states.[3] For those in the public sector, tuition is usually much higher than the price charged to state residents, with a national average for 2016–17 of $24,930.

2. Data on prices are from Ma and others (2016).
3. NCES (2016, table 309.10).

Dollars

Table 4-1. *Tuition and Fees and Other Expenses by Sector, 2016–17*

Sector (percentage of students in each sector)	Tuition and fees	Room and board	Books and supplies	Transportation	Other expenses	Total budget
Public two-year in-district	3,520	n.a.	1,390	1,760	2,270	17,000
Public four-year in-state	9,650	10,440	1,250	1,160	2,110	24,610
Public doctoral in-state (57%)	10,510	10,840	...	...	...	...
Public master's in-state (36%)	8,340	9,680	...	...	...	...
Public bachelor's in-state (6%)	7,110	9,990	...	...	...	...
Public four-year out-of-state	24,930	10,440	1,250	1,160	2,110	39,890
Private nonprofit four-year	33,480	11,890	1,230	1,060	1,650	49,310
Private nonprofit doctoral (28%)	40,980	13,580	1,390	...	...	...
Private nonprofit master's (38%)	28,890	11,220	...	...	...	...
Private nonprofit bachelor's (29%)	32,400	11,040	...	...	...	...
For-profit	16,000	n.a.	n.a.	n.a.	n.a.	n.a.

Source: Ma and others (2016).

Note: Percentages in parentheses report the proportion of full-time students in each sector enrolled in the specified subcategory of institutions.

n.a. = not applicable.

Figure 4-1a. Average Tuition and Fees at Public Two-Year Colleges by State, 2016–17

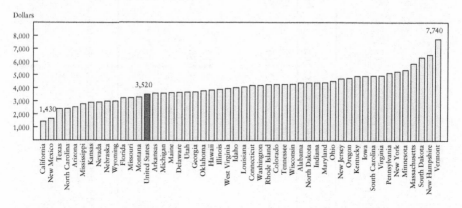

Figure 4-1b. Average In-State Tuition and Fees at Public Four-Year Institutions, 2016–17

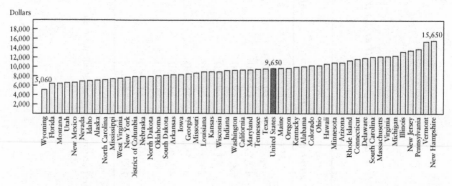

Source: Ma and others (2016).

The variation in sticker prices for public colleges across states is striking. In 2016–17, as figure 4-1a indicates, tuition and fees at public two-year colleges ranged from $1,430 in California and $1,660 in New Mexico to $6,530 in New Hampshire and $7,740 in Vermont. In the four-year public sector (figure 4-1b), the range was from $5,060 in Wyoming and $6,360 in Florida to $15,450 in Vermont and $15,650 in New Hampshire. Because of the price differential for out-of-state students, it is not possible for students who live in high-tuition states to escape the high prices by going elsewhere.

These price differentials are not driven by recent rates of change. In the nation as a whole, public two-year college tuition increased 11 percent after adjusting for inflation between 2011–12 and 2016–17. California, with the lowest current price, saw an increase of 20 percent over these five years. In contrast, New Hampshire, with current prices second only to Vermont, lowered its community college tuition by 9 percent between 2011–12 and 2016–17.

Tuition Price Increases

Concerns about college prices are not just about the price itself, but about the rate of increase. Historically, public college prices have risen most rapidly when the economy is weak and state budgets are strained. The recession of the late 2000s was no exception. The average published tuition and fees at public four-year institutions rose by 9 percent (in inflation-adjusted dollars) in 2009–10, by another 7 percent in 2010–11, by 5 percent in 2011–12, and by 3 percent the next year. In the public two-year sector, tuition and fees rose by 10 percent in 2009–10 and by 5 percent in each of the three succeeding years. However, both sectors saw only 1 percent real increases in 2013–14 and 2014–15, followed by real increases under 3 percent in 2015–16 and under 2 percent in 2016–17.

To put price increases into context it is helpful to look at a longer time frame. Tuition prices have been rising faster than average prices in the economy for decades, and as figure 4-2 indicates, growth since the mid-2000s has, if anything, been slower than in the past. If tuition is not growing rapidly by historical standards, why is there so much concern about college becoming unaffordable? One issue is that the percentage increases are on higher and higher bases. The 3.5 percent average annual increase from 2006–07 to 2016–17 in the public four-year sector represents an increase of $2,790 in 2016 dollars over the decade. The 4.2 percent per year increase the preceding decade added up to an increase of $2,300.

But another problem is the stagnation of incomes. Median family income in the United States did not recover to its 2007 level until 2015, when it reached $70,697, just 4 percent above its level a decade

Figure 4-2. Average Annual Percentage Increases in Inflation-Adjusted Published Prices by Decade, 1986–87 to 2016–17

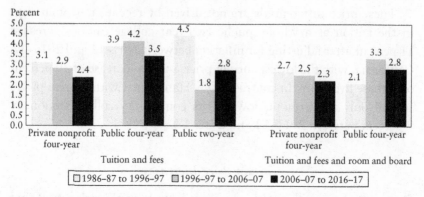

Source: Ma et al. (2016), figure 4.

Note: Each bar shows the average annual rate of growth of published prices in inflation-adjusted dollars over a ten-year period.

earlier.[4] Moreover, income inequality continued its long-term increase over the decade from 2005 to 2015, with lower shares of income going to families in the middle and at the lower end of the income distribution.[5] In other words, outside of the highest-income families, people have had less to spend on everything—including college—in recent years.

Financial Aid

The sticker prices charged by colleges and universities do not represent what students and families actually pay for postsecondary education. As table 4-2 indicates, 59 percent of all undergraduates, including 72 percent of those enrolled full time, received grant aid averaging $6,200 in 2011–12. Over 90 percent of full-time dependent students from families with incomes below $40,000 received an average of over $11,000 in grant aid—more than the average tuition and fees at public four-year colleges.[6] In other words, sticker prices significantly overstate the financial barriers to college enrollment for disadvantaged students.

4. U.S. Census Bureau (2016a, table F-6).

5. U.S. Census Bureau (2016a, table F-2).

6. Radwin and others (2013).

Table 4-2. *Undergraduate Grant Aid, 2011–12*

Aid recipients	Students receiving grant aid (percent)	Average grant aid per recipient (dollars)
All undergraduates	59.1	6,200
Full-time	72.4	9,200
Part-time	50.8	3,400
Public two-year	50.5	3,200
Public four-year doctoral	55.3	6,800
Public four-year nondoctoral	59.9	4,900
Private nonprofit four-year doctoral	74.7	16,100
Private nonprofit four-year nondoctoral	78.1	13,500
For profit four-year	70.7	4,100
For-profit two-year	64.7	3,800
For-profit<two-year	77.5	4,000
Full-time undergraduates		
Dependent	69.9	10,600
Independent	78.1	6,500
Dependent by income		
<20,000	95.1	11,200
20,000–39,999	89.0	11,500
40,000–59,999	83.9	10,000
60,000–79,999	64.1	9,700
80,000–99,999	54.5	9,900
100,000 or more	51.4	10,300
Independent by income		
<10,000	87.6	7,500
10,000–19,999	87.3	6,200
20,000–29,999	77.2	5,500
30,000–49,999	67.3	5,700
50,000 or more	41.9	4,700

Source: Radwin and others (2013).

Table 4-3 shows the sources of this grant aid for students in different types of institutions. Private nonprofit college students, and to a lesser extent, public four-year college students, get much of their grant aid directly from their institutions. In contrast, students enrolled in public two-year and for-profit institutions rely primarily on the federal

Table 4-3. *Sources of Grant Aid for Undergraduate Students, 2011–12*

Percent distribution within sectors

Source	Private nonprofit four-year	Public four-year	Public two-year	For-profit
Federal government (nonmilitary)	11	38	68	64
Department of Veterans Affairs / Department of Defense	3	5	6	21
State	6	20	10	4
Institution	67	25	7	2
Private and employer	13	13	9	9

Source: Baum and others (2015), based on NPSAS data.

government for their aid. Federal Pell Grants provide about two-thirds of the grant aid for these students; and for those in the for-profit sector, military and veterans aid is also very important.

In recent years, the federal government has significantly increased its commitment to funding college students. In the years after the Great Recession states slashed their funding to public institutions; in response, schools rapidly raised their prices, and the federal government has filled part of the resulting gap. In just one year, between 2008–09 and 2009–10, federal Pell Grant expenditures rose from $18 billion to $30 billion; grants to veterans and active duty military grew from $5 billion to $9 billon; and federal education tax credits and deductions for undergraduate students increased from $11 billion to $16 billion. Undergraduate enrollment surged by 8 percent that year, as job opportunities became scarce. Nonetheless, as table 4-4 reveals, the federal government's contribution to the average student increased sharply, by 84 percent (after adjusting for inflation), over the decade from 2005–06 to 2015–16—from $2,510 (in 2015 dollars) in 2005–06 to $4,630 per student in 2015–16.[7]

7. Baum and others (2016).

Table 4-4. *Federal Grant Aid and Tax Benefits per Full-Time Equivalent (FTE) Undergraduate Student, 2005–06 to 2015–16*

In 2015 dollars

	2005–06	2010–11	2015–16	Ten-year change (%)
Pell Grants	1,370	2,860	2,220	62
Veterans and military	360	800	1,000	178
Federal work-study and FSEOG[a]	180	130	120	–33
Education tax benefits	590	1,410	1,290	119
Total federal aid, excluding loans	2,510	5,290	4,630	84

Source: Baum and others (2016).

a. FSEOG=Federal Supplemental Educational Opportunity Grant.

Allocating Need-Based Aid

In order to assess the financial gaps facing low-income students, it is important to have a reliable way of evaluating their capacity to pay. A policy of free tuition and fees might eliminate the barriers of paying the direct costs of higher education for all students—or at least for those who attend public colleges. However, even in the presence of such a broad-based policy, many students would struggle to meet their living expenses while in college. Since it is neither sensible nor feasible for public funds to cover the housing, food, and other living expenses of everyone enrolled in postsecondary education, strategies for distinguishing among students are necessary regardless of pricing policies.

The allocation of need-based federal student aid—and of the grant aid awarded by most states and many institutions—is based on the Federal Methodology (FM). This formula uses information about income, assets, family size, taxes paid, and number of family members in college collected on the Free Application for Federal Student Aid (FAFSA) to calculate an expected family contribution (EFC). The EFC determines eligibility for Pell Grants, as well as some other forms of federal student aid and much state and institutional aid.

The eligibility formula is far from perfect. Its complexity and the difficulty of allowing students to predict their aid in advance are widely criticized. Although the formula was developed to evaluate the ability of parents to contribute to the funding of their children's college education, over half of all Pell Grant recipients—and many of the students seeking associate degrees and certificates—are not dependent students for financial aid purposes. Students are considered independent if they are age twenty-four or older, graduate students, married with dependents of their own, active duty military or veterans, emancipated minors, orphans, in foster care, unaccompanied homeless youth, or wards of the court. For these students, parental financial circumstances are not relevant.

Historically, the FM formula has based eligibility for aid during an academic year on income the preceding year. For example, aid applicants for 2015–16 reported their 2014 incomes. Beginning with applications for aid in 2017–18, the system now relies on income information that is one year older—2015 incomes will determine eligibility for that year. For parents, relying on incomes earned in previous years might be a reasonable way of predicting available resources while the student is in college. But for older independent students, it is not. An adult who goes back to school cannot reasonably continue to earn at his or her precollege level and succeed in college. First-year independent students in 2011–12 who had earnings the year before they enrolled had an average income of about $28,000. During their first year of college, fewer had earnings, and when they did, the average was about $14,000.[8] Moreover, differences in earnings among undergraduate students are likely to be at least as much a function of work effort and personal choice as of actual earnings capacity. The FM formula imposes a tax rate of 50 percent on the earnings of independent students without dependents. (Those with dependents are treated more generously.) Mitigating the financial difficulties facing adult students is likely to require a revision of this approach to financial aid allocation.

8. NCES (2012, PowerStats calculations).

Table 4-5. *2011–12 Undergraduate Students within Sectors
Who Did Not Apply for Federal Financial Aid*

Percent

Student type	Institution type		
	Public two-year	*Public four-year*	*For-profit*
All	38	27	12
Independent			
All	40	31	13
Full-time, full-year[a]	18	13	5
Low-income dependent[b]			
All	36	24	12
Full-time, full-year	15	9	5

Source: NCES (2012, Power Stats calculations).

a. Full-time full-year includes only those students enrolled at one institution for the entire academic year.

b. Low-income is defined as parent income of $30,000 or less.

Moreover, many students who would be eligible for federal financial aid do not complete the application process. As table 4-5 shows, 40 percent of independent students and 36 percent of dependent students from families with incomes of $30,000 or less did not apply for federal aid for the 2011–12 academic year. Students who enrolled full-time full-year in one institution were more likely to apply for aid, but even among this group, 15 percent of full-time low-income community college students did not apply for aid. Only 5 percent of similar students enrolled in for-profit institutions did not apply.[9]

Many of the students who do not apply for aid would be eligible and their financial struggles could be ameliorated by helping them through the application process. But for many others, the available funds might not be adequate to prevent finances from interfering with their academic success.

9. NCES (2012, PowerStats calculations).

Total Postsecondary Expenses

Students seeking associate degrees and certificates at public two-year colleges face very different financial demands than those enrolled at for-profit institutions. In the mid-1980s, the maximum Pell Grant was three times the average tuition and fees at a public two-year college. It was twice as high as the sticker price in 2000–01 and again in 2008–09, and 1.7 times as high in 2015–16, when the maximum Pell Grant left the recipient at the average community college with more than $2,300 to put toward other expenses. In contrast, the maximum Pell Grant covered less than 40 percent of the average for-profit college tuition that year, leaving a recipient with about $9,800 of charges to cover—in addition to living expenses.

Even at public two-year colleges, low-income students frequently struggle to meet all of their expenses. On average, total grant aid for full-time community college students, when combined with federal tax credits, covers their tuition and fees.[10] That said, tuition and fees are a relatively small part of the budgets of community college students. According to data from the National Postsecondary Student Aid Study (NPSAS), in 2011–12, for 80 percent of full-time and 57 percent of part-time community college students, total grant aid was insufficient to fill the gap between their budgets, as estimated by institutions, and the amount the federal government estimated they could afford to pay. The average full-time community college student had to fill a gap of $5,800 with a combination of loans and work exceeding expected earnings, and the average part-time student was short $2,800.[11] For students in the for-profit sector, the gaps are, not surprisingly, much larger. In 2011–12, 95 percent of full-time students could not cover their budgets without work exceeding expected earnings and/or loans, with the average student facing a gap of $16,100.

In order to partially fill these gaps, many students, particularly older students, attend college part time. But 86 percent of part-time

10. Because federal tax credit funds are not available until students or parents file their taxes in the calendar year following the tuition payments, they do not help to solve short-term liquidity problems.

11. These averages are for all students, including those with no gap between grants plus expected contribution and total budget.

students in the for-profit sector still faced gaps averaging $7,600 in 2011–12. Moreover, part-time attendance and working many hours while enrolled interfere with academic progress. As we noted in chapter 2, students who enroll part time have much lower completion rates than full-time students. According to the National Student Clearinghouse, which has data tracking individual students across institutions over time, only 18 percent of public two-year college students who first enrolled in 2010 and enrolled exclusively part time earned a credential anywhere within six years. In contrast, 35 percent of those with mixed enrollment patterns and 55 percent who enrolled exclusively full time completed a degree or certificate. Although completion rates are higher at public and private nonprofit four-year colleges and universities, the patterns are the same everywhere.[12]

It is difficult to know how many students would switch to full-time enrollment if more of their expenses were covered or how much impact this would have on completion rates. The Connecticut Community College system is finding that just informing students of the increased financial aid they would receive if they enrolled full time has the potential to change enrollment patterns for some students.[13] And while it might be possible to increase somewhat the percentage of expenses met by grant aid for low-income students, the funding gaps facing these students are unlikely to disappear in the foreseeable future.

Student Debt

Given rising college prices, financial aid that has not kept up with these prices, and stagnant wages and family incomes, it is not surprising that an increasing number of college students borrow to help finance their education.

Many discussions of student debt focus on the aggregate amount of debt outstanding, which includes funds borrowed over time by graduate students and parents, in addition to undergraduates. Discussions of the amount of debt with which students graduate frequently

12. Shapiro and others (2016a, appendix C, table 22).
13. Klempin (2014).

focus on bachelor's degree recipients. We look instead at the borrowing patterns of associate degree and certificate recipients, in addition to the debt levels of students who leave community colleges and for-profit institutions without a credential.

As table 4-6 reports, both the percentage of students borrowing and the average debt levels at for-profit institutions far outstrip those at public two-year colleges. In 2011–12, when for-profit institutions awarded 14 percent of all associate degrees, 88 percent of these students graduated with debt and 55 percent had borrowed $20,000 or more. In contrast, 41 percent of public two-year associate degree recipients graduated with debt and only 9 percent had borrowed $20,000 or more.

Certificate recipients, 55 percent of whom came from for-profit institutions in 2011–12, have less debt because they are in school for shorter periods of time. Only 35 percent from public two-year colleges, in contrast to 86 percent from the for-profit sector, graduated with debt in 2011–12. Even in the for-profit sector, most students borrowed less than $20,000; in the public two-year sector, only 13 percent borrowed as much as $20,000.[14]

These debt patterns reveal that with the notable exception of for-profit institutions, relatively few individuals completing sub-baccalaureate credentials emerge with high levels of debt. However, as Table 4-6 shows, these 2011–12 debt levels far exceed those that prevailed less than a decade earlier. The percentage of associate degree recipients who graduated with $30,000 (in 2012 dollars) or more in debt increased from 1 percent in 2003–04 to 8 percent in 2011–12. The percentage of for-profit graduates with this much debt skyrocketed from 1 percent to 28 percent over these years, and the percentage of all associate degrees that were granted by that sector rose from 7 percent to 14 percent.

Whether or not debt is manageable depends on postgraduation earnings, a subject we discussed in detail in chapter 3. Default rates are actually highest among those with low levels of debt, who tend to have been in school for a short period of time and to have poor labor

14. NCES (2012, PowerStats calculations).

Table 4-6. *Distribution of Cumulative Debt Levels of Associate Degree and Certificate Recipients over Time in 2012 Dollars*

Percent of graduates in sector

Year	No debt	Less than $10,000	$10,000–$19,999	$20,000–$29,999	$30,000 or more
Associate degree recipients					
For-profit					
2003–04 (7%)[a]	10	33	49	8	1
2007–08 (14%)	7	23	37	21	13
2011–12 (14%)	12	13	20	27	28
Public two-year					
2003–04 (79%)	70	24	4	2	1
2007–08 (70%)	62	25	9	3	1
2011–12 (67%)	59	20	12	5	4
Total					
2003–04	63	26	9	2	1
2007–08	52	25	14	6	3
2011–12	50	19	14	9	8
	No debt	Less than $10,000	$10,000–$19,999	$20,000–$29,999	$30,000 or more
Certificate recipients					
For-profit					
2003–04 (48%)	15	75	9	1	0
2007–08 (53%)	12	51	29	6	2
2011–12 (55%)	14	36	37	9	4
Public two-year					
2003–04 (32%)	82	15	3	0	0
2007–08 (31%)	69	22	6	1	1
2011–12 (28%)	65	22	7	3	3
Total					
2003–04	46	47	6	1	0
2007–08	37	37	19	4	2
2011–12	34	30	25	6	4

Source: Baum and others (2015).

a. Percentages in parentheses report the percentage of associate degrees or certificates awarded by the sector in the specified year. These include students who were U.S. citizens or permanent residents. Percentages may not sum to 100 because of rounding. Undergraduate certificate programs vary in length from less than one year to two years.

Table 4-7. *Distribution of Cumulative Debt Levels of Noncompleters: Students Beginning in 2003–04*

Did not earn a degree or certificate by 2009 percent

Institution type (percentage of students in sector)	Did not borrow	$1–$10,000	$10,001–$20,000	$20,001 or more
For-profit (17)[a]	13	51	24	12
Private nonprofit four-year (8)	31	30	22	17
Public four-year (17)	41	33	14	12
Public two-year (56)	71	22	5	2
Total	52	30	11	7

Source: NCES (2009, Power Stats calculations).

a. Percentages in parentheses report percentage of noncompleters who were enrolled in the specified sector.

market outcomes.[15] This makes debt levels of students who leave school without a degree or certificate a particular concern.

Debt of Noncompleters

Starting college and leaving without completing a degree has significant implications for job opportunities and earnings. Students who leave school with debt but no degree are particularly vulnerable. These students tend to borrow less than those who complete their programs, partly because they are in school for a shorter period of time, but possibly also because a higher fraction of noncompleters were part-time students, likely devoting more time to the labor market and earning more while they were in school.

As table 4-7 indicates, among 2003–04 beginning students, almost half of the noncompleters left with some amount of education debt. Consistent with the patterns among graduates, 87 percent of those from the for-profit sector, and 29 percent of those who were enrolled in public two-year colleges, left with debt. More than one-third of the for-profit noncompleters—but only 7 percent of the community college students—had borrowed over $10,000.[16]

15. Brown and others (2015).
16. NCES (2009, PowerStats calculations).

Student Loan Default

New evidence on student debt and default patterns raises serious concerns for disadvantaged students enrolling in community colleges and for-profit institutions for the purpose of improving their labor market options. Data merging Department of Education information on student loans with Internal Revenue Service data on earnings reveal that the recent increase in federal student loan default rates is largely explained by growth in the number of borrowers in the for-profit sector and, to a lesser extent, public two-year and less-selective four-year institutions. The combination of low levels of financial resources with weak academic and labor market outcomes creates the perfect storm of increasing levels of borrowing and limited capacity for repayment.

Among borrowers who began—or should have begun—repayment on their student loans in 2011, 70 percent of those who defaulted within two years had attended either for-profit or two-year public institutions. These defaulters constituted 21 percent of the students from these sectors who entered repayment. Only 8 percent of other undergraduate borrowers and 2 percent of graduate borrowers—who tend to have much larger loan balances—defaulted during this time period.[17]

One key reason for higher default rates among borrowers from the for-profit and two-year public sectors is their relatively weak labor market outcomes. Borrowers leaving school in 2010 and 2011—during years of high unemployment—experienced unemployment rates ranging from 21 percent for those from for-profit institutions and 17 percent for community college students to about 7 percent for those from four-year public and private nonprofit institutions. Median earnings for those who worked were $21,000 for for-profit borrowers and $24,000 for community college borrowers—significantly lower than the earnings of those who attended other types of institutions. Median earnings declined far more during the recession for borrowers from for-profit and two-year colleges than for those from four-year colleges and universities.[18]

It is not surprising, then, that student loan default rates are consistently much higher for borrowers from for-profit and two-year colleges

17. Looney and Yannelis (2015).
18. Looney and Yannelis (2015).

Figure 4-3. Federal Student Loan Default Rates Two Calendar Years after Beginning Repayment, 1995–96 to 2011–12

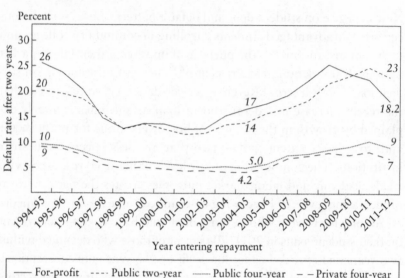

Source: Baum and others (2015).

than for those from four-year public and private nonprofit institutions. Figure 4-3 shows this pattern over time.

A significant part of the explanation for the differences in default rates relates to differences in completion rates across sectors, as discussed in chapter 2. Among borrowers entering repayment in 2011, 24 percent of those who had not completed a credential had defaulted within two years—compared with only 9 percent of those who had earned a degree or certificate.[19]

But even students who complete their academic programs yet have difficulty finding well-paying work can face hardship servicing the debts they accumulate. This phenomenon was exacerbated by the Great Recession, which took a big employment toll on new college graduates.[20] As labor markets recover from the recession, this problem is less prevalent, though it will not totally disappear.

19. Baum and others (2015).
20. Kahn (2010); Dahl, DeLeire, and Schwabish (2013).

Because of the provisions that allow borrowers to defer their payments on federal loans when they have low earnings, many borrowers are in good standing, even though they are not making any progress toward retiring their debt. Among borrowers entering repayment in 2012, 74 percent of those from for-profit colleges and 64 percent from community colleges owed more after two years than when they entered repayment. The same was true of 36 percent of borrowers from selective four-year colleges, with those from less-selective four-year institutions falling in between.[21]

The implementation in 2009 of a widely available income-driven repayment plan for federal student loans and continued strengthening of that form of insurance has significantly reduced the risks associated with student loans. But we are concerned not just with how students fare after they leave college, but how the prospect of debt, as well as other financial issues, affects whether students succeed in postsecondary education.

Funding Community Colleges

The funding of community colleges is critical to the success of the low-income and adult students seeking valuable credentials for the labor market. In 2013–14, when public four-year institutions received $7,110 per full-time-equivalent student in state and local appropriations, public two-year colleges received $5,210 (table 4-8). Because of the much lower tuition at community colleges, total per student revenues at two-year public colleges were $10,130—about 43 percent of the $23,760 at public four-year colleges and universities. Community colleges have not been able to raise tuition as much as four-year institutions have, and their dependence on state and local appropriations has made them particularly vulnerable to declining per-student revenues in difficult economic times.

The different institutional missions complicate comparisons of these figures across sectors. Community colleges offer only the first two years of undergraduate education. Educating upper-level under-

21. Looney and Yannelis (2015).

Table 4-8. *Institutional Revenues per Full-Time Equivalent (FTE)
Student at Public Institutions by Revenue Source,
2003–04, 2008–09, and 2013–14*

2013 dollars

Year	Net tuition revenue	State and local appropriations	Federal appropriations and federal, state, and local grants and contracts	Total revenue per FTE student	Revenues from state and local appropriations (%)
Public four-year					
2003–04	6,640	9,010	7,190	22,840	39
2008–09	7,710	8,380	7,110	23,200	36
2013–14	9,740	7,110	6,910	23,760	30
Public two-year					
2003–04	2,690	5,780	1,640	10,110	57
2008–09	2,840	5,550	1,490	9,880	56
2013–14	3,530	5,210	1,390	10,130	51

Source: Ma and others (2016).

graduates, a critical mission of all four-year institutions, is more expensive because of the specialized curriculum and smaller classes. Educating graduate students and conducting research skews the picture
even more. A commonly used estimate is that it costs about one and a
half times as much to educate upper-level undergraduates as it does to
educate lower-level undergraduates and about three times as much to
educate graduate students.

Community colleges also offer many noncredit programs. Although
revenues and expenditures for these programs are part of measured
totals, their students are not included in the enrollment count. If they
were included, revenues per full-time equivalent student would be
quite a bit lower.[22]

Because of these measurement problems, it is not possible to compare precisely the resources devoted to community college students

22. Baum and Kurose (2013).

with those devoted to students enrolled in public four-year institutions. That said, the large gap in revenues across sectors makes it clear that students enrolled in public two-year colleges have significantly fewer resources available to them than those attending most four-year institutions.

Students tend to arrive at public two-year colleges in need of developmental education and social and academic supports that more privileged students may not require. Providing these types of support is expensive. Better-prepared students from well-resourced high schools and college-educated families are more likely to be able to fend for themselves than are typical community college students. Institutional funding shortfalls combined with the resources available to individual students surely contribute to the limited success of community college students.

Financial Barriers and College Completion

Given the rising price tag on a college education, the cost of taking time out of the labor force, and the liquidity issues surrounding paying for living expenses while in school, it is reasonable to ask to what extent financial problems contribute to low completion rates for low-income and adult students. We examine the evidence on this issue here.

The evidence about the impact of prices and aid on college enrollment is compelling. There is broad consensus that lower net prices increase enrollment, and that price sensitivity is greatest for those with lower incomes. The specific evidence about the effectiveness of Pell Grants is not strong. Studies early in the program's life found no measurable impact.[23] A more recent study found a significant impact on the enrollment of adult students, but not of recent high school graduates.[24] One explanation for the weakness of the evidence is the difficulty of measuring the impact of a broad-based program available to all students in similar circumstances. Moreover, the complexity of the Pell Grant program appears to limit its impact.[25] Students and

23. Hansen (1983); Kane (1995).
24. Seftor and Turner (2002).
25. Mundel (2008).

families lack information about the benefits they might receive and have to complete a complex application process in order to get specific information and access to funds.

There is, however, convincing evidence that simpler grant programs do significantly increase postsecondary enrollment. For example, merit-based state grant programs in Georgia and other states that promise free college tuition to high school graduates who meet specific academic requirements increase overall college enrollment, although they disproportionately subsidize middle- and upper-income students; elimination of college benefits under the Social Security program led to a measurable decline in enrollment among the eligible population; and the implementation of a generous grant program for residents of Washington, D.C., led to higher college enrollment rates.[26]

But the impact of financial constraints once students enroll in college has attracted less research attention and is difficult to measure reliably. The evidence about the relationship between finances and persistence is suggestive rather than definitive. A study of the Georgia and Arkansas state merit scholarship programs found an increase in degree completion rates of around three to four percentage points, with a larger impact on the persistence of students who would have entered college even in the absence of the programs, but noted that many students who do not have to pay tuition drop out.[27]

Some studies of Pell Grants and other broad-based subsidies for students find a measurable impact on degree completion, but others do not.[28] Several studies have found that lower net tuition prices have a greater positive impact on persistence and enrollment among low-income students than among higher-income students.[29]

A recent study examined a private scholarship program in Nebraska that randomly assigned generous grant aid to undergraduate students in the state and found significant positive impacts on enrollment, on students choosing more selective institutions, and on second-year retention. Because the impact on students with lower levels of high school

26. Dynarski (2003); Kane (2007); Deming and Dynarski (2010).
27. Dynarski (2008).
28. Bettinger (2004); Turner (2004).
29. Paulsen and St. John (2002); Bowen, Chingos, and McPherson (2009).

achievement and minority students was largest, the aid significantly narrowed the gaps between these students and those with lower risk factors. However, the implications for disadvantaged students who are focused on occupational preparation are less clear. The study did not find significant effects on the enrollment and persistence of students who targeted community colleges rather than applying to both two-year and four-year institutions. Follow-ups to the study will provide more evidence on the impact of the additional grant aid on degree completion.[30]

Reviews of the literature on this subject usually conclude that the evidence is inconsistent but that well-designed student aid programs hold promise for improving college completion.[31] In addition to a growing consensus that simplicity and transparency are important in financial aid programs, evidence is accumulating that the incentives embedded in grant programs have a measurable impact on the accumulation of college credits and perhaps on eventual completion. Careful statistical analysis of programs that provide additional funds to students who complete prescribed numbers of credits each semester reveal that, structured properly, with attention to the behaviors required for academic success, financial aid programs can help raise persistence rates, not just relieve immediate financial pressures.[32]

But the evidence is strong that even if money can improve completion rates, it is most effective when combined with support services.[33] Financial barriers do not entirely explain students leaving school without degrees. The importance of the college environment and the support services provided is consistent with the well-documented finding that students who attend poorly funded institutions are less likely to complete degrees than similar students attending better-resourced institutions.[34]

30. Angrist and others (2015).

31. Goldrick-Rab (2010); Haynes (2008).

32. Scott-Clayton (2011a); Patel and others (2013).

33. Angrist, Lang, and Oreopoulos (2009); Deming and Dynarski (2010).

34. Bowen, Chingos, and McPherson (2009); Bound, Lovenheim, and Turner (2010); Roderick and others (2008).

Low-income students tend to arrive in college with lower levels of academic preparation, having grown up with limited resources in their families, neighborhoods, and schools. As discussed in chapter 3, they are more likely than others to enroll part time and, of particular significance, they lack the social capital—the information, connections, and experience—that helps many more privileged students overcome the hurdles of postsecondary education.

It is clear that some students who would otherwise complete credentials leave school because of money problems. There is little doubt that providing students with more resources to cover their expenses while in school would relieve strain and have a positive impact on completion rates. But it is not at all obvious how much of the completion problem or of the gap in completion rates between low-income and higher-income students could be eliminated by lowering tuition prices or increasing financial aid. Additional funding cannot eliminate differences in academic preparation, expectations, support networks, and life circumstances

Conclusion

Tuition and fees have risen rapidly across the nation in recent years. Variation across states means that access to low prices is uneven for students in different geographic locations. And among students seeking associate degrees and certificates to improve their labor market opportunities, those enrolling in for-profit institutions face dramatically higher prices than those who attend public two-year colleges. Students leave the for-profit sector with high levels of debt, increasing the struggle of finding postcollege financial success.

Tuition and fees are a small component of many students' expenses, particularly in community colleges. Despite the availability of need-based grant aid from the federal government and other sources, many students struggle to make ends meet while they are in college. Those who must attend college part time are less likely to complete their programs of study and be rewarded by the labor market afterward. For these students, as well as for those who do complete their programs but then have difficulty finding well-compensated work, paying back even small amounts of debt can be onerous.

While it is difficult to quantify the impact of financial barriers on college completion, there is no doubt that more money would make it easier for many of these students to succeed.

While high prices and high debt are central issues for students in the for-profit sector, institutional resources may be the most serious problem for two-year public college students. Because colleges in this sector have much lower per-student revenues than other types of institutions, they are too often unable to offer students the strong guidance and support they need to succeed in college.

PART II

Programs and Policies to Improve Student Outcomes

5

Policies and Practices Aimed at Students

In the previous chapters, we documented the low rates of college completion, especially among disadvantaged students, and the difficulties many have earning credentials with labor market value. Rising tuition levels and student debt loads certainly deserve attention, but solving other problems is likely even more critical for improving outcomes for these students. What kinds of policies and practices have the potential to improve the futures of disadvantaged, minority, and older students, as well as those with weak academic preparation?

In this chapter we review a range of efforts that are—or could be—provided at limited cost to at-risk *students* to increase their completion of a postsecondary credential with strong labor market value, examining available evidence about which strategies are most effective. In chapter 6, we consider efforts to change the characteristics of *institutions*, especially those at which disadvantaged students are concentrated, to improve these outcomes. And in chapter 7, we discuss alternatives for students for whom a postsecondary institution may not be the best option, at least right after high school.

It is not, of course, possible to draw a definitive line between student-focused and institution-focused policies. But providing better guidance and other student support services and improving financial aid fall into the first category. Reforming remedial education is also crucial, although some of the most compelling ideas for improvement would affect the structure of course offerings. Creating more structured curricular paths for students and strengthening partnerships with local employers are institution-based policies addressed in chapter 6.

Disadvantaged students are hampered both by their own personal or family characteristics and by weaknesses in the institutions they attend. Accordingly, it is useful to divide the approaches that target students into two categories: (1) efforts to improve the *access* of disadvantaged students to postsecondary programs and institutions that generate stronger outcomes; and (2) efforts to improve student *success* in programs that provide credentials with market value, wherever they enroll.

Reliable evidence indicates that we can reduce the number of disadvantaged students who enroll in institutions that do not serve them well and, to a lesser extent, increase the number who enroll in more selective institutions and programs by:

- improving the personalized *information and guidance* available to students when they apply to college;

- strengthening *financial aid* to reduce the impact of limited resources on college choice; and

- giving some *preference in recruiting and admissions* at selective institutions to applicants from disadvantaged backgrounds.

We can generate improvements in outcomes for disadvantaged students at *all* institutions by:

- improving *remediation* for students who are not academically prepared for college-level work;

- providing *supports and services* such as counseling, tutoring, and coaching to improve success rates;

- strengthening *financial aid* to diminish financial barriers to retention and completion once students are enrolled; and

- providing *nudges* to college students to keep them on track and thus improve performance.

All of these programmatic and policy changes, especially the supports and services provided to students, can improve completion rates in both liberal arts and occupational programs, while helping students make more informed and realistic choices among the options.

Improving Institutional Choice

Improving postsecondary outcomes for disadvantaged students by modifying enrollment patterns means one thing for recent high school graduates with strong academic records and something quite different for those who are less well prepared academically, are older, or have concrete short-term occupational goals.

For the first group, those with strong academic records, the problem is that many low-income and first-generation students do not apply to selective institutions. In addition, institutional admissions policies or finances may prevent those who do apply from attending these high-quality schools.

But the more pervasive problem is that too many less-exceptional disadvantaged students enroll in institutions with shockingly low graduation rates, in programs that do not lead to available jobs, or in high-priced institutions in the for-profit sector that cause them to accumulate inordinate amounts of debt. We begin by addressing institutional choice among the large majority of disadvantaged students. We then consider policies and practices to improve the access of the disadvantaged to more selective public and private colleges and universities. We conclude with a discussion of improving performance wherever students enroll.

Improving Information

The wide array of postsecondary choices in the United States expands opportunities by providing options suitable for people with diverse interests, capacities, and goals. But the range of choices available also requires individuals to make an overwhelming series of decisions. For students whose parents have no experience in and knowledge of the system and who do not have access to well-trained counselors, making informed decisions can be close to impossible.

Low-income and first-generation students have very little information about the complex world of postsecondary education in the United States. They often know nothing about colleges other than those closest to their homes, and many have no idea that it matters *where* they go, as opposed to *that* they go. Many potential college students are unaware of the availability of financial aid and believe that the published sticker price of tuition is what they will have to pay if they attend. As a result, they do not investigate their options.

Any state or federal efforts to provide personalized information and assistance to students must address a wide range of disadvantaged students. Efforts to improve the information available to these students are more likely to be effective if they involve outreach to staff in a variety of locations and contexts who can provide direct personal assistance to individual students. In addition, students should receive at least broad information about potential *careers* as well as *colleges*, so they have some notion of which programs of study at different colleges would suit their needs—even if they are not yet ready to make a career choice.

The federal government has made considerable effort in recent years to expand the information available to students facing the choice of where to enroll. Since 2011, Congress has required every college to post a net price calculator on its website, providing an estimate of how much students in different circumstances would be likely to pay for a year at that institution, after taking grant aid into consideration. The federal government has long had a College Navigator website[1] with detailed information about the prices, enrollment, graduation rates, financial aid, and other aspects of every college participating in federal student aid programs. It recently developed a user-friendly site that added information about postcollege earnings.[2] Some nonprofit organizations also have websites providing detailed information about individual colleges.

Oregon senator Ron Wyden's proposed Student Right to Know before You Go Act would require states to make very detailed data on academic and earnings outcomes for each public college or university

---

1. See College Navigator at https://nces.ed.gov/collegenavigator/.
2. See College Scorecard at https://collegescorecard.ed.gov/.

available.[3] But such information alone is not likely to have a large effect on where students apply and enroll. Many students have geographic constraints that limit their options, and many other personal factors influence whether and where they go to college.[4] Experimental evidence confirms the importance of customizing information for individual students and of direct contact with and assistance from advisers. An experiment in which students got assistance with filling out financial aid applications at their local H&R Block offices when they went to get help on their tax returns provides a compelling example. Merely providing information about financial aid availability had no effect on application and enrollment outcomes; but when H&R Block staff filled out the forms with potential students or their parents, more students applied to and enrolled in college.[5]

Just making general information available is unlikely to significantly improve the college decisions of students from less-privileged backgrounds. When the Department of Education added to its College Scorecard website information about the average earnings of students from different colleges, more students sent their SAT scores to the colleges whose students had higher postcollege earnings. But the impact was only on students from private and affluent public high schools. The behavior of those from high schools with large populations eligible for the Free and Reduced Price Lunch program did not significantly change.[6]

For high school students, guidance counselors are the most logical providers of these support services. However, low-income high schools, where few students traditionally go to college and where guidance counselors have large caseloads and little time or training for college advising, would require considerable additional resources to implement an effective strategy. As we will discuss in chapter 7, more options for career and technical education in high school might be a different way of providing information about careers and the pathways that can lead to them.

3. For the text of the proposed act, see Student Right to Know before You Go Act of 2015 at www.congress.gov/bill/114th-congress/senate-bill/1195/text.

4. Akers and Soliz (2015).

5. Bettinger and others (2012).

6. Hurwitz and Smith (2016).

For older adults and those younger students who have specific career goals in mind, the most sensible location for advising may be American Job Centers, funded by the U.S. Department of Labor (DOL) through its Workforce Innovation and Opportunity Act (WIOA).[7] The roughly 3,000 such offices are where workers go to receive any services or assistance from the DOL—including Unemployment Insurance as well as job search assistance. Any worker can obtain "core" assistance at these offices—staff-assisted help perusing online postings of job vacancies. Some workers also obtain "intensive" services, which include testing and counseling about job opportunities. And small numbers of workers receive Individual Training Account (ITA) vouchers funding limited amounts of training.

The intensive services include some limited information about colleges at which certain kinds of occupational training are provided; but the centers could also provide more information about college quality and programs, as well as local labor market information. Since adult workers rarely travel far from home to attend college, these students would likely be helped by specific information about nearby occupational programs and the labor market rewards they generate, as well as about odds of completion and costs of attending.

Most of these offices currently provide little such information, and staff would need additional training to fill this need. The centers would need additional funding, and users would need to view the centers as providing routes to better labor market opportunities, not just to jobs for the unemployed. Some proposals for funding this process suggest using a small portion of federal student aid dollars; if well designed and implemented, the program could significantly improve postsecondary and employment outcomes.[8]

7. American Job Centers were called One-Stop Centers before the 2014 implementation of WIOA, to replace the previous Workforce Investment Act (WIA). A 2013 report by the College Board on needed Pell Grant reforms proposed that all recipients of these grants above the age of twenty-four be required to obtain labor market counseling at a One-Stop office or other venue.

8. Rethinking Pell Grants Study Group (2013); Baum and Scott-Clayton (2013).

Additional expenditures on this service could be quite modest, while likely generating substantial benefits. Even after students enroll, they could continue using the centers, especially if the offices were located on community college campuses.[9] In the following discussion we consider some rigorous evaluation evidence on structured guidance and counseling beyond the simple provision of additional labor market information to low-income job trainees receiving vouchers. The combination of personalized advice and effective communication is critical. Strong evidence from behavioral economics and the cognitive sciences suggests that it is not sufficient just to make information available, and expect that the people who need it most will be aware of it and have the time and wherewithal to take advantage of it. Although having a wide array of choices can be a good thing, people frequently have difficulty making decisions that require comparing many criteria.

Weighing the importance of several schools' graduation rates, geographic location, programs offered, size, price, and many other factors can be a daunting task. In circumstances like these, people tend to resort to simplifying strategies that may not lead to optimal choices. All human beings share these basic characteristics, but for teenagers, whose capacity to plan ahead and process information is not fully developed, and for students from disadvantaged backgrounds, who may be addressing immediate survival issues, the problem may be more severe.[10] Moreover, students who lack direction when they decide to go to college need much more than a list of options to guide them toward constructive choices.

Matching Students to Selective Institutions

Disadvantaged students are often "undermatched," attending less-selective colleges and universities than students with similar qualifications from more affluent backgrounds. And some students may be "overmatched," attending institutions where they struggle to compete

9. According to conversations with Labor Department officials, as many as one-fourth of American Job Centers / One-Stop offices are now located on community college campuses.

10. Castleman (2015).

with their classmates. But disadvantaged students are more likely to be under- than overmatched.[11] They are heavily concentrated in public two-year and for-profit colleges, even when they have strong high school achievement. Most of those who attend four-year institutions enroll in broad-access regional public universities. In any case, even overmatched students at selective colleges and universities can benefit from the higher completion rates at those institutions and higher earnings afterward.

Increasing the flow of disadvantaged students into highly selective colleges and universities is not likely to transform the role of higher education in improving the lives of individuals from low-income backgrounds, since too few meet admission standards for this very limited number of slots. About 3 million students graduated from high school in 2004. About 18 percent of these students (539,000) were in the top mathematics achievement quartile and had an overall high school grade-point average above 3.0. But only 5 percent of those from the lowest socioeconomic quartile (34,000 students) met these criteria, whereas 35 percent (285,000) of high school graduates from the highest socioeconomic quartile did so. Two-thirds of high school graduates from the highest SES quartile, but only one-quarter of those from the lowest SES quartile, had either a GPA exceeding 3.0 or placed in the top mathematics quartile.[12]

Moreover, only 20 percent of four-year college students attend institutions that accept less than half of their applicants.[13] The number of slots for students at highly selective institutions is fixed and fairly limited relative to the size of the cohort of entering students. For every additional disadvantaged student who is matched to a selective college, another student will be turned away. Those turned away may not be from much more privileged backgrounds and may be no more likely to succeed at less-selective institutions than those who have replaced them.

Nonetheless, improving educational opportunities and outcomes for the most academically successful low-income students is critical,

11. Smith, Pender, and Howell (2013).
12. NCES (2002, PowerStats calculations).
13. Ma and others (2015).

and the case for improving access of the disadvantaged to more selective colleges and universities is strong.

Information about Selective Colleges

In a 2013 experiment, researchers focusing on very high-achieving low-income high school students developed a program called Expanding College Opportunity to improve access to highly selective colleges and universities. They provided students with a set of highly ranked colleges for which they might qualify, as well as a list of others that would be very likely to accept them—much as a guidance counselor would. They also provided the students with information about attainable financial aid, based on their family income, as well as a waiver of the usual application fee at each college. This very low-cost intervention ($6 per student) dramatically changed application patterns and increased the probability that students would enroll at an institution matching their qualifications by 46 percent. On average, students who received the mailing enrolled in colleges with graduation rates that were 15 percent higher, instructional spending that was 22 percent higher, and student-related spending that was 26 percent higher than schools chosen by similar students who did not receive the information.[14]

It is important to note that this strong response to personalized information delivered through the mail may be specific to the targeted group. These students represented a very small segment of the population, all scoring in the top 10 percent of SAT and ACT takers; they were applying to colleges with generous enough financial aid to make these highly selective institutions less expensive for them than most other options. This may help to explain the difference between the effectiveness of information alone in the H&R Block study and the information provided in this experiment.

In any case, changes in enrollment choices might be limited because many factors other than school quality affect where students enroll. Among lower-income students, price and location are very large factors. Indeed, the median student travels just fifty miles from

14. Hoxby and Turner (2013).

home to college or university; for first-generation students the median is just twenty-five miles.[15] Older students and those who need to work or take care of children do not have the luxury of traveling far to attend school. And a modest change in institutional quality is unlikely to change student outcomes very much; only if a student is moved from a broad-access to a very selective school are the institutional effects likely to change substantially.

Admission policies are not relevant to the majority of disadvantaged students who attend open-access or nonselective institutions, including most for-profit and public two-year colleges, as well as many regional public four-year universities. But admission policies can affect the access of disadvantaged students to selective institutions. Increasing enrollment of disadvantaged students in selective institutions is not just a matter of providing more information. Many will need to modify their admission procedures and spend considerable resources to enroll more low-income students.

When high-achieving low-income students apply to highly selective colleges and universities, they have a good chance of being admitted. But many simply never apply.[16] These schools' recruitment efforts could target high schools with high proportions of low-income or minority students and reach out to nearby community colleges to help students who want to transfer.

Admission policies and practices are also important. Constructive efforts could include waiving application fees for low-income students; deemphasizing ACT and SAT scores, which are highly correlated with family background; reviewing disadvantaged student files more holistically to note special talents and accomplishments as well as mitigating factors; and putting a "thumb on the scale" in favor of disadvantaged students in the evaluation process (Bowen, Kurzweil, and Tobin 2005).

Because they have so many more available spaces, public flagship universities have the potential to make a bigger impact than the highly selective private colleges and universities. In 2013–14, twice as many first-year students enrolled in public institutions that accept less than

15. Akers and Soliz (2015).
16. Hoxby and Avery (2013).

half of their applicants (986,000) as in private institutions with this level of selectivity (491,000).[17] For both sectors, however, resources are a critical issue. Low-income students do not just need to be encouraged to apply and be accepted. They must have generous enough financial aid to make attending these institutions a realistic possibility. Both higher tuition and the need, in most cases, to live away from home mean that students require significantly more grant aid than they would at a local two-year or regional public four-year institution.

Selective institutions are making efforts to recruit and admit more disadvantaged students. A number of highly selective and wealthy private colleges have for many years offered free tuition and living expenses to qualified students from low-income families. An increasing number of institutions have announced test-optional policies, welcoming applicants who do not report SAT or ACT scores, a strategy that may or may not increase socioeconomic diversity.[18] Another example of efforts to transform the admission process is the Coalition for Access, Affordability and Success, through which eighty selective schools are reaching out to ninth graders around the country with a website that offers personalized information and feedback. The idea is to facilitate the early accumulation of evidence of accomplishments that could help students at admission time.[19] Despite the inclusive intentions, it remains to be seen whether this innovation will significantly benefit low-income students.

There is wide variation in the representation of low-income students at selective colleges and universities across the country, and efforts to publicize these differences may have some impact. The *New York Times* publishes a College Access Index for about 180 colleges and universities, both public and private, with graduation rates of 75 percent or higher. The index is based on the percentage of students who are Pell Grant recipients and the net prices facing

17. NCES (2015b, table 305.40).

18. At least one study suggests that test-optional policies increase perceived selectivity but do not raise the number of low-income students enrolled (Belasco, Rosinger, and Hearn 2014).

19. Bruni (2015).

lower- to middle-income families.[20] It is a crude index that is often misinterpreted as a reliable measure of the "effort" colleges make to recruit needy students, but no school wants to be at the bottom of this list.

The wide variation in this measure of institutional access is striking. For instance, at several state universities in California, as well as the University of Florida, Pell grantees account for 20 to 40 percent of all new first-year students. In contrast, at the flagship universities in many other states, only 10 to 12 percent of students receive Pell Grants. Many of the state differences are likely due to differences in the demographics of their low-income populations, the geographic locations of universities and the relevant populations, and varying selectivity in admissions. But some of the variation is surely due to recruitment and admission practices. David Leonhardt notes, for example, that the University of California at Irvine, ranked highest of all the institutions on the list, with 40 percent receiving Pell Grants, has a strong program to help community college students transfer in.

Another important policy that affects the admission of at least some disadvantaged students is affirmative action. To date, affirmative action policies in the United States have focused much more on racial and ethnic identity than on socioeconomic status, though the share of students from low-income families is somewhat higher in institutions practicing affirmative action because of the correlations between low-income and minority status in the population.

The use of race in university admissions at public institutions is very controversial and has been restricted in some states by a series of court rulings and popular referendums.[21] As state flagship institutions have become increasingly limited in their ability to use race as a factor in admissions, many have begun to encourage the admission of socioeconomically disadvantaged students as a way of indirectly preserving at least some of the racial diversity that affirmative action had generated.

For instance, after California passed Proposition 209 in 1996, forbidding the use of race in individual admission decisions, the Uni-

20. Leonhardt (2015).
21. Alon (2015).

versity of California instituted some additional practices to recruit and admit more disadvantaged students. A program known as Eligibility in the Local Context allows the university to reach out to the top 9 percent of students in each public California high school early in their senior years to encourage them to apply and to follow up with them if they show interest (Perez 2012). Comprehensive review of candidates is allowed in the admission process for disadvantaged students who otherwise might not be admitted; partnerships with K–12 schools and community colleges have been designed to enhance the academic preparation of low-income students as well as their application flows. These practices have only partially restored the presence of underrepresented minorities at Berkeley and UCLA in the wake of Proposition 209.[22]

The narrowing scope of affirmative action for racial diversity need not interfere with creative efforts by universities to enroll more socioeconomically disadvantaged students, and may even increase efforts in this direction. A major hurdle, however, is the cost of enrolling and supporting large numbers of students with limited financial means. While admission preferences are relevant for a small segment of the college population, making enrollment and success financially feasible is critical for students in all segments of postsecondary education.

Tuition and Financial Aid: Improving Access and Guiding Choice of Institution

Financial strains affect both the enrollment patterns and the success rates of disadvantaged students. The perception that tuition levels at selective colleges and living expenses far from home are out of reach may discourage students from low-income backgrounds from applying to the institutions that could serve them best. Even among those who enroll, many struggle to make ends meet, and unexpected events can derail their studies. Strengthening the financial aid system—or

---

22. For instance, Berkeley's minority enrollment went from 27 to 12 percent of the total after Prop 209 passed, and then back to 17 percent after these alternative procedures were instituted. At UCLA minority enrollment went from 28 to 13 percent and then back to 21 percent (Perez 2012).

lowering tuition prices—can, therefore, have a measurable impact on the college success of students of limited means.

Recent discussions about removing financial barriers to college access have focused on tuition levels and modifying federal and state-level financial aid programs. We discuss these issues here.

Tuition

Tuition and fees increased by 41 percent in inflation-adjusted dollars at public four-year colleges and universities and by 31 percent at public two-year colleges between 2006–07 and 2016–17.[23] These prices do not reflect financial aid, and most students do not pay the full published price. Nonetheless, rapid price increases in an era when family incomes have been stagnant or declining have brought college affordability issues to the forefront of public discussions. The Obama administration proposed a national policy known as America's College Promise to make community colleges tuition-free, and several states have implemented or are planning to implement similar policies. Other politicians, including Bernie Sanders and Hillary Clinton, have supported this idea, in addition to proposing that all public colleges, both two-year and four-year, be tuition-free for most families.[24]

These proposals would communicate clearly to potential students that they will be able to afford the payments. However, eliminating tuition would not remove the financial barriers facing many disadvantaged college students, for whom it is covering their living expenses that presents the biggest problems. In 2011–12, 85 percent of dependent full-time community college students from the lowest income quartile and 66 percent of independent students paid no net tuition and fees. But they had to cover an average of about $8,000 and $12,000 in additional living expenses, respectively, to get through the year.[25] Free tuition might increase enrollment rates, but once

23. Ma and others (2016, table 2).

24. Candidate Bernie Sanders proposed free public college tuition for all. Candidate Hillary Clinton proposed that it be free for students from families with incomes below $125,000.

25. Ma and others (2016, figure 14).

students are enrolled they need adequate financial aid in order to succeed.

Proposals for free tuition are structured differently, and the details are significant. For example, the widely discussed Tennessee Promise program makes community college free for selected students by filling in the gap between federal and other state grant aid and published tuition levels.[26] In other words, low-income students must apply their Pell Grants to tuition and fees and are unlikely to receive any incremental funding from the program. They will not have an easier time covering their living expenses because of this new policy.

In contrast, President Obama proposed America's College Promise to eliminate tuition and fees, allowing low-income students to keep their Pell Grants to help cover other expenses.[27] The administration's approach was more expensive, but it would more effectively address the financial difficulties of disadvantaged students. However, since it would apply only to community colleges, it could have the unintended consequence of pushing into this sector more lower- and middle-income students who would likely achieve better academic outcomes if they enrolled in a four-year institution.[28] Since many community colleges already have limited classroom and teaching capacity, especially in high-demand fields such as nursing, the potential negative consequences of drawing so many students into two-year colleges without addressing these issues could be pronounced. Also, since this policy would likely attract students who otherwise had not planned to attend college at all—including many with poor academic

26. See the terms of the Tennessee Promise program at http://tennessee promise.gov/about.shtml.

27. See information about the America's College Promise proposal at www .whitehouse.gov/the-press-office/2015/01/09/fact-sheet-white-house-unveils -america-s-college-promise-proposal-tuitio.

28. There are other problems with the idea of free community college tuition. In particular, these institutions are already underresourced. As noted throughout this book, completion rates are disturbingly low and students need more academic and social supports to help them succeed. These supports are expensive and might well become less available in an environment where community colleges received no tuition revenues at all.

preparation—completion rates and other academic outcomes in this sector might decline.

Another approach to diminishing financial barriers that is gaining popularity is the local "college promise." Following the example of Kalamazoo, Michigan, some communities around the country are promising to pay the tuition of local residents at any public college or university. Preliminary evidence suggests that the simple message that college will be paid for has a significant impact among students who might not otherwise enroll.[29] Unless accompanied by a strong advising component, however, these programs are unlikely to improve students' choice of school and course of study.

As long as tuition is required, there may be strategies for making it less burdensome. One approach that can ease the burden without diminishing the cost to the student is to allow students to pay their tuition over the course of the term, instead of requiring it up front. Third-party vendors offer this service to institutions, but colleges can implement the practice on their own. Even if students are charged a small fee or required to make an early first payment, this flexibility could be helpful to students living on tight budgets or facing money management issues.

Another set of strategies for easing the burden of high tuition prices is to expand income-driven repayment (IDR) schemes for education loans, through which students repay their loans in the future as a fixed percentage of their incomes.[30] If the educational investment provides big returns in the future, they pay back their entire debt; if not, they pay much less in programs that forgive unpaid balances after a specified number of years, like those currently in effect for federal student loans in the United States. IDR bases subsidies on ability to pay *after* college—an approximation of the payoff students

29. Miller-Adams (2015).

30. Income-share agreements are an even more dramatic version of these loans. In these agreements, students are obligated to repay a share of their future incomes for specified periods of time, beyond just what they might owe to cover the amount of the loan they received. Purdue University, among others, is planning to expand its use of this type of agreement (Douglas-Gabriel 2016).

receive—rather than on their financial circumstances *before* college, which determine traditional need-based aid. Federal IDR plans have become more generous and more widely available, with 25 percent of borrowers with outstanding federal direct loans and 43 percent of the total balances in these programs as of fall 2016.[31] We do not yet have evidence that these programs have a significant impact on college enrollment or success, but they do mitigate the risks for students.

Federal Student Aid

More generous grant aid to low-income students would, of course, make paying for college easier for them by diminishing the amount they have to pay. In 2016–17, students with no estimated ability to pay for college could receive $5,815 in federal Pell Grant funding if they enrolled full time—enough to more than cover the average community college tuition, but equal to only about 60 percent of the average public four-year college tuition and less than 40 percent of the average price at a for-profit institution. While every dollar helps, small increases are not likely to transform the experience, and a doubling of the maximum Pell Grant is not feasible in the current fiscal environment. But there are other modifications to the financial aid system that could make a real difference for students.

In 2015–16, the federal government distributed $28 billon in Pell Grants to low- and moderate-income students.[32] Despite the evidence that reductions in the net price they pay has a significant impact on enrollment rates of low-income students, as discussed in chapter 4, researchers have not been able to clearly document the effectiveness of the Pell Grant program.[33] The consensus is that the difficulty of predicting how much aid will be available and the complexity of the application process and the eligibility formula interfere, making the program less effective. This reality and the fact that the program was designed only to increase access to college, without much consider-

31. Baum and others (2016, figure 10A).
32. Baum and others (2015).
33. Page and Scott-Clayton (2016).

ation given to supporting student success, have led to proposals to reform the program.[34]

Strong evidence indicates that the complexity of the entire student aid system creates significant challenges for disadvantaged students. In order to pay for college, students must piece together aid from the federal government, state governments, colleges and universities, and other sources. There is grant aid—sometimes called grants, sometimes scholarships, sometimes tuition waivers or discounts. But there are also refundable tax credits, subsidized student loans, and work-study aid. In order to apply for most of this aid, students and parents must complete the Free Application for Federal Student Aid (FAFSA). Although most applicants complete the form online and "skip logic" allows them to avoid answering questions that do not apply to them, the form is long and asks for detailed financial information that might not be easily accessible to applicants.

A simpler application process that relies more on data already provided to the Internal Revenue Service rather than asking students and parents again for financial information would mitigate this problem and give disadvantaged students access to the funds to which they are already entitled.[35] A more challenging but interesting idea is to automatically determine Pell Grant eligibility for students about to graduate from high school, informing them of the support they could receive and of the funds they would leave on the table if they decided not to pursue postsecondary education.[36]

Another central issue is how the federal government determines which institutions are eligible for federal student aid. Federal aid is distributed in the form of vouchers. Students are informed of their eligibility for grants and loans, and they can use their aid at any postsecondary institution that is accredited by an organization recognized by the Department of Education and that meets some general requirements about programs offered. Schools lose eligibility for federal aid

34. National Association of Student Financial Aid Administrators (2013); Rethinking Pell Grants Study Group (2013); Baum and Scott-Clayton (2013).

35. See Rueben, Gault, and Baum (2015) for a review of simplification proposals.

36. Baum and Scott-Clayton (2013).

if their students have extraordinarily high loan default rates, but only a small number have been penalized.[37] In recent years the department has sanctioned a few schools for fraudulent practices, including exaggerating job placement numbers, and two large for-profit chains closed their doors as a result.[38] But the violations must be egregious before the government takes action to protect students.[39]

Students could be better guided into institutions where they have a reasonable chance of succeeding if the criteria for institutional participation in federal student aid programs were more stringent. The triad of the U.S. Department of Education, state governments, and higher education accrediting agencies is responsible for monitoring the quality of postsecondary institutions. But there is broad consensus that this system is not working well to protect students. The Obama administration made progress in this direction through the 2015 implementation of the Gainful Employment regulations, which apply to all for-profit programs and to certificate programs at public and private nonprofit institutions. Under the new regulations, a program risks losing aid eligibility if the annual loan payments of typical graduates exceed 20 percent of their incomes above a basic living allowance or 8 percent of total earnings. The Department of Education estimates that about 1,400 programs serving 840,000 students—of whom 99 percent are at for-profit institutions—would not meet these standards.[40]

These standards, implemented after a long legal battle, represent a step in the right direction. But much work remains to be done in developing effective strategies to prevent students from enrolling in institutions where they have little chance of graduating or, if they do graduate, of finding remunerative employment based on their credentials.

37. Stratford (2015).

38. Blumenstyk (2016).

39. Smith (2016).

40. U.S. Department of Education (2015), "Fact Sheet: Obama Administration Increases Accountability for Low-Performing For-Profit Institutions," July 1 (www.ed.gov/news/press-releases/fact-sheet-obama-administration-increases-accountability-low-performing-profit-institutions).

State Grants

State grant programs vary quite a bit across the nation. Fourteen states award more than half of their grant aid without considering the financial circumstances of the recipients. Grant aid to middle- and upper-income students with high levels of high school achievement may ease financial burdens, but it does little to improve access and success.[41] Moreover, many states limit their grant aid to recent high school graduates, leaving out older adults who go back to school to improve their labor market opportunities.[42] Including older students and those who did not excel in high school is critical to increasing opportunities and success among disadvantaged students.

Improving Success Rates at *All* Institutions

Most disadvantaged students will continue to enroll at nonselective institutions, many of which have very limited resources. Directing students to institutions that will serve them best and providing the financing that makes it possible for them to enroll there are critical. But it is also vital to find effective strategies for improving the success rates of all students—and particularly of disadvantaged students—wherever they enroll. At community and for-profit colleges, where the disadvantaged are most concentrated, money is only part of the problem, and often not the biggest factor. A range of other supports and services matter a great deal, and could potentially play a more positive role.

Filling the Gaps in Academic Preparation: Better Remediation

U.S. colleges and universities provide a range of supports and services to disadvantaged students in addition to financial aid. These services include developmental education (sometimes called remediation), in addition to academic or career counseling and child care.

41. Heller (2001); Heller (1997); Bowen, Chingos, and McPherson (2009).
42. Baum and others (2012).

Sixty-eight percent of students beginning at two-year public colleges in 2003–04 and 40 percent of those beginning at four-year institutions took at least one remedial class between 2003 and 2009.[43]

There is a growing consensus that too many students are placed in developmental classes, and that these classes do not accomplish their goal of increasing the chances that students will succeed in college. Instead they discourage students and divert them from college-level programs. Most colleges have used a standardized test such as ACT's Computerized Adaptive Placement Assessment and Support Systems (COMPASS) or Assessment of Skills for Successful Entry and Transfer (ASSET) to determine which newly enrolled students will be required to take developmental classes. Many scholars question whether a single standardized test can accurately predict students' potential for success in the very broad range of programs in which they enroll; in fact, ACT discontinued COMPASS at the end of 2016 because of its questionable effectiveness. The evidence indicates that placement tests cause a significant number of students who could succeed in for-credit college courses to be diverted into developmental classes. Basing placements on high school performance would be more appropriate.[44]

Furthermore, the research suggests that, as currently structured, remediation is not successful at improving student skills and postsecondary success.[45] Indeed, some studies find negative effects of developmental coursework on credit and degree attainment.[46]

In some ways, this is not surprising. Many students placed into remediation cannot take courses in their degree programs for academic credit until they successfully complete the developmental courses and can pass a test in Algebra I or English. If they also need to work and support a family, the time they can devote to college classes is limited, and the time spent in developmental courses might well discourage them from continuing.

43. Chen (2016).
44. Scott-Clayton, Crosta, and Belfield (2014).
45. Bettinger, Boatman, and Long (2013); Clotfelter and others (2013).
46. See Jaggars and Stacey (2014) for an accessible summary of the literature.

As a result, there have been calls for reform of every phase of the remediation process (Long 2014)—including how placement into developmental coursework is determined and how the remediation is delivered. Of particular importance are efforts to increase the number of high school students who graduate prepared to do college-level work.

A constructive approach may be to move away from general policies applying the same requirements to all students, instead determining the need for developmental coursework in the context of what students intend to study.

Recent evidence indicates that allowing students to enroll in college classes at the same time that they get the assistance they need to develop their skills improves outcomes. Complete College America found that this strategy, dubbed "corequisite remediation," dramatically increases the number of students who complete college-level courses.[47]

Similarly, the Accelerated Learning Program (ALP) at Baltimore County Community College allows students to take college-level English classes concurrently with remediation. Evaluations show large improvements in completing college-level classes and greater persistence.[48] In Virginia, community college students take nine one-credit modules of developmental coursework while also enrolled in classes for credit; students in STEM programs are required to pass all nine while others have fewer requirements. At Austin Peay State University in Tennessee, enrolling students in specially structured for-credit math courses with different levels of remediation embedded has also proven to be relatively effective.[49]

In 2013, Florida responded to skepticism about the effectiveness of its developmental education strategies by making developmental education entirely voluntary. It is too soon to know what the effects of this policy change will be, but it would be wise for researchers and policymakers to keep track of all such state-level changes and to analyze the resulting impact on education outcomes for low-achieving students.

47. Complete College America (2015).
48. Bettinger, Boatman, and Long (2013).
49. Boatman (2012).

Abandoning remediation for all college-bound students may not be a constructive approach. It is likely to be more successful with students with moderate gaps in preparation than with those whose skills are far below those required for college-level work. The CUNY Start program at the City University of New York, instituted in 2009, illustrates reform of precollege developmental education. Students with large gaps in preparation postpone matriculation into college programs for one semester and, paying only $75, participate in intensive instruction in reading, writing, and mathematics, combined with active academic advising, tutoring, and skill building. The results are promising and rigorous analysis of the program is under way.[50]

The Carnegie Foundation's Statway and Quantway models and the Dana Center's Mathway model allow students to proceed along different paths to remediation, with fewer topics covered on each pathway but more emphasis placed on understanding concepts and contextualizing them in real-world situations. Descriptive studies show successful outcomes for these approaches.[51]

Some promising approaches also use new technologies in the developmental education process.[52] In some models, students take online classes in learning labs and proceed at their own pace through the remediation. Little rigorous evidence yet exists on the effectiveness of this approach, but it does reduce costs.

Some states are experimenting with testing students much earlier, while they are still in high school, to determine their remediation needs and to supply the needed support before they apply to and enroll in college. For example, the California Early Assessment Program and the Florida College and Career Readiness Initiative assess the college readiness of eleventh graders.[53] The idea is that if schools, students, and parents know in advance about gaps in preparation, they can address these problems before students get to college.

A different approach, which is especially appropriate for youth or adults enrolling in college for limited career education, is the state of

50. Scrivener and Logue (2016).
51. Bailey, Jaggars, and Jenkins (2015).
52. Long (2014).
53. California Department of Education (2015).

Washington's Integrated Basic Education and Skill Training (I-BEST) model. It is designed primarily for students who are not high school graduates and who lack basic skills or English-language proficiency. I-BEST provides two teachers in the same class, one to deliver the regular course material and the other to provide remediation as needed. The I-BEST model thus embeds remediation in applied job training classes, rather than relegating it to stand-alone math or English classes, providing context for the remedial material and thereby increasing student motivation and understanding. Nonexperimental evaluations have shown strong positive impacts on student persistence and credit attainment, though more rigorous evaluation is needed to definitively establish the effects.[54] Still, Maryland and other states are now trying to apply the I-BEST model to their own remedial efforts.[55]

Of course, preventing the need for remediation among adult job trainees at community colleges might be a better option, just as it is for students still in high school. "Bridge" courses offered before students begin college are designed with this goal, but existing evidence about their impact suggests caution.[56] A program at LaGuardia Community College in New York integrated instruction to help students pass GED exams with introductions to health care and business programs, applying the idea of embedding remedial instruction within material relevant for job training and the labor market. Rigorous evaluation showed positive impacts of this program on GED pass rates and on community college enrollment.[57] But, as is frequently the case with programs designed for high-risk populations, the overall success rates remained low.[58] A central challenge to developing strategies for im-

54. Zeidenberg, Cho, and Jenkins (2010) use nonexperimental matching and difference-in-difference methods to show that I-BEST participants had substantially higher college credit and certificate attainment than nonparticipants. But the relatively high cost of assigning two instructors to each course might make it difficult to scale up this program.

55. Jobs for the Future (2014).

56. Barnett and others (2012).

57. Martin and Broadus (2013).

58. For instance, even for the treatment group just 24 percent enrolled in community college afterward, and 12 percent enrolled for a second semester.

proving outcomes among disadvantaged students is determining the cost-effectiveness of programs that have significant positive impacts but leave the vast majority of the target population behind.

Nonfinancial Supports and Services

Other approaches to increasing college success provide a range of supports, both inside and outside the classroom. Examples include comprehensive system redesign; "learning communities," where a group of students take all classes together in order to strengthen peer connections and the sense of belonging; and counseling and guidance that can be more or less intensive and voluntary or mandatory.

The Accelerated Study in Associate Programs (ASAP) at the City University of New York provides a comprehensive set of supports and imposes strict requirements on students.[59] Even after taking developmental courses, students receive intensive academic advising and tutoring plus career services while being required to attend college full time. Students participate in blocked courses with their ASAP peers, thus creating learning communities, while also receiving additional financial supports (such as free metro cards and textbooks). They are strongly encouraged to complete their associate degree programs within three years.

The impacts demonstrated in a rigorous evaluation of ASAP were extremely strong: graduation rates of students nearly doubled from about 22 to 40 percent as a result of receiving ASAP treatment. Costs per *student* were high, since ASAP cost about $16,000 more than programs for nonparticipants over three years.[60] But costs per *graduate* were relatively low because of the significant increase in graduation rates.[61]

The large positive impact of ASAP on college completion, especially among students needing developmental education, dwarfs results from

59. Scrivener and others (2015).

60. For nonparticipants, total costs over three years averaged nearly $26,000; for participants, they averaged about $42,000.

61. ASAP raised costs per participant by about 62 percent but raised completion rates by over 80 percent.

any other program that has been rigorously evaluated. The requirement that students attend college full time likely contributed substantially to its impacts, showing that the combination of intensive
supports plus full-time attendance can generate dramatic results.
Whether similar programs can be effective for students who must
attend part time because of their work and family responsibilities
remains unclear.

Still, the dramatic improvement in completion rates observed in
ASAP among full-time students strongly suggests that it should be
considered a model to replicate. Finding the necessary resources up
front to implement this expensive program is very challenging, though
it is likely to be cost-effective in the long run. Figuring out which components of ASAP are most critical for its success among different populations, through rigorous program evaluation, should also be high
on our list of priorities.

Other programs with academic supports and counseling have also
generated positive impacts in rigorous evaluations, though much
smaller in magnitude and less likely to persist until program completion. For instance, learning communities can create a sense of belonging within a larger institution and generate peer support. The National
Center for Postsecondary Research conducted rigorous evaluations
of these interventions at several community colleges. Overall, they
showed positive but very small effects. Notably, the effects were larger
when the learning communities were combined with broader support
services.[62]

Institutions have tried a variety of approaches to improving counseling and guidance for students. The counseling may be purely academic, or it may focus on potential labor market opportunities.
"Intrusive" counseling, in which coaches or counselors reach out to
students frequently, is gaining support because it is consistent with
insights from the behavioral sciences into how people make choices.

In its Opening Doors study, MDRC evaluated two efforts focused
on academic counseling. Students at community colleges receive relatively little advising or mentoring whether they need remediation or
not. But just offering advising to students does not ensure that they

take advantage of such services, or that the services are effective in improving student outcomes. One approach, tested at Lorain County and Owens Community Colleges in Ohio, paid students $150 to meet with academic advisers at least twice each semester. The other, at Chaffey College in California, offered students on academic probation a student success course focused on time management, study skills, and college expectations. Students were expected to meet with instructors outside of class and visit the success center for additional help. Initially, students took the success course for just one semester and attending it was voluntary, but program modifications increased the course to two semesters and made it a requirement.

All of these interventions had some significant impact on educational outcomes, but the effects were mostly short term. In the Ohio programs, both student persistence in college and credit attainment were higher in the semester during which counseling was paid for and in the next one, but the effects dissipated soon afterward. In the California program that required counseling, the percentage of students who moved off probation over two semesters rose to 30 percent from 16 percent, but there was no effect on persistence.

These studies suggest that counseling can have positive impacts, but there must be strong incentives or requirements that struggling students participate. Although the observed impacts dissipated, they likely would have remained stronger had the counseling lasted longer. We should also note that counseling and tutoring were among the comprehensive support services provided in the highly successful ASAP program. Not surprisingly, any single short-term intervention will be less successful than a more comprehensive and lasting set of supports.

Coaching is a form of intrusive guidance for college students. In this intervention, the coach proactively reaches out frequently to students to remind them of academic requirements, provide information, and help with time management and study skills. In one randomized trial focusing on older students in a variety of institutions, coaches contacted students regularly and helped them to connect their daily activities to their long-term goals. Coached students were about five percentage points (9 to 12 percent) more likely than others to return to school the following year. The effects of the coaching persisted after the activity ended, suggesting that students were able to develop skills that stayed with them. Although individual attention may be costly, the results of this study suggest that the coaching was more effective in fostering student success than a similar amount of financial aid would likely be.[63] Coaching is one form of a "nudge" to student behavior that we consider in more depth below.

But academic counseling and coaching alone are not enough. Few students receive labor market counseling, through which they could learn more about job opportunities and training paths toward stable and remunerative careers. We do not have a great deal of evidence from community colleges about this type of counseling, though the career services through ASAP helped students choose academic or occupational paths that were most appropriate for them.

One additional study has analyzed the effectiveness of providing guidance in conjunction with individual training accounts (ITAs), short-term job training vouchers available in the American Job Centers funded by the Department of Labor. The earnings increases of ITA recipients rose by almost $500 per quarter when the trainees were required to obtain guidance.[64] Requiring labor market guidance is a more successful way to convey market information to disadvantaged students than simply making the information available on a website. In the past few years, college/career "navigators" have also been more frequently used to help older college trainees choose appropriate programs of study and even specific courses, and practitioners believe these navigators can help these students achieve success.[65]

Nonacademic Services and Supports

Many students seeking to improve their labor market opportunities are parents. In 2011–12, 26 percent of all undergraduate students had dependent children. Thirty percent of community college students and 50 percent of those enrolled in for-profit institutions had children. Forty-four percent of these children were under the age of

---

63. Bettinger and Baker (2014).
64. McConnell, Perez-Johnson, and Berk (2014).
65. Aspen Institute (2014).

five and 76 percent were under the age of 12.[66] Inadequate child care options can prevent these students from succeeding in college, regardless of their motivation or academic qualifications. Focus groups conducted at six community colleges revealed child care issues as a key obstacle.[67] Many community colleges have child care centers on campus, but there is usually not enough capacity or funding for all student-parents to benefit.[68] Some institutions have used funding from the federal Child Care Access Means Parents in School (CCAMPIS) program to help meet child care needs.[69] Not all colleges can provide on-campus care, but providing referral services or other information may be a constructive, lower-cost alternative.

Because low-income college students often have difficulty meeting basic food, housing, and other needs for themselves and their families,[70] another useful supplementary service is assistance with access to publicly funded income assistance programs. Some students are eligible for food, housing, child care, and other subsidies but do not know about them or are unsure how to access them. The Benefits Access for College Completion program, a partnership between the Center for Law and Social Policy (CLASP) and the American Association of Community Colleges, with funding from multiple foundations, supported seven community colleges around the country in setting up services to help students receive public benefits.[71]

The Single Stop program, operating in seven states, provides community colleges with the resources and training to connect students to public financial assistance and financial coaching. There is no rigorous evidence about the impact of these efforts, but Single Stop reports helping students receive an average of almost $2,000 in benefits, and preliminary data indicate that those students who use Single Stop services are more likely to stay in school.[72]

66. NCES (2012, PowerStats calculations).
67. Matus-Grossman and Gooden (2002).
68. Nelson, Froehner, and Gault (2013); Schumacher (2013).
69. University of North Florida (N.D.).
70. Goldrick-Rab (2010); Goldrick-Rab, Broton, and Eisenberg (2015).
71. Duke-Benfield (2015).
72. Single Stop (2014).

Programs like Single Stop offer nonfinancial services to help students gain access to both cash and in-kind benefits. Simply providing more cash specifically designated for these needs can also make a difference. An Opening Doors intervention in Louisiana provided low-income student-parents with a $1,000 cash stipend if they maintained at least a C average and earned at least six credits in a semester.[73] The program improved credit attainment and persistence among these students, who reported using the cash for basic living expenses. Another experiment found that allowing Pell Grants to pay for child care increased enrollments of women with children but not their college attainment.[74]

In short, a range of primarily nonfinancial supports and services for disadvantaged students can contribute to better academic performance. However, programs must be well designed and carefully implemented. Though each service on its own is likely to have modest effects, the combined impact of multiple interventions may be quite substantial.

Tuition and Financial Aid: Improving Student Performance and Success

Most financial aid programs are designed primarily to increase access to college. But both tuition and financial aid policies can also help enrolled students succeed.

American college students are taking longer to complete their studies than students in earlier generations. Additional time to degree adds dramatically to the cost of a college education. If a student spends three full-time years earning an associate degree instead of two years, she not only pays an extra year of tuition, but also loses a year of labor market participation at the college-graduate earnings level.

How tuition prices are structured has the potential to affect student success. For example, many community colleges and broad-access public four-year institutions charge by the credit hour. Students pay more

73. Scrivener and Coghlan (2011).
74. Simmons and Turner (2003).

if they enroll for more courses. The alternative is "block" or "flat-rate" tuition pricing, under which students pay the same price regardless of the number of credit hours for which they register, within specified limits—commonly twelve to eighteen credit hours per semester. Because institutions that use block pricing frequently implement other strategies to encourage students to enroll in fifteen credit hours per term, it is not clear what the impact of this policy on its own might be. However, Adams State University in Colorado and Oklahoma State University are among the institutions that have moved in this direction to encourage students to earn their degrees as quickly as possible. This policy, combined with modification of the twelve-credit definition of full time embodied in the federal student aid system, and communication efforts promoting the importance of averaging fifteen credits per semester, could reduce time to completion for many students.

In addition to putting money in students' pockets, financial aid programs can provide incentives and opportunities to spur academic progress. There is considerable evidence that financial aid is more effective when combined with access to academic and other student support services and when some portion of the aid is attached to evidence of progress toward a degree.[75]

Some of the financial aid policies that have the potential to increase student success rates must be implemented at the federal and state levels. In addition to providing larger grants, the Pell Grant system could improve the incentives for on-time completion. Under current policy, in order to be considered full time and receive the maximum award, students must be enrolled for twelve credit hours per semester. But the typical associate degree requires sixty credits—an average of fifteen credits a semester for two years. The typical bachelor's degree requires 120 credits—an average of fifteen credits a semester for four years. Not surprisingly, many students sign up for twelve or thirteen credits, understanding this to be a full-time schedule. In fact, a student who takes twelve credits a term for five semesters to earn an associate degree will receive two-and-a-half full Pell Grants. The same student who completes those sixty credits in four semesters will receive just

75. Page, Castleman, and Sahadewo (2016).

two full Pell Grants—even though both might pay the same amount of tuition if their institutions charge by the credit hour.

A Pell adjustment that would award more aid to students who enroll for more credit hours, possibly by fixing the amount of aid available for the entire program, to be distributed according to the intensity with which the student enrolls, would better support timely completion. The Obama administration proposed a $300 Pell Grant premium for recipients who sign up for fifteen credit hours, which would be a positive step in this direction. Another approach is to allow students to receive additional Pell funding for summer enrollment even if they have used up their annual allotment by enrolling full time in the fall and spring. Congress eliminated a summer Pell provision in effect from 2008 to 2011 in order to save money, but the Obama administration and lawmakers on both sides of the aisle in Congress have supported restoring a similar program.

Supplementary Aid

There is considerable evidence about the design of effective grant programs that supplement federal and state aid. This assistance may be funded by institutions or other private entities or be an add-on to basic need-based federal and state grant programs. Rigorous experimental testing of programs that provide extra funds to students based on their timely and successful completion of coursework indicates that at-risk students respond positively to these financial incentives, completing more course credits than similar students not offered these potential rewards.[76]

Rewarding postsecondary academic progress among high-need students is quite different from basing financial aid on merit rather than need. Awarding aid to high-achieving high school graduates subsidizes students likely to enroll and succeed in college even without the aid, and fails to serve many with severe financial constraints and potential to benefit from postsecondary education. Providing supplementary aid that increases the incentives of high-need students to progress more quickly through their programs cannot

76. Mayer and others (2015); Scott-Clayton (2015).

solve all the problems these students face, but it can measurably improve their outcomes.

Institutions with limited funds—like the institutions most disadvantaged students attend—can develop creative financial aid strategies to improve student outcomes even within their budget constraints. Tying a component of available need-based aid to academic progress, Adams State University in Colorado and the University of Texas-Arlington are examples of institutions that have acted on evidence about the positive impact of performance-based scholarships by incorporating rewards for credit completion into institutional scholarship programs.[77]

Experimental evidence also supports the effectiveness of tying a component of aid to needy students to participation in academic and other support services on campus.[78] Examples of the implementation of programs to motivate students to use these services include the Higher Education Opportunity Program in New York State, which has been successful in graduating disadvantaged students for many years; Western Oregon University, which ensures that students receiving financial aid also get supplementary academic support services; and the Indiana State University Center for Student Success, which provides personal guidance and community service opportunities in addition to financial assistance.[79] The Carolina Covenant, through which the University of North Carolina at Chapel Hill has provided a mix of grants, loans, and work-study plus academic supports and services to low-income students, also shows some evidence of success at improving student outcomes.[80]

No general need-based grant program is designed to handle unforeseen emergencies. Need-based aid is, by definition, allocated on the basis of students' financial circumstances at the time they apply. It is not possible to know in advance whose car will break down, whose child caregiver will become incapacitated, or who will have a medical or other emergency requiring extra resources. Some institutions have

77. Baum, McDemmond, and Jones (2014).
78. Angrist, Lang, and Oreopoulos (2009); Patel and Rudd (2012).
79. Baum, McDemmond, and Jones (2014).
80. Clotfelter, Hemelt, and Ladd (2015).

set up emergency aid programs in the form of supplemental grants, advances on financial aid, or short-term loans.

Although more rigorous study of emergency supports is needed, reports on several of these efforts provide suggestive evidence that they can prevent disadvantaged students from dropping out of school in the face of short-term problems.[81] Georgia State University has found that a supplementary grant program supporting students who are progressing successfully but are unable to pay their tuition and fees in full has increased persistence rates; Austin Community College has a fund to help students who have completed at least fifteen credit hours and are facing an unforeseen financial emergency; and Pasadena City College offers short-term emergency loans for unexpected expenses, books, and supplies.[82] These programs must be carefully designed to avoid abuse, but have the potential to diminish some very real challenges to student success.

"Nudging" Student Behavior

Even students who have affordable college options, and adequate academic skills and preparation, too frequently do not enroll in college. Many who do enroll attend institutions where they are unlikely to succeed or likely to leave school before earning a credential. As discussed above, as insights from the cognitive sciences increase our understanding of human behavior and decisionmaking, it is becoming increasingly clear that changes in the way information and options are framed can have a significant impact on choices. Moreover, small and subtle pushes or "nudges" can measurably improve student outcomes. Very few students make decisions by simply weighing the long-term costs and benefits, and going down the path that leads to the outcome they desire. We should be guiding students in constructive directions, without unduly limiting their autonomy.

Recent experimental studies yield important results about modifying student behavior. For example, one study found that an auto-

81. Geckeler (2008).
82. Baum, McDemmond, and Jones (2014).

mated, personalized text-messaging campaign to remind high school graduates of important summer tasks significantly increased the number of disadvantaged students accepted to college who actually enrolled in the fall.[83] In an experiment described above, in which H&R Block tax assistants filled out financial aid applications at the same time they completed tax forms for some low-income filers, high school graduates who received this service were eight percentage points more likely than others to enroll in college.[84]

A key understanding behind the effectiveness of these behavioral interventions is that people tend to take the path of least resistance when faced with difficult or complex choices. A seminal study showed that switching pension plan registration from requiring new employees to check a box if they wanted to join the plan to requiring them to actively opt out if they did *not* want to join significantly increased participation.[85]

The idea of making the "default option" one that is mostly likely to lead to success is behind the creation of structured curriculum pathways in community colleges. Leaving students to choose without guidance among thousands of courses is less effective than designing a set of courses they will take unless they actively choose to make substitutions.[86]

Low-cost, low-touch interventions can affect both behaviors and attitudes. Many first-generation students are unfamiliar with college norms and expectations. Simply informing them that people like them who succeed attend all class sessions, or that their peers typically participate in study groups, can induce them to adapt to those norms. Similarly, brief exposure to positive descriptions that increase their sense of belonging in college can increase the academic performance of first-generation and minority students. For example, one experiment showed that a small amount of reading and writing about how students adjust to college dispelled the concerns of African American students that they were not suited to the

83. Castleman and Page (2013).
84. Bettinger and others (2012).
85. Madrian and Shea (2001).
86. Scott-Clayton (2011b).

college environment enough to markedly increase their grades over the coming year.[87]

Variations on a combination of personalized attention and automatic nudges have the potential to move the needle on student success. Time management is a serious problem for students facing the unfamiliar demands of college, particularly for those who have work and family responsibilities. The evidence from behavioral sciences about the impact of reminders, of asking people to commit in advance to carrying out tasks at a specified time, and of simplifying their options is mounting.[88] Applying these insights to supporting student success holds great promise.

More experimentation will improve understanding of the optimal amount of structure and the optimal design of nudges and reminders for students. But rather than just trying to pound basic quantitative and verbal skills into students with weak academic preparation, institutions should focus on straightforward ways to improve their self-confidence and their organizational skills, keep them on track to complete the required daily tasks, and make it easier for them to make choices that will serve them well.

In a different vein, a small number of states have begun requiring that all high school seniors register for and take the SAT or ACT college entrance exam. Careful studies analyzing changes in college application and enrollment behavior in these states, relative to those that do not require the tests, find notable increases, particularly in four-year and more selective institutions.[89]

A Troubling Question: Should We Raise Admission Requirements at Some Open-Access Institutions?

Many of the policies discussed above, such as programs to make community college free, could substantially expand the numbers of students who attend these institutions—even among those who are

---

87. Walton and Coehn (2007).
88. Thaler and Sunstein (2008).
89. Goodman (2012); Goodman (2013); Hurwitz and others (2015).

not well prepared academically for postsecondary education and who do not now enroll in any college or university. Yet we already admit large numbers of poorly prepared students, creating significant expenses for remediation and academic support services while ultimately generating very low rates of college credit attainment and completion. Indeed, one might argue that tens of billions of public and private dollars and millions of hours of student and instructor time are wasted each year when so many students attend college with virtually no chance of having anything concrete to show for it.

Yet many would justifiably find it troubling if we suggested that access to postsecondary education for weakly prepared students should be reduced or denied through more rigorous admission requirements. As we noted in the introduction, postsecondary education has become the single most important determinant of success in the labor market and of potential upward mobility for individuals from low-income backgrounds. In other words, access to higher education for all who can benefit is a critical source of opportunity in America.

Perhaps a better approach would be to provide a wider range of pathways to success for at-risk students, including some where their chances of achieving labor market success are higher. For instance, if more students had access to high-quality career and technical education (CTE) in high school, where they were prepared for rewarding routes into the labor market as well as for postsecondary education, fewer might choose immediate entry into open-access college programs where their odds of success are so low.

In addition, if many students who currently enroll in associate degree programs with low completion rates and low labor market rewards could be guided into more promising paths at community colleges, such as certificate programs with labor market value, whether for academic credit or not, they might be better off. Making students in such programs eligible for federal financial aid, as we discuss in chapter 6, could facilitate this outcome.

Before raising the admission bar at broad-access public institutions of higher education, we should widen other pathways to success in education and the labor market. We discuss these possibilities more fully in chapter 7.

Conclusion

Many students enter college in America with relatively weak academic preparation, ill-equipped to choose the institutions and programs that match their interests and abilities. Helping high school graduates and older adults returning to school to select the most appropriate institutions and programs is the first step toward improving their labor market opportunities.

High-achieving students from low-income backgrounds frequently enroll in colleges and universities where their academic skills far exceed those of most other students. The evidence is strong that these students would have better outcomes if they enrolled in more selective institutions. Improving this situation is important, but improving the outcomes of the vast majority of disadvantaged students who are not eligible for highly selective institutions will make a bigger difference for many more students.

Graduation rates at broad-access institutions are disturbingly low, while many who graduate obtain credentials with little labor market value. Finding successful and cost-effective strategies that help students reach their goals is critical to higher education's mission as a path to upward mobility. Some of the solutions involve diminishing the financial challenges faced by low- and moderate-income students. But helping students compensate for inadequate academic preparation by providing effective academic remediation and other support systems is even more critical. Helping students choose the right programs for themselves, whether in the liberal arts or in an occupational sector, is critical as well. For this to occur, there is no substitute for tailoring information, guidance, and academic programs and structures to the specific needs of students.

No single innovation will, on its own, make an enormous difference in college success rates. There is no silver bullet to success. The ASAP program for full-time students at CUNY is our greatest success story to date; it roughly doubled completion rates among full-time students who entered with weak academic performance. But it is expensive to administer and we do not know to what extent its success can be replicated around the country, especially for part-time students.

Our top priority, then, should be to *help community colleges implement the supports and services provided in ASAP, including career services, but in ways that are affordable and suited to their own populations and institutional characteristics.* More experimentation with and evaluation of programs like ASAP, in different locations and with different student bodies, will advance our knowledge of what works and for whom. More broadly, federal and state government policies should facilitate the array of proposals discussed in this chapter, and institutions should make a concerted effort to implement them for their students.

Regardless of which policies and practices are implemented, students from disadvantaged backgrounds and with weak academic preparation will face an uphill battle without some fundamental changes in the structures and practices of their postsecondary institutions. Many of the institutions in which these students enroll do not now have frameworks in place that maximize opportunities for student success.

Broad-access public institutions, in particular, need major structural changes that would more effectively direct students onto successful pathways. And, in order to ensure good labor market outcomes for their students, they must offer a range of programs and credentials, including nontraditional certificate programs—either for credit or not—along with curriculums that are more closely integrated with workplace needs. They will need ample resources to strengthen their teaching capacity in key fields and stronger incentives to spend those resources effectively.

Public colleges will likely remain the route for most of the students on whom we focus. But ensuring that for-profit institutions also provide reliable paths, and that other providers offer innovative but proven learning and training strategies, will increase the number of students who can achieve their goals. In addition, a range of alternative paths beginning in secondary school and reaching into higher education or the labor market would offer all students better chances for success. We turn to these issues in chapters 6 and 7.

6

Policies and Practices for Institutions

In the previous chapter, we reviewed policies and programs targeted to individual students applying to or attending college. In this chapter we consider major structural changes and new practices that postsecondary institutions could undertake to improve the success rates of disadvantaged students, especially those seeking occupational preparation. Although these categories overlap considerably, the distinction is useful for distinguishing between offering services and supports to students within existing institutional structures and significantly modifying those structures. We also review public policies that could support those innovations. Our focus is again on increasing the number of students who earn credentials with strong labor market value.

Evidence from research on these issues indicates that the institutional structures, policies, and practices that promise to improve postsecondary and labor market outcomes for disadvantaged students include:

- building more *guided pathways* within academic and occupational programs in public two-year colleges; and

- expanding the scale of *sector partnerships* among industry, colleges, and intermediaries and related *career pathways* to provide more high-quality occupational training.

The policies and practices that have the greatest potential to incentivize and facilitate these and other institutional improvements include:

- ensuring that broad-access public institutions have enough resources to implement structural improvements—perhaps by making higher education subsidies more equitable across institutions;

- modifying internal institutional structures to increase performance incentives;

- holding public institutions of higher education more accountable for the academic and subsequent employment outcomes of their students, by basing state subsidies partially on these outcomes; and

- reforming and expanding the reach of federal student aid.

In addition, strategies for improving opportunities in the for-profit sector and encouraging innovation include:

- strengthening the regulation of private for-profit colleges; and

- supporting innovations tailored to disadvantaged students, while ensuring quality and accountability.

The discussion below focuses primarily on community colleges. This sector provides more occupational training programs and credentials, including nondegree certificates, than public four-year institutions. But many of the suggestions below would also apply to programs in broad-access four-year institutions and to the for-profit sector, which has distinct problems that we address separately.

Building More Guided Pathways

The internal structure of community colleges can have a significant impact on student success. In their recent book, Tom Bailey, Shanna Jaggars, and Davis Jenkin call for large-scale redesign of community college curriculums and practices.[1] They argue that most community colleges now use a "cafeteria" model of course and program offerings to students, who must choose from hundreds of different classes and dozens of programs with little structure or guidance from counselors.[2] These authors present a strong case for more structured pathways within community colleges; the discussion that follows draws heavily on their work.

The cafeteria approach reduces success rates among students for a variety of reasons. Students have too many options, too little information about the alternatives, and too little insight into their own skills and preferences when choosing courses and majors. Academic counselors are in short supply at most community colleges. New students usually have just one mandatory face-to-face session with an adviser who has little individualized information and who is swamped with responsibility for hundreds of students.

Instead of gathering sufficient information to make sensible choices, students defer difficult choices like choosing a major and fall back on default options, taking the path of least resistance. They struggle to complete the degree or credential they seek, with too little guidance about what courses to take and in what sequence. Students have particular difficulty transferring into other programs and to other institutions because the credits they have earned are frequently not accepted.[3]

Community colleges should develop a set of "guided pathways" that would replace the cafeteria model. In contrast to "career pathways," the guided pathways concept refers to the structure of programs within and across academic institutions. The central issue is how students can efficiently complete the programs in which they enroll, accomplishing clearly defined learning goals. The guided pathways approach suggests that students begin in broad fields of interest (sometimes called "meta-majors") such as allied health, business, education, or social sciences, and then focus on more specific programs of study. It guides students toward selecting a major as they learn more about these fields, available

1. Bailey, Jaggars, and Jenkins (2015).
2. Bailey, Jaggars, and Jenkins draw arguments from behavioral economics and from previous work by Judith Scott-Clayton, James Rosenbaum, and others.
3. Jenkins and Cho (2012).

opportunities, and their own strengths and preferences. "Maps" show them how to proceed along the pathways and where they lead. The maps clarify how each community college pathway aligns with workforce opportunities or with a major at a four-year college. If successful, the guided pathways approach will improve the rate of associate degree completion and improve students' successful transfer to four-year institutions.[4]

Along with the carefully developed pathways and maps, Bailey and his coauthors would require changes in the intake procedures and supports for students when they first arrive in college; reforms in the process of who is selected for developmental education and what they must accomplish to complete it; and changes in instructional processes, with professional development and support for faculty. Students would have mandatory meetings with advisers and take online surveys and tests to determine whether their skills and preferences match their intended fields of study.

As discussed in chapter 5, many students are forced into developmental classes and required to pass an algebra or basic English exam before being allowed to take for-credit classes, even when the programs in which they are interested do not require these skills. With the proposed reforms, requirements for remediation would not be applied uniformly but would instead depend on any sign of mismatch between students' skills and their chosen fields. Particularly for students with only moderate skill deficits, developmental education would be accelerated and often integrated into the teaching within these fields, along with other reforms discussed in chapter 5. A "learning facilitation" model of instruction would stress important broad concepts and tools, rather than specific content, to better motivate students.[5]

4. For more information about how students choose a major and successfully switch from one major to another, see EAB Student Success Collaborative (2016). For more discussion of how transfers can be made more successful, see Jenkins and Fink (2016) and Wyner and others (2015).

5. See Bailey, Jaggars, and Jenkins (2015) for more description of learning facilitation models.

Some of these proposed changes might be effective even in the absence of broader guided pathways. But, as Bailey and his coauthors argue, implementing an integrated system will raise the odds of success. There could be large initial costs to institutions that choose to restructure themselves in this fashion, particularly for mandatory advising and other supports for faculty and students. But the increases in retention and completion rates would eventually reduce the cost per completed degree. Institutional revenues over time might well exceed the higher up-front costs, as students persist in their studies. Some case studies of community colleges and of public universities in Florida, Arizona, and elsewhere that have aligned their programs with changes in two-year colleges suggest that implementation of the model is feasible on a large scale.[6]

The arguments for guided pathways are convincing on a number of grounds. They are based on strong evidence of how a lack of structure and information impedes student outcomes at community colleges, and they rely on insights from behavioral economics as to why the proposed structure and guidance should improve these outcomes. The proposed package of structures, supports, and instructional changes is consistent with the most recent evidence on what works.[7]

There are some interesting case studies of colleges that have adopted the guided pathways approach. City Colleges of Chicago is a notable example, with fundamental restructuring funded by savings generated through operational efficiencies. The completion rate in this system of urban community colleges is rising rapidly—from a startling 7 percent in 2009 to 17 percent in 2015.[8]

But we have no rigorous evidence to date about the impacts of these structural changes on college completion rates or subsequent earnings. It should therefore be high on the evaluation agenda to analyze the impacts of these pathways—and particularly to compare

6. Bailey, Jaggars, and Jenkins (2015).

7. For example, the proposed changes in developmental education assessments, assignments, and remedial activities are consistent with a separate evaluation literature on this topic (Bettinger, Boatman, and Long 2013).

8. Kazis (2016).

the outcomes at institutions that adopt the entire package of reforms with those where only some or none were adopted.

It is not possible to randomly assign students to different community colleges, but other rigorous evaluation methods could be applied to colleges with similar student bodies following different models.[9] Studies should assess the value of the benefits relative to the fixed institutional transition costs and the added up-front costs per student of the guided pathways model to determine whether the benefits are large enough and persistent enough to outweigh the costs.

Even in the face of convincing evidence of the cost-effectiveness of the guided pathways model, it is not clear that institutions have sufficient incentives and resources to implement this promising strategy. In addition to the short-run costs and the higher long-run costs of focusing on technical fields for which there is strong demand in the labor force, implementation of instructional reform requires the cooperation of faculty, administrators, and staff who have a strong vested interest in maintaining the status quo.

Finally, even if the evidence shows that guided pathways significantly increase students' completion of certificates and associate degrees, as well as their ability to transfer to four-year institutions and earn a bachelor's degree, many students will need additional support. Reaching satisfactory success levels will require a variety of policies and practices to help students choose programs that they can complete that will lead to labor market success.

Scaling Sector Partnerships and Building Career Pathways

Another promising approach for improving both completion and labor market outcomes, which can be integrated with guided pathways for students in occupational training programs, involves the

---

9. Researchers could apply difference-in-difference or interrupted time-series methods to analyses of community colleges, comparing student outcomes at colleges that implement structured pathways to outcomes at colleges that previously had similar outcomes or were trending similarly over time but did not introduce structured pathways.

sector partnerships that have proliferated across the country in recent years. These partnerships structure training in an industry sector, focusing on organizing groups of firms to work together to identify employment needs.[10] They usually include multiple employers within an industry or industry association; community colleges; local workforce boards; and an intermediary, usually a community-based organization. The goal of the partnerships, which usually operate at the local or regional level, is to improve employment opportunities for the students the colleges are training.

Sector partnerships are designed to serve the dual interests of employers, who often have difficulty filling jobs on their own, and of workers, who otherwise might not get the education or training needed for well-paying jobs. The training is typically provided by community colleges, through courses and credentialing programs, to meet the specifications of employers. Because participants earn a postsecondary credential, these partnerships tend to generate stronger labor market returns than did previous job training programs. The goal is to move trainees into positions where there are well-paying jobs by linking the training to the needs of employers. Third-party intermediary organizations bring together the employers, workers, and training providers, and provide support to all of these groups. The Workforce Innovation and Opportunity Act (WIOA), which was reauthorized by Congress in 2014, explicitly requires the creation of more such partnerships by state and local workforce boards.

In order to prepare students for local labor markets, community colleges are also partnering with employers to provide career pathways in high-demand occupations across multiple industries. Workers can advance toward a career or occupation on a path that includes one or more credentials plus appropriate work experience along the way.[11] Steps on a career path toward a nursing career, for example,

10. National Governors Association (2013); Conway and Giloth (2014).
11. Fein (2012). The workforce literature defines career pathways as structured sets of credentials attained in the classroom and related work experiences that allow progression to high-paying careers over time. This concept can be thought of as a specific version of the guided pathways within community colleges, or directly between community and four-year colleges, that puts particu-

might begin with a nurse's aide certificate (CNA), which leads to a licensed practical nurse (LPN) associate degree and ultimately to a registered nurse (RN) bachelor's degree. State and local educational agencies and workforce boards are defining a number of such career paths in many states, beginning at either the secondary or postsecondary level, with multiple on and off ramps to accommodate students at different stages.[12]

The sector partnerships and career pathways now being developed are more frequently associated with workforce programs for older adults seeking certificates than with degree programs for younger students. But this distinction is not rigid. Older students earning certificates can sometimes "stack" them to achieve an associate degree, and younger students entering community college from high school sometimes enroll in a certificate program in the workforce area, from which they may or may not move to an associate degree program. Some sector-based training programs are beginning to focus more on associate degrees, such as those for technicians in health care and advanced manufacturing, that are in high demand in their industries, although to date they have focused primarily on certificate attainment. The usefulness of the partnerships and related career pathways is, therefore, not limited to the shorter-term workforce programs or to older adult student populations.

Both career pathways and sector partnerships are designed to address some of the market failures and other problems we discussed in chapters 2 and 3. As we noted, workers might have weak basic skills; face personal financial challenges that are difficult to overcome; have too little information about college and/or the job market—or social capital; and feel pressure to work full time to support their families. On the supply side, many public colleges provide too little counseling or structure to guide student choices and have few incentives to improve outcomes or respond to labor market needs. Some for-profit colleges have incentives and agendas that are inconsistent with social goals. Sector partnerships and career pathways are designed to over-

---

lar emphasis on occupational credentials and obtaining work experience in the short run.

12. See, for instance, the Alliance for Quality Career Pathways (2014).

come these challenges, ensuring that educational institutions are responsive to demand-side trends and improving the flow of labor market information and services to students and workers.

Of course, employers could also provide some of the training people need—either by paying for their workers to obtain postsecondary education or by providing it on the job. But as Gary Becker (1964) argued decades ago, employers will hesitate to invest their own resources in *general* training that can be used at other firms, since workers who leave will take the firm's investments with them. The more *specific* training is, and the less useful it is to nearby competitors, the more employers should be willing to share in the costs of providing it. Firms also have little incentive to provide training to young workers whose basic cognitive or job-readiness skills are weak.[13] While American employers apparently invest hundreds of billions of dollars in training their workers,[14] such training is very heavily skewed toward professional and managerial employees, in whose underlying skills employers have more confidence and whose tenures with the firm will likely be longer than those of less-educated workers.

In the middle-skill job market, where many jobs require postsecondary skills but not a bachelor's degree, employers complain about their inability to find appropriately trained job applicants.[15] Such complaints may seem inconsistent with the notion that the middle of the job market is shrinking but, as we noted in chapter 3, a "new middle" where jobs require postsecondary education in health care, advanced manufacturing, IT, financial services, hospitality, and other parts of the service sector is actually growing—and it is here that employers seem to have the most difficulty finding skilled applicants.

In any event, career pathways built in stages are becoming important mechanisms for overcoming inadequate training. Employers often coordinate and share fixed costs within sector partnerships and

13. Heckman (2008) develops and emphasizes the notion that "skill begets skill," or that early strength in cognitive skill is necessary for subsequent human capital investments. For a broader discussion of how investments in on-the-job training drive wage growth over time, see Mincer (1974).

14. Carnevale, Strohl, and Gulish (2015).

15. See, for instance, Manufacturing Institute (2015).

provide information to colleges and their students about the general and specific skills they seek when hiring. Because of their potential to help employers find workers with the necessary skills, governors and their workforce boards in many states view sector partnerships and career pathway strategies as a core part of their economic development plans, through which they convince major employers to remain in or relocate to their states.

The popularity of sector strategies has been enhanced by rigorous evaluation evidence.[16] One carefully designed study of three well-known local sector-based programs serving employers and disadvantaged workers found that, despite the fact that many of the jobs were low level, these workers had roughly 30 percent higher earnings after six months of sector-based training, at least through the end of the second year after training began.[17] More rigorous evaluations of a variety of sector-based or career pathways models are under way, with funding and support from the U.S. Departments of Education, Health and Human Services, and Labor.[18]

16. Maguire and others (2010).

17. The three sector-based programs whose impacts were evaluated are the Wisconsin Regional Training Partnership in Milwaukee, Jewish Vocational Services in Boston, and Per Scholas in New York. Among the sectors on which these partnerships have focused are construction, manufacturing, health care, and IT. There has also been positive evidence of impacts from Year Up, a sectoral program focusing on youth (Roder and Elliott 2012); and from Work Advance, a model that combines sector-based training with a range of other support services, at Per Scholas in New York (Hendra and others 2016).

18. The Office of Policy Research Evaluation (OPRE) in the Department of Health and Human Services is conducting RCT evaluations of career pathway models in health care through its Health Professional Opportunity Grants (HPOG) to roughly sixty organizations around the United States (www.acf.hhs .gov/programs/ofa/programs/hpog/what-is-hpog), and in other industries in its Pathways for Advancing Career Education (PACE) project for disadvantaged workers. The Departments of Education and Labor have provided $2 billion in competitive grant funding over several years to community colleges and other state or regional entities to build innovative sector-based or career pathway models through their Trade Adjustment Assistance Community College to Career Training (TAACCCT) grants. In addition, MDRC is currently evaluating its

It is important to note that because they are designed to serve employer needs, sector partnerships carefully screen out many applicants at the admission stage, and again before sending them onto jobs, in order to maintain the confidence of employers that they will deliver highly skilled employees. Students with poor cognitive achievement will have more difficulty enrolling in or completing these programs, especially in STEM and other technical fields. Because employers are also reluctant to hire individuals with weak backgrounds without clear evidence of strong work habits and skill attainment, there is some tension between employer needs and those who seek to help the hard-to-employ.

In addition, we do not yet have good evidence about the extent to which the impacts of this fairly specific type of training persist over time.[19] It will require rigorous review over a longer period of time to know how much of the initial gains remain when workers change jobs and economic sectors. More generally, in a very dynamic labor market where employer demands fluctuate, students must develop strong skills that can be used in a variety of types of employment, not just in a specific set of jobs in one sector. This is a motivation for some training programs that have begun to provide "stackable credentials" that signal a worker's specific competencies.

Despite some remaining uncertainty, the combination of positive impacts on disadvantaged workers' employment outcomes and the support of both employers and state policymakers has generated widespread interest in replicating the best programs and scaling them up. One important operation seeking to replicate the best practices of earlier sector-based programs is the National Fund for Workforce Solutions (NFWS), funded by a team of private philanthropies and now operating in over thirty localities. Although the evidence is not quite as rigorous as that generated from the studies cited earlier, re-

---

WorkAdvance program in several sites that combines sector-based training with a range of other pre- and postemployment supports.

19. One example of a program in which more specific training has lasting effects on worker earnings, even after they change jobs, is the Career Academy program, which is described more fully in chapter 7. There is some evidence of fadeout in the impacts of Year Up (Roder and Elliott 2012).

cent evaluations once again suggest strong program outcomes and impacts.[20]

By "braiding" funds from disparate federal or private education funding streams, participating states often seek to improve alignment between the community college curriculum and the skills demanded by local employers. They are building state-level data systems to identify sectors where demand is expected to remain strong and generate well-paying middle-skill jobs in the future.[21] States are also trying to generate more systemic paths from their colleges to the labor market, to avoid the creation of fragmented individual programs.[22]

Even selective four-year colleges and universities are stepping up their efforts to partner with employers, creating more internships and other forms of work-based learning for their undergraduate students. Georgia Tech and Northeastern University have built innovative programs, including both online and in-person experiences, to expand student involvement in the private sector during the college years.[23] Although these efforts are fundamentally different from the occupational training and credentials described above, they share the goal of providing real-world work experience while students are enrolled in college.

The integration of employers into the development of postsecondary programs and of actual work experience into college curricula is quite different from programs that pay tuition for employees. About 6 percent of undergraduate students receive at least partial funding from their employers;[24] and partnerships between employers and individual colleges, such as the much-publicized Starbucks arrangement with Arizona State University, are proliferating.[25] But these programs just provide greater access to college, not structured pathways for occupational preparation.

20. Michaelides, Mueser, and Mbwana (2014).

21. California Chancellor's Community College Office (2015); Reamer (2015).

22. Alliance for Quality Career Pathways (2014).

23. Stokes (2015).

24. NCES (2012, PowerStats calculations).

25. Blumenstyk (2016).

The widespread support for integrating postsecondary occupational preparation with employer needs and workplace experience is
encouraging. Efforts around the country to implement strategies that
appear to be successful are promising. But while some states boast
dozens or even hundreds of sector partnerships, labor market and
institutional failures continue to limit the willingness of many employers and some community colleges to participate in these programs. Many employers, especially small ones, are reluctant to spend
time and financial resources on training exercises, and community
colleges limit the scale of the training provided, largely because they
lack incentives to respond to the labor market and because of the
high costs of instruction and equipment in high-demand technical
fields. Overcoming these hurdles is vital to getting more disadvantaged students on the path to remunerative skilled careers.

Modifying Internal Institutional Structures to Increase Performance Incentives

Some structural changes within public colleges have the potential to
help students meet the challenges they face, and improve incentives for
offices and departments to implement programs that will improve student outcomes. Florida State University, for example, in a data-driven
systemic reform effort, strengthened communication and planning
among academic departments and other offices, such as the registrar
and student affairs. Regular meetings to discuss retention issues, along
with proactive advising, have contributed to dramatic increases in
completion rates.[26]

Structural changes can be implemented from above or, with
proper incentives, might bubble up across campuses. Growing financial pressures could facilitate some constructive structural changes.
For example, declining subsidies from states and rising tuition levels
at public colleges and universities may make it more difficult to
maintain cross-field subsidies, through which revenues are redistrib-

26. Kurzweil and Rossman (2016).

uted from high-demand fields to those facing lower demand and/or higher costs.[27]

As students and parents pay higher prices and demand more economic value from their credentials, institutions may seek additional revenues by letting market forces have more influence on tuition levels. Some institutions now charge more for programs in business, engineering, and nursing, where both demand and the costs of instruction are relatively high. More institutions may also embrace administrative models that give more power to individual departments and colleges to control the higher revenues they generate; some of these resources are "taxed" by central authorities to pay for the institution's general costs—and to support critical academic departments in, for example, the humanities and social sciences.[28] The state of Texas has already granted its public institutions a great deal of autonomy in setting tuition levels differentially across fields, both across and within institutions.[29] These strategies could potentially increase capacity in fields with high labor market value and high program costs.

As economists, we tend to agree that market forces should play a relatively greater role in how expenses are covered within public colleges and universities, especially in an era when public resources will grow increasingly tight. This notion is also consistent with our goal of expanding the attainment of credentials with strong labor market value, especially for disadvantaged students.

But differential pricing risks shutting out the very students about whom we are most concerned. Rising tuition in high-demand and high-cost fields will reduce the ability of disadvantaged students to enroll in and complete credentials in these fields, unless scholarship assistance is also made more generous. Providing grants and scholarships that differ by field of enrollment is complicated but possible at the institutional level. But allowing state or federal grant aid to be a

27. Fethke and Policano (2012). See also an excellent review of the book by Ronald Ehrenberg (2014).

28. This structure, sometimes known as "revenue-center management," already prevails at many research universities.

29. See Kim and Stange (2016).

function of tuition prices is not just complicated; because it provides incentives for institutions to raise their prices, it is not a viable policy direction.

Moreover, too much reliance on market forces would diminish the capacity of public colleges and universities to fulfill the public-good component of their missions. As a society, we subsidize public education at all levels for both equity and efficiency reasons. Individuals should not be excluded from the opportunity to invest in their futures because they are unable to pay. Moreover, the benefits of higher education extend to the economy and the society as a whole. Not all of the benefits are monetary. For example, higher education leads to greater civic engagement, more open minds, and better opportunities for the next generation.[30] It is quite likely that liberal arts education contributes more to these public gains than does education in narrowly defined, well-compensated fields.[31] These social benefits might be diminished if short-term market forces were to divert resources within higher education away from the general analytical, critical thinking, and communication skills generated in language arts, the social sciences, and the humanities toward more concrete career-building fields.

Achieving the right balance between market-driven and more traditional determinants of college and university teaching will be a challenge for the foreseeable future. Movement of broad-access colleges and universities toward internal funding models that allow high-demand departments and programs to keep more of the revenues they generate and strengthen the responsiveness of postsecondary institutions to the job market, while maintaining at least some redistribution toward important liberal arts programs, has the potential to improve students' labor market outcomes. Differential tuition levels across units is a riskier strategy because of the impact on lower-income students.

30. Baum, Ma, and Payea (2013).
31. See Glaeser (2013) and Moretti (2012) for evidence that high average levels of education in a region generate higher earnings, even for those who do not have the education themselves. It is likely that general analytical and communicative skills provide more spillovers than narrower technical skills.

Creating and expanding both high-quality sector partnerships and guided pathway programs requires addressing the forces that currently limit employer engagement with these programs. But it also requires strengthening the teaching and support services capacity of community colleges—and their incentives to improve completion rates and labor market outcomes. For the rest of this chapter, we focus on policies and practices that could help overcome these limitations.

Holding Public Colleges Accountable for Performance

As per-student state subsidies for public higher education decline over time in most states, it is imperative that public institutions find ways to spend their resources efficiently. One key goal is to maximize the attainment of credentials with strong labor market value, especially among disadvantaged students.

Making data on student outcomes at different institutions more widely available to prospective students might strengthen institutional incentives. In chapter 5, we discussed the use of publicly available data on the costs, completion rates, and average earnings of students from different institutions to better inform students about their choices. While these efforts are worthwhile, and could well be cost-effective in guiding students toward appropriate colleges, students do not typically respond to information in ways that make this strategy a sufficient solution to the problem.[32]

Evidence from behavioral economics makes it clear that students, like all people, have difficulty making complicated decisions, misjudge their own probabilities of success, and frequently choose the options that require the least active decisionmaking. Moreover, it is challenging to produce information tailored to individual characteristics and needs. For example, knowing an institution's completion rate will not tell students how others like them fare in that institution or in the program they are considering. In addition, most students are geographically constrained and must choose from a small number of

32. See evidence on differential responses to information about postcollege earnings across demographic groups in Hurwitz and Smith (2016).

institutions.[33] We are skeptical that consumer information alone can sufficiently change where students apply, and thus create strong enough incentives for institutions to dramatically change their educational practices, guiding students into optimal pathways.

To strengthen the incentives of public institutions to improve student outcomes, states should base a portion of their subsidies to public colleges and universities on these outcomes. Indeed, the use of *outcomes-based funding* (OBF) in higher education has been spreading rapidly; by late 2015, thirty-two states allocated at least a portion of their higher education funding through a form of OBF, and at least five more states were planning to do so.[34]

Most state OBF systems appropriately base subsidies to institutions at least partially on the attainment of credentials and degrees; but how to measure the labor market value of the credentials attained so far remains elusive.[35] Many disadvantaged students enroll in higher education primarily to increase their earnings potential. If the funding metrics place substantial weight on the earnings of graduates seeking occupational preparation, colleges will have greater incentive to expand teaching capacity in high-demand areas such as the allied health fields and engineering, even though both the salary and equipment costs of providing instruction are higher in these areas. The system would also give institutions an incentive to provide career counseling, which would likely improve the subsequent earnings of their students.

The ability of states to base subsidies on performance depends on their ability to use their administrative data to measure academic outcomes at individual colleges and universities. Most states that employ OBF put considerable weight on metrics of student academic

33. Akers and Soliz (2015).

34. Kurzweil and Rossman (2016). Martha Snyder (2015) distinguishes between earlier "performance-based funding" (PBF) systems and "outcomes-based funding" (OBF) systems, which are more explicitly connected to state attainment needs, focus on student completion, and have more sophisticated designs and implementation processes.

35. The Texas State Technical College system does have a funding system that incorporates labor market outcomes.

outcomes, including institution-level retention rates, credit attainment, and credential completion rates, but the percentage of total funding linked to performance varies considerably from state to state. North Dakota, Nevada, and Tennessee base over 80 percent of their subsidies to institutions on performance, while in many states less than 10 percent of funding is affected by the performance metrics.[36]

Few states put any weight on the earnings of graduates in their outcomes measures.[37] Some indirectly reward high earnings among graduates by placing some weight in their subsidy designs on the attainment of degrees in high-demand fields such as STEM and allied health.[38] New York rewards colleges for enrolling students in work-based learning programs, including apprenticeships.[39]

Including earnings measures requires linking student records to data from the Unemployment Insurance (UI) system. Most states are developing this capacity, often with grant assistance from the federal government.[40] To be useful, the earnings measures must follow students for at least five to ten years after they leave college. Measures based on shorter time periods will not account for extended periods of job shopping and lower earnings immediately after graduation, or for the higher earnings of students who go on to earn graduate degrees.[41] In addition, some adjustments in earnings calculations should be made for students who are not observed in the UI data, usually because they leave the state for work. Moreover, the goal should not

36. Snyder (2015).

37. Florida and Louisiana are exceptions.

38. Examples include Hawaii, Kansas, Maine, South Dakota, and Texas.

39. National Conference of State Legislatures (2015).

40. Zinn and Van Kleunen (2014). The federal government's State Longitudinal Data Systems (SLDS) Workforce Data Quality Initiative (WDQI) grants assisted states in the development of these data.

41. While allowing for at least five or six years of earnings after college completion seems important, Rothwell (2015) points out that correlations in average earnings across colleges measured at six-year and ten-year intervals are very high. For a recent analysis of how long youth live at home, the amount of time it takes them to find full-time work, and the later age of marriage, see Danziger and Rouse (2007). The very weak labor market for young college graduates after the Great Recession (Kahn 2010) likely reinforces this trend.

be maximizing average earnings, but ensuring that as many students as possible have strong career options.

Designing effective OBF systems is not simple, and incorporating labor market outcomes increases the challenge.[42] Institutions have a variety of missions, all of which need support. Flagship universities and other institutions that produce many liberal arts degree holders or train people for careers in social work or teaching should not be penalized. Nonetheless, the urgency of improving the employment outcomes of disadvantaged students seeking better labor market opportunities makes this process well worth the effort.

It is appropriate, however, to be cautious about implementing outcomes-based metrics, and about overestimating the impact these systems are likely to have. Any system that measures student success rates risks unintended consequences. It is all too easy to meet goals for completion rates by denying admission to at-risk students. Although this is less likely in open-access institutions like community colleges, institutions can attempt to improve their measured performance by "cream-skimming"—reducing their admission of students with weaker levels of academic preparation.[43]

But discouraging institutions from admitting disadvantaged students, and from making strong efforts to improve their outcomes, would be counter to the purposes of performance-based funding and to the fundamental goals of public higher education. The best way to avoid excessive cream skimming is to use value-added measures of student academic and employment outcomes, which statistically control for the characteristics of enrolled students.[44] However, the difficulty of administering such a system and the importance of transparency have discouraged states from adopting this strategy.

Many states do place added weight on positive outcomes among minority students or Pell Grant recipients. However, this approach does not counter creaming within these demographic categories. Weighting outcomes for specific groups of disadvantaged students is a step in the right direction, but developing true value-added or

42. Deming and Figlio (2016).
43. See, for example, Dougherty and others (2016).
44. HCM Strategists (2012).

input-adjusted measures that can be easily understood but not easily gamed is an important goal.

Another potential unintended consequence of rewarding outcomes is the watering down of the standards for credentials. There is evidence that these programs in some states have increased the number of short-term certificates awarded, without any measurable positive impact on retention rates or associate degree production.[45] Experimentation with alternative strategies, such as external monitoring or quality metrics, would be useful. Including employment and earnings outcomes in the evaluation process for colleges should help mitigate the problem of colleges watering down standards, since low-quality credentials are unlikely to generate significant labor market returns over time.

An additional challenge is distinguishing between inadequate resources and inefficient use of resources. Reducing the funding of underfunded institutions because they are unable to provide the supports students require to succeed could exacerbate the problems facing the many disadvantaged students who enroll in these institutions.

Although states do and should have discretion over their funding of postsecondary institutions, it might be appropriate for the federal government to encourage states to meet national goals. One option could be a higher education version of "Race to the Top," the competitive grants program used by the Obama administration to encourage the use of test-based accountability and other reforms in the K–12 years.[46] In such a program, the federal government would inject some carefully targeted new resources into community colleges and broad-access four-year colleges and universities in states that strengthen performance incentives in their higher education subsidies. Another possibility might be to include incentives of this sort within the Higher Education Act, which will likely be reauthorized in the next few years. We consider both possibilities in the concluding chapter.

In the meantime, we applaud state-level experimentation with outcomes-based subsidies for higher education and encourage rigorous

45. Hillman, Tandberg, and Fryar (2014).
46. Holzer (2015c).

evaluation of the impacts through cross-state analysis of academic and earnings outcomes, especially among disadvantaged students.

Improving Equity in Financing Higher Education

The students we are most concerned with in this book are those from disadvantaged backgrounds. Many have weak academic preparation and they disproportionately postpone postsecondary education, enrolling after spending some time after high school in the labor market. As the data in chapter 1 report, these students are concentrated in community colleges and for-profit institutions and, to a lesser extent, in broad-access public four-year institutions. Unfortunately, the institutions enrolling better-prepared, more privileged students tend to have far greater resources to work with than those enrolling at-risk, less privileged students.

As noted in chapter 4 and detailed in table 4.8, in addition to charging lower tuition prices, on average public two-year colleges receive much lower state and local appropriations per student than public four-year institutions. Simple comparisons of funding per student across sectors can be misleading because of differences in institutional missions. Funding covers other expenses in addition to direct educational costs. But looking just at direct educational expenditures paints a similar picture. Because of their limited resources, educational spending per community college student increased by only 4 percent in inflation-adjusted dollars between 2003–04 and 2013–14; in the public four-year sector it increased 16 percent.[47]

The gap is not as large as it appears because community college students are typically seeking a short-term certificate or associate degree, working to transfer to a four-year institution, or just taking a few courses for personal enrichment or to gain a specific skill. At the other end of the spectrum, research universities enroll beginning undergraduates, but also educate upper-level undergraduates in many academic fields, as well as graduate students. While it is not possible to determine the precise ratios because of data limitations, it clearly

47. Ma and others (2016).

costs more to educate upper-level than lower-level undergraduates, and even more for graduate students.

Estimates of how much different types of institutions spend per lower-level undergraduate reach varied conclusions. A 2013 Century Foundation paper reviewing the evidence concludes that public master's institutions probably spend about as much as community colleges on these students, but public doctoral institutions likely spend considerably more.[48]

Even equal per-student spending would not, however, generate equal experiences. On one hand, because community colleges are teaching institutions, their full-time faculty devote less time to research and more to teaching, teach more courses than university faculty, and are less likely to hold a PhD. On the other hand, the mix of programs significantly affects costs. Instructional costs in technical fields, for example, are much higher than those in the humanities.[49] In other words, the occupational preparation programs in community colleges are likely to be much more expensive to offer than the typical courses taken by bachelor's degree students at four-year institutions.

Another question is how to account for the disadvantaged educational backgrounds of many community college students in considering an equitable and efficient distribution of resources. There is broad consensus that at the elementary and secondary levels it takes more resources to foster success among disadvantaged students than among those from more affluent backgrounds.[50] It is not easy for schools to compensate for differences in home environments and early education. The same principle might hold for college students.

Delving into this issue is beyond the scope of this book, but the limited level of resources dedicated to community colleges and broad-access four-year public universities has to be part of any discussion about how to improve success rates for students in these sectors. Current discussions of making community colleges tuition free do not adequately address how these institutions, which are already

48. Baum and Kurose (2013).

49. Middaugh, Graham, and Shahid (2003); Romano, Losinger, and Millard (2010).

50. Krueger, Hanushek, and Rice (2012); Mosteller (1995).

underfunded, will provide the instruction and support necessary to improve the success rates of their students if their resources are even further constrained.

If the states are to meet their workforce needs, and if the nation is to meet its goal of increasing educational opportunities and developing a highly skilled labor force, the institutions serving disadvantaged students will have to be adequately funded. Increasing efficiency and finding lower-cost methods of providing quality education and training for all students, including those who come to college poorly prepared, is critical. Technology holds promise, but there is no silver bullet that will make it possible to provide the necessary education and training without increased resources.

Expanding the Reach of Federal and State Student Aid

Pell Grants, federal student loans, and other financial aid authorized under Title IV of the Higher Education Act are available to students enrolled in accredited institutions, in programs leading to certificates or degrees, and meeting the minimum time and credit-hour requirements. Critics argue that the current accreditation system is too lenient, allowing too many existing institutions to enroll students; and that it is too restrictive, admitting too few new providers.

Providing students with funds in the form of vouchers, and sending them off to make their own decisions about where and what to study, is a recipe for widespread failure. The stricter regulation of for-profit institutions is one necessary step. Instead of just handing out money, the federal student aid system should also incorporate better guidance and should tailor that guidance to the needs of different student populations. The advice most recent high school graduates need differs from the guidance that will be most useful for older independent students and students seeking specific occupational training.[51] Students need guidance *before* they enroll. That guidance

51. The College Board's Rethinking Pell Grants Study Group (2013) proposed adding this component to the Pell Grant program, and Baum and Scott-Clayton (2013) further developed the idea.

should be personalized and should be from a disinterested party, not from an institution hoping to recruit them.

With better guidance for students and clear criteria for outcomes, it should be possible to extend federal student aid to some programs not now covered. Currently, Pell Grants can only be used for for-credit courses in programs that last at least fifteen weeks and involve at least 600 hours of classroom time in accredited institutions. But there is growing interest in relaxing some or all of these restrictions. Although a significant number of for-profit institutions do enroll and train students without the benefit of financial aid—and they charge much lower prices than the for-profit institutions whose students receive Pell Grants and federal loans[52]—paying tuition and covering living expenses is a real challenge for many disadvantaged students, and is even more difficult without federal grants and loans.

The distinction between credit and noncredit programs at community colleges is sometimes arbitrary, and very similar courses in neighboring community colleges within the same state may be categorized differently. Only students in for-credit programs have access to federal grants and loans.[53]

Evidence about the labor market rewards of short-term certificates is mixed, but some of those in high-demand fields appear to pay off well.[54] Accordingly, there are legislative proposals to allow Pell Grant funding for short-term and/or noncredit certificate programs. Some advocates suggest including nonaccredited institutions, as long as there is evidence that the credential provided is "industry-recognized" and therefore generates a labor market reward.[55]

52. Cellini and Goldin (2014).

53. McCarthy (2014).

54. Jepsen, Troske, and Coomes (2014); Stevens, Kurlaender, and Grosz (2015); Carnevale, Rose, and Hanson (2012) find positive average returns to short-term certificates, but Bahr and others (2015) and Dadgar and Trimble (2015) do not. Xu and Trimble (2016) find considerable variation in returns across fields, program length, and location.

55. See, for instance, Hanks (2015). Senator Tim Kaine has proposed the "Jumpstart Our Businesses by Supporting Students (JOBS) Act," which would allow Pell funding for short-term certificate programs that provide an industry-recognized credential.

Experiments under way through the Department of Education will test the impact of allowing Pell Grants to finance noncredit and short-term certificate programs deemed useful for local or regional workforce skill development. Careful testing of these programs with a focus on labor market outcomes is important, given the mixed evidence about the payoff to these certificates. But ending the credit/noncredit distinction for occupational training, and aiding students in a broader range of programs that award credentials recognized by industry and valued by the labor market, could help many students prepare for remunerative employment.

The Obama administration also experimented with other ways of expanding access to Pell Grants. For example, Educational Quality through Innovative Partnership (EQUIP), launched in 2015, will allow partnerships between accredited and nonaccredited institutions, such as companies operating online courses or teaching specific skills. Third-party evaluations of these experiments will test whether this is a productive route for training disadvantaged youth and adults.

There is also growing interest in using Pell Grants to finance innovative approaches to obtaining certain postsecondary credentials, such as the *stackable credentials* that are frequently part of the career pathway partnerships discussed earlier, or *competency-based education* (CBE). Stackable credentials are gaining popularity in workforce circles as a way for adult trainees, who must work at least part time, to accumulate skills gradually. These credentials indicate mastery of specific skills and tasks; they can be earned over time and combined with work experience to generate forward movement on a career path.[56]

56. The ACT and the Manufacturing Skills Standards Council are building a set of stackable credentials to indicate general career readiness as well as production or logistics technical skills for use by advanced manufacturers (McCarthy 2015). The Texas State Technical College awards certificates for Industrial Systems Technology (IST) and Management (ISM), though efforts to scale the program have been limited. The U.S. Department of Education's Mapping Upward Project will publish research on stackable credentials and provide technical assistance to colleges designing these programs in 2016–17 (http://cte.ed.gov/initiatives/community-college-stackable-credentials).

Similarly, CBE programs award credentials for the mastery of specific skills, rather than for defined coursework and formal instruction time. In some cases, institutions certify prior learning through formalized assessments, rather than actually supervising the acquisition of skills and knowledge. Western Governors University and the University of Southern Vermont have been pioneers in the area, and the Department of Education has already granted several institutions waivers to the standard aid eligibility requirements.[57]

Stackable and competency-based credentials are sometimes awarded outside of traditional postsecondary institutions; some observers see them as examples of innovations that can counter rising prices and poor outcomes in traditional higher education. Industry certifications are not new, but "boot camps" that teach computer coding (which attract many students who already have college degrees), stackable short-term credentials in manufacturing, and other variations on the model could be promising routes for individuals seeking specific skills. It is worth asking what standards should be relevant for determining which, if any, of these programs should be eligible for federal student aid. Expanding federal financial aid to cover this variety of programs is not simple. It is, for example, hard to argue that either an institution/organization or a student should receive as much funding for the certification of prior knowledge as for providing instruction or learning something new.

Denying students financial aid because their programs do not fit into traditional models limits opportunity and innovation. But our troubling recent experience with for-profit colleges demonstrates that we need to move very carefully in opening up access to these funds. Exactly how to demonstrate that specific credentials are recognized by industry or have market value is not always clear. The approach of running experiments with rigorous testing of the results is sensible, but requires considerable time and resources.

Some of these innovations, including stackable and competency-based credentials, may be appropriate for developing and measuring the specific skills required for certain occupations, but not for

---

57. For an analysis of best practices in CBE programs supported by TAACCCT funds, see Person (2015).

bachelor's or more advanced degrees. The certification of skills is not a substitute for the broad education and degrees that signal a wider range of analytical and communicative capacities. There is a danger that we could move too far in the direction of quick certifications, and deprive students seeking workforce training of the kind of education that will allow them the flexibility to move into new jobs as the labor market evolves.

More and better labor market research, using survey or administrative data on the wide array of available credentials, is sorely needed to give us a better sense of which credentials employers value and why.

Regulating For-Profit Colleges

This chapter focuses primarily on community colleges because they serve a large fraction of postsecondary students, provide specific occupational preparation, and are central to public policies that promote access to higher education for disadvantaged students. But many of those students enroll in for-profit colleges. These institutions charge more than public two-year or four-year colleges and universities, and the observed outcomes of their students are no better, and are frequently worse, than those of students in public colleges.

The characteristics of the students who attend each type of institution do not fully explain the poor outcomes at for-profit institutions.[58] These institutions receive large public subsidies through the federal student aid system and account for a high percentage of student loan defaults.[59] They lobby successfully against many of the efforts to regulate them.

There are weaker and stronger institutions in all sectors, and for-profit institutions have, in general, been more successful than community colleges in creating the types of guided pathways discussed

---

58. See Deming and others (2015) for experimental evidence comparing employer responses to applicants with for-profit and other kinds of degrees. Also see Chaudhary and Cellini (2012) and Darolia and others (2014) for evidence on returns to for-profit degrees relative to others.

59. Federal Student Aid (2015).

above (Rosenbaum 2011). But the sector deserves targeted attention in any discussion of improving outcomes for disadvantaged students. The closing of the large for-profit Corinthian Colleges in 2015 and of ITT Tech in 2016, and the many students there who were stranded with large debts but no degrees, illustrates the potential severity of the problem.

Despite rhetoric about the for-profit sector representing the free market in higher education, this sector is very much a product of federal subsidies to low-income students. These institutions raise their tuition substantially in response to increases in the availability of public financial aid.[60] They receive a high percentage of their revenues from Pell Grants, aid to veterans, and federal student loans. Their outcomes are consistent with major market failures. Students have inadequate information about the value of different options; most of the payment for tuition at for-profit institutions comes from the government—a third party—which diminishes price sensitivity; and by the time students become aware of the shortcomings of their institutions, they have already invested their time and money and cannot easily switch to another provider.

State governments exert some degree of control over public institutions. But for-profit institutions respond overwhelmingly to the bottom line. The federal government should play a stronger role in regulating for-profit colleges. Outcomes-based funding is not relevant, since these institutions do not directly receive public funding. But their reliance on publicly funded grants and loans does provide significant leverage for influencing outcomes.

The Obama administration developed and, after legal challenges, implemented "gainful employment" regulations for for-profit institutions and other institutions that provide occupational training leading to a certificate rather than a degree and that participate in federal student aid programs.

The Obama administration issued its first round of gainful employment regulations in 2011, attempting to limit the percentages of annual total and discretionary income that could be used for loan repayment, and putting a floor under the percentage of former students

60. Cellini and Goldin (2014).

successfully paying off their loans.[61] Colleges would lose Title IV eligibility only if they failed to meet all three conditions. But a federal court in 2012 found the required minimum successful repayment rate arbitrary and struck down the entire regulation.

The administration issued new gainful employment regulations in 2015 that limit the fraction of income the average program graduate can be required to spend to repay student loans. A federal district court upheld these rules in June 2015. The for-profit sector considers the regulations discriminatory, since they apply to all for-profit programs, but only to nondegree programs in nonprofit institutions. Critics on the other side are concerned that the regulations focus only on graduates, not on the many students who enroll in for-profit institutions but never complete a degree or certificate.

We do not yet know whether the new regulations will improve student outcomes in for-profit colleges. We also do not know if stricter rules would pass legal muster. Some for-profit colleges appear to have responded to the threat of greater regulation by changing their recruiting practices, requiring trial enrollment periods, or taking other steps to improve student outcomes.[62] But the problems still loom large. New accusations about for-profit college transgressions emerge frequently.

The problems with student debt highlight the problems of the for-profit sector. A quarter of all federal borrowers attend for-profit institutions. About half of the for-profit borrowers default on their loans within five years.[63] Low completion rates and weak labor market outcomes even for those who do graduate are serious problems in this sector.

Given the large role for-profit colleges play in providing occupational skills to disadvantaged students, we strongly support attempts by the federal government to regulate them more aggressively, while we await some analysis of the outcomes of existing regulations. Whether Pell Grants and other forms of federal aid should remain as fully available to the for-profit colleges as they are today is an open question, especially as the Higher Education Act is up for reauthorization.

61. Hamilton (2011).

62. Pope (2012).

63. Looney and Yannelis (2015).

Other Higher Education Innovations

The number and range of innovations being proposed and developed in higher education and workforce development go well beyond those we have surveyed here. Many are designed to enable students to obtain postsecondary degrees faster and at lower cost. Most are not specifically focused on low-income students or credentials with labor market value. We also have limited evidence to date on their cost-effectiveness and how the private sector reacts to and rewards them. Yet, if they ultimately prove to be successful, some of these innovations could significantly improve the ability of low-income students to obtain postsecondary credentials leading to labor market success.

It is important to note in this context that lowering the cost of providing high-quality postsecondary experiences is an important goal. We discussed tuition pricing in chapter 4, but the distinction between prices charged and educational expenditures is critical. While it is expensive to provide valuable college experiences, some of the approaches we mention here do have the potential to lower costs. Passing any cost savings on to students will require maintaining public funding levels.

The spread of online learning options creates opportunities for students to earn credentials despite geographic and schedule constraints. Online courses take a variety of forms, from the large-scale, impersonal massive open online courses (MOOCs) to intense personalized interactive learning. Although it is reasonable to be optimistic about potential cost savings, these savings have yet to materialize.[64] Moreover, the pedagogical qualities and educational successes of online efforts are very mixed, with less classroom engagement weakening persistence rates and grades, especially among students with weak academic preparation and performance.[65]

Another set of innovations is designed to let students begin their postsecondary studies earlier and complete them more rapidly. Early-college high school and dual enrollment programs are proliferating around the country, enabling students to obtain college credits while

64. McPherson and Bacow (2015).
65. Xu and Jaggars (2013, 2014).

still in high school.[66] One of the better studies of these efforts shows mixed effects on subsequent academic enrollment and attainment—with community college enrollments rising but four-year enrollments falling.[67]

We are more dubious about proposals that push colleges and universities to squeeze BA programs into three years.[68] Among students who received bachelor's degrees in 2014–15, the average length of enrollment was 5.2 academic years and the average time elapsed between initial enrollment and degree completion was 5.6 years.[69] Attempts to accelerate might result in even lower completion rates or less mastery of material. Encouraging year-round enrollment could reduce the time that elapses between initial enrollment and degree completion, but a thinning of general education requirements in bachelor's degree programs might well diminish the development of the writing and critical thinking skills that many employers clearly value.[70] Given that the market continues to reward those who complete a BA in its current form, arguments for dramatically restructuring and shrinking the contents of these degrees are not compelling. Students can certainly save money, both in tuition and forgone earnings, if they graduate more quickly. But the appropriate goal would appear to be increasing the number of students who earn an associate degree in two years and a bachelor's degree in four years.

Another approach would be to offer more bachelor's degrees at community colleges, with paths to these degrees beginning with occupational training at the certificate or associate level (McCarthy 2015). Only about 25 percent of community college students transfer to a four-year college, and only about half of those who transfer complete a BA. The guided pathways approach, which in many cases would lead students directly from their community colleges to four-year schools, could ease the transfer process. But creating more bachelor's degree programs at community colleges would completely eliminate

66. Hoffman, Vargas, and Santos (2009); ACT (2015).
67. Goldhaber and Cowan (2014). See also Xu and Jaggars (2013, 2014).
68. Weinstein (2014).
69. Shapiro and others (2016b).
70. Trilling and Fadel (2009); National Research Council (2012).

the need to transfer to another school, potentially increasing BA attainment rates. On the other hand, the labor market might not value the new degrees as highly as those offered by four-year colleges; some evidence to date from Florida is not encouraging in this regard.[71]

Moreover, efforts to create another set of paths to a bachelor's degree would further dilute the attention and resources that community colleges devote to their primary mission. When community colleges push to be permitted to offer bachelor's degrees, they may really be seeking to increase educational opportunities for their students. But striving for greater prestige is pervasive among academic institutions, and this is also likely to be part of the motivation. Moreover, the limited success rates of students in this sector in earning shorter-term credentials raises questions. Does it make more sense to put resources into diminishing the barriers limiting transfer from two-year to four-year institutions, or on extending the options for the relatively small segment of students who would benefit from bachelor's degree programs? The community college sector is critical to providing certificate and associate degree programs of high quality and value. Adding a new component to its already crowded agenda could diminish its effectiveness in achieving this core mission.

Overall, innovations designed to increase access to higher education through technology, and to shorten the path to a postsecondary credential, are promising and worthy of further experimentation and evaluation. But before directing many more students, along with public subsidies, in these directions, we should gather more evidence about their labor market value among disadvantaged students.

71. Backes and Velez (2014) find that students earning BAs who start at a community college suffer substantial earnings penalties of 10 to 30 percent relative to those who start in a four-year institution, even controlling for previous achievement levels. Those who earn their BA at the community college instead of transferring to a four-year college or university suffer additional penalties.

Conclusion

Given the weak academic preparation and other challenges that impede progress for many disadvantaged students, it is not enough to increase their access to colleges and universities through efforts to reduce or eliminate tuition. We must also improve the academic experiences of disadvantaged college students and their labor market outcomes. To accomplish these goals, it will be necessary to go beyond the set of programs and practices identified in chapter 5 that provide services and financial aid directly to individual students. Both programs and practices at the institutions themselves and public policy must undergo major changes to meet these challenges.

We identify two strategies as our top priorities for achieving these goals: (1) the *restructuring of community colleges to create more structured or "guided" pathways* to help students make appropriate choices between liberal arts and occupational programs, and to guide them more effectively through these choices to their goals; and (2) the *expansion and scaling of sector partnerships and career pathways* in community colleges, to provide occupational training for well-paying jobs in sectors with strong demand.

Both strategies are integral to improving the capacity of community colleges to support student success. The pathways guiding students directly to workplace opportunities will involve sector partnerships, but the more structured environment should also reduce the barriers on the path to transfer. These strategies will strengthen the routes available to disadvantaged students for obtaining credentials with labor market value, both in traditional for-credit academic programs and in a range of occupational programs, including those that are not-for-credit. But we need both *more resources and stronger incentives* for colleges to undertake this costly restructuring.

The increasing reliance on outcomes-based subsidies from states to their public colleges and universities is promising. Systems should measure both academic and labor market outcomes, with appropriate adjustments for the characteristics of incoming students. Along with effective regulations for private for-profit colleges, these efforts should generate more accountability and improve colleges' performance incentives. Providing targeted federal funding to public colleges in states that agree to expand accountability would provide additional resources to institutions that sorely need them, while creating new incentives to ensure that those resources are well spent. There is also likely a federal role in creating incentives for states to fund community colleges more generously, making postsecondary funding more equitable across public institutions.

Incentives within colleges and universities to be more responsive to the labor market could also be strengthened by allowing the units with market value to keep more of the revenues they generate. While there are reasonable arguments for allowing differential tuition levels to cover the higher costs of some programs, the potential for excluding low-income students gives us pause about this strategy. But both expanding eligibility for federal financial aid to include more of the programs that provide students with valuable credentials for the workforce, and creating new types of credentials with labor market value that are attainable by disadvantaged students and informative to employers, hold strong promise.

The lack of rigorous evidence to date on the impacts that would be generated by most of these approaches is sobering. Opening the spigot of federal aid to a range of new programs is risky, given the negative experiences with for-profit colleges that rely on federal student aid revenues. But it is also important to expand support for new approaches to increase the attainment of postsecondary credentials with market value. Ongoing experimentation and evaluation to determine what works and what doesn't is critical before we commit major new federal resources.

In addition to improving postsecondary pathways for disadvantaged students, we must also expand the range of options outside of colleges that can prepare people to enter the labor market with both skills and work experience. We consider a range of additional paths to student success in chapter 7.

7

Alternative Pathways to Skills and Higher Earnings

Completion rates at U.S. colleges are disturbingly low. They are particularly low for students from disadvantaged backgrounds and for those who enroll at nonselective postsecondary institutions. Students with weak academic preparation are frequently assigned to noncredit developmental education courses, from which most never go on to take classes for academic credit. Even among those who manage to earn a degree or certificate, too many obtain credentials with very low labor market value.

The preceding chapters have discussed a variety of reforms designed to improve postsecondary completion rates in fields with market value. In this chapter we focus on alternative paths to successful careers. Strong career and technical education (CTE) options in high school have the potential to create constructive paths directly to the labor market for some students, and to improve the postsecondary experiences of others. The goal of preparing all students for both the workforce and postsecondary education is appropriate—but not all students can be prepared for every option. Ensuring that there are constructive pathways for the students who struggle most after high school requires strengthening CTE for high school students.

Career and technical education is not limited to preparing students for a narrow range of occupations. Rather, all high school students need exposure to information about different potential career directions and opportunities to become familiar with workplace norms and expectations. Concrete workplace skills such as problem solving and teamwork should be part of their academic programs.

For some high school students, the opportunity to prepare for a specific occupation, possibly earning a certificate more commonly available at the postsecondary level, could open the door to high-wage jobs immediately after high school. For others, integration of more traditional academic courses with carefully designed CTE will provide stronger grounding for making good postsecondary choices.

As the 2011 report *Pathways to Prosperity* emphasized, increasing opportunities for work-based learning and concrete occupational preparation at both the high school and postsecondary levels can improve outcomes for many students.[1] However, concerns over closing doors to students from disadvantaged backgrounds and racial and ethnic minorities have for many years diminished the extent to which high schools provide career and technical training. Moreover, despite the fact that more than half of the undergraduate degrees awarded in the United States are certificates and associate degrees,[2] it is common for people to think of "college" as a four-year institution and a "college degree" as a four-year degree, diminishing the attention and resources devoted to occupational pathways that require shorter-term postsecondary credentials.

But attention to alternatives to a purely academic curriculum is growing.[3] Ideally, these efforts at the secondary level should improve students' "college and career readiness," enabling them to take a wide range of paths into the labor market as well as higher education.

In this chapter we review the evidence about these paths, with a heavy focus on CTE that starts in high school or earlier, and on models of work-based learning, such as apprenticeship. We review the difficulties with this type of education in the past and what newer

1. Symonds, Schwartz, and Ferguson (2011).

2. NCES (2015b, table 318.40).

3. Rosenbaum (2002) makes a similar argument about the value of proprietary occupational colleges, as we described earlier. K. Newman and H. Winston (2016) decry the stigma attached to occupational education in the United States and advocate learning from European apprenticeship models.

high-quality models of CTE look like. We consider the empirical evidence of CTE's impacts and close with some policy implications.

Vocational Education and CTE: Weighed Down by the Past

Historically, most CTE in the United States—which was called vocational education or "voc ed"—was low in quality.[4] The academic content was weak, the skills imparted were limited, and the jobs for which students were prepared were often low-wage and low-skill. Voc ed was where students went if they were not "college prep," and it was clearly seen as a last-resort option. Indeed, many of the skills taught were for declining occupations and industries, taught by instructors far from the frontier of knowledge of the contemporary labor market.

Even worse, there was a long tradition of tracking those with lower perceived achievement into voc ed. In many cases, race and class, as opposed to measured achievement through test scores, determined the tracks into which students were sorted. Minority and lower-income children were tracked into voc ed much more often than whites and middle-class students. Voc ed and tracking came to be viewed as mechanisms through which historical patterns of social stratification were maintained or even strengthened in secondary schools.

During the 1960s this type of tracking became politically controversial. Both parents and advocates for minorities and the poor fought against it. Unfortunately, opportunities for needed career preparation in high school were eliminated, along with the often pernicious tracking system.

Reviving occupational preparation in high school, but making it appropriate for all students and integrating it with college preparation, is not a new idea. The School-to-Work Opportunities Act of 1994 promoted similar goals, and the associated efforts to provide work-

---

4. "Vocational education" began to be called "career and technical education" in the early 2000s, and the change was made formal through the latest iteration of the Carl D. Perkins Career and Technical Act of 2006; it was intended to indicate a strong break with the past in terms of skill attainment quality and relevance to industry needs.

based learning and prepare students for a rapidly evolving labor market appeared to be making a difference.[5] Other directions for reform prevailed in later years, but the incomplete efforts of the past should not prevent us from pursuing more sophisticated efforts in the future.

In recent years the evolution of occupational education into CTE has entailed major efforts to improve both its academic quality and its job market relevance. Gaps remain between the academic rigor of CTE and other high school courses taken, and CTE students are less likely than others to enroll in college. But these gaps have declined in magnitude. In 2015, 45 percent of students taking four or more CTE classes completed the coursework necessary for four-year college attendance; 74 percent of non-CTE students completed similar coursework; comparable numbers for 1990 were lower for both groups, but especially for CTE concentrators.[6] Moreover, the expectation is that now those in CTE are there by choice, not because they have been offered limited options, although guidance counselors and teachers still help shape those choices based on their own subjective perceptions of student ability and potential, which are too often influenced by racial stereotypes.[7]

There is some evidence that the lower average academic level of CTE students reflects their earlier academic achievement, rather than weaker standards in CTE programs. More generally, it is still true that more CTE students come from low-income families and have lower postsecondary expectations than other students, but these gaps have also narrowed over time.[8]

Attitudes are changing, but negative perceptions of CTE among students and parents persist, based both on historical legacy and on the ongoing reality that CTE students tend to have weaker academic preparation and lower performance levels than other students. For CTE courses and programs to represent viable alternative pathways

5. Stull and Sanders (2003); Bailey and Merritt (1997).

6. U.S. Department of Education (2014); Stern (2015).

7. See Card and Giuliano (2015) for insights into the role of teachers in sorting students into alternative tracks.

8. Stern (2015).

to college and careers, the quality must continue to improve, and students and parents must come to respect this alternative approach. Attracting higher-performing students to these courses might be an important component of improving CTE quality.

It is worth noting that CTE and apprenticeships in Germany, the Netherlands, Switzerland, and other European countries provide high school graduates with broad analytical skills as well as the technical skills for specific occupations. Partly for this reason, high school graduates in many of these countries do not lag as far behind college graduates in earnings as they do in the United States.[9] European countries seem more comfortable with tracking students permanently away from universities. Given the history of tracking in the United States and its negative consequences for minorities and youth from low-income families, our own view is that we must keep a variety of options alive for students choosing CTE pathways in high school.

High-Quality CTE in High Schools: What Does It Look Like?

Most of the discussion in this book focuses on the weak postsecondary experiences and outcomes of disadvantaged students. A significant part of the problem is the lack of academic preparation among students from disadvantaged backgrounds, the lack of opportunities for labor force preparation outside of postsecondary institutions, and the perception that occupational preparation is a second-class pathway. A system more tailored to the diverse needs, preferences, and capacities of all students would improve the lives of many of the individuals with whom we are most concerned.

Among education researchers and analysts who focus on secondary education, there is a growing consensus on what constitutes high-quality CTE. Analysts consider the following attributes to be most important.[10]

9. Hoffman (2011); Newman and Winston (2016).
10. This discussion draws heavily from Holzer, Linn, and Monthey (2013). See Southern Regional Education Board (2015) for similar concrete proposals for CTE.

Universal Career Education

Historically, career and technical education has been stigmatized, at least partially because it was considered a lower-quality alternative to a college preparatory curriculum. As long as it remains a separate entity, it will continue to be viewed as an inferior alternative to college prep. Accordingly, many analysts believe that the silos that keep college prep and CTE curricula separate should be broken down. In this view, all students should be exposed to at least some information about different career paths and their academic requirements. Even students determined to attend liberal arts colleges and those actively taking Advanced Placement courses could benefit from some career exploration and perhaps some career education. No students, whatever areas they choose to explore, should be locked into any area of career education. Those who study careers in health care, for instance, should be prepared for and free to apply to any college—including liberal arts colleges—and ultimately to choose any major.

An additional benefit of universal early exposure to information about the labor market is that students would be much better informed about the requirements for pursuing various careers. They might be more motivated to learn math, science, and English when they understand the relevance of these subjects to their career aspirations. Indeed, exposure to information about potential employment paths might start in middle school, before students begin to disengage from these academic fields.

Strong and Integrated Academic Content

In order to avoid stigmatization, the academic content of CTE classes must be strong. It must be *relevant* to the jobs and careers for which students are preparing and set high standards. The way to accomplish both is to integrate the building of academic skills, wherever possible, into more applied contexts, such as student projects and work-related environments.

Another argument for *contextualized* learning—such as project-based or work-based instruction—is that some students learn better in applied rather than purely abstract academic situations.[11] They may be more motivated to study and learn when they can directly see the relevance of their studies, and might be better able to understand concepts if they are applied to the real world.

Technical and Employability Skills

In addition to rigorous academic content, CTE students must learn technical skills that are relevant to specific careers in key industries such as health care, finance, or information technology (IT). They also need to learn a set of general employability skills that employers value, including communication skills, the ability to work in teams, and general workplace knowledge. The combination of applied classroom instruction and work experience can help students attain the right mix of academic, technical, and employability skills, much as students can gain these skills in the postsecondary career pathways described earlier.

Paths to Future Postsecondary Studies and Employment

A number of approaches to contemporary CTE are designed to make sure that the mix of academic, technical, and employment skills students receive will ultimately lead to postsecondary education and/or remunerative careers. For instance, the National Association of State Directors of Career Technical Education Consortium (NASDCTEC) defines sixteen "career clusters" for CTE and associated programs of study that contain pathways to more specific careers within each cluster.[12] These programs are designed to increase the relevance of CTE to employers while maintaining strong academic standards. Employer

---

11. Resnick (1987).

12. There are seventy-nine defined "programs of study" associated with the sixteen "career clusters" as defined by NASDCTEC. The clusters are: Agriculture, Food, and Natural Resources; Architecture and Construction; Arts, A/V Technology, and Communication; Business Management and Administration; Education and Training; Finance; Government; Health Science; Hospitality and Tourism; Human Services; Information Technology; Law, Public Safety, Cor-

involvement ensures that the curricula and work experiences are up to date and relevant to the current job market.

To ensure access to postsecondary institutions, CTE programs can rely on a variety of approaches that should be available to all high school students, including articulation agreements with state and local colleges, which guarantee that high school classes will meet requirements for admission and might even count toward some college credit. Other promising strategies include allowing students to take college courses, earn college credit, and learn more about postsecondary education while still in high school.

Secondary school district administrators have gotten more directly involved in developing connections with local and state colleges. High schools are providing CTE students with guidance about postsecondary admission requirements, as well as help with their admission and financial aid applications.[13] These approaches can promote career pathways that begin as high school CTE programs of study and continue into the college years.

Student and Teacher Supports

One of the strongest arguments for reforming CTE is to improve access to colleges and careers for disadvantaged students. Despite the evolution of CTE, with more required exposure for all students and more rigorous academic content, students who concentrate in CTE still have lower average achievement and are more likely to come from more disadvantaged backgrounds than those on traditional college prep paths.

The tension between increasing academic standards and attracting more well-prepared students on the one hand, and improving opportunities for disadvantaged students on the other, creates some dilemmas. The more rigorous standards designed to prepare students for successful pathways and eliminate stigma might well move CTE beyond the academic reach of students with limited achievement in the

---

rections, and Security; Manufacturing; Marketing; Science, Technology, Engineering, and Math; and Transportation, Distribution, and Logistics.
    13. Stern (2015).

K–8 years. Academic support and effective counseling will become increasingly important.

Other sources of support for CTE students include the creation of learning communities, where a group of students take all of their high school classes together, to provide better social and academic supports for one another. Career and Technical Students Organizations (CTSO), such as SkillsUSA, which bring together CTE students with similar goals, can also provide support.[14]

High-quality, up-to-date teaching is a critical component of successful CTE education. To remain effective, CTE teachers will also need ongoing career development and support. An explicit commitment of principals and school districts to high-quality CTE can help generate the supports that these teachers need.

Curriculum, Assessment, and Accountability

The development of the Common Core State Standards for school curricula around the country, as well as the increasing role of testing in assessing secondary schools, teachers, and students, has implications for CTE and its integration into a mainstream high school curriculum.[15] All CTE students must take courses that reflect the new learning goals and participate in the assessment of their academic skills as defined by the Common Core; but it may also be advisable to develop similarly rigorous guidelines for CTE, along with new ways to assess the technical and employability skills that CTE is designed to foster.

NASDCTEC has developed a Common Career and Technical Core (CCTC), attempting to apply levels of rigor in math and English to the CTE curriculum that are comparable to the Common Core standards. The CCTC also includes standards for the content of the career clusters and programs of study that CTE programs now

14. Holzer, Linn, and Monthey (2013).

15. Almost every state agreed to implement the Common Core when it was first presented, but it has become much more controversial. Parents often demand the right of their students to opt out of tests that measure the attainment of these skills, as nearly 20 percent did in 2014–15 in the state of New York (Singer 2015).

include, and some new assessment tools for student success in these areas are being developed.[16] States are implementing these new curricula and assessments, though likely with very different levels of commitment and fidelity to the CCTC.

CTE Effectiveness: What Does the Evidence Show?

We have a body of data on the impacts of CTE in general and rigorous evaluation evidence on one particular model of CTE—the Career Academy. Other specific models seem promising in a number of ways, but we cannot endorse them without stronger evidence that they are effective.

A report on CTE by the U.S. Department of Education summarized the research literature at that time and found that:[17]

- on average, CTE programs in high school clearly improve the employment and earnings of participants for several years afterward, especially among disadvantaged students;[18] and

- although the evidence has been mixed, CTE programs might also increase high school graduation rates.

More recent evidence on whether CTE improves high school graduation rates remains mixed. When the numbers of applicants exceeded available slots in five CTE high schools in Philadelphia, a lottery was used to determine who was admitted; such lotteries can be used to replicate impact studies using random assignment. Results showed an increase in high school graduation rates among those who enrolled in the CTE high schools. But these results may not be externally valid—applicable to other CTE programs within high schools or to CTE outside Philadelphia more generally. In fact, a credible

16. See Advance CTE (N.D.).

17. U.S. Department of Education (2004).

18. Ryan (2001) provides a cross-country analysis of effects of occupational education and finds similar impacts on employment and earnings for a number of years.

nonexperimental study of CTE using survey data found no positive impacts on high school completion.[19]

What does the evidence show about specific CTE models that incorporate some of the principles and characteristics of high-quality CTE? The one proven model of CTE is the Career Academy. These are schools within broader high schools that link students with training for and jobs in particular industries, such as health care and IT. The Career Academy concept has three key elements:

- a small learning community (SLC);

- a college-prep sequential curriculum with a career theme; and

- an advisory board that forges partnerships with employers, higher education institutions, and the community.

Teams of high school teachers work across several academic and technical subjects, grouping students in cohorts to follow a program of study. The advisory board helps to identify a sequential set of experiential components that show students the applications of academic subjects to the chosen field and deliver work-based learning experiences, including shadowing, community service, mentoring, internships, and apprenticeships. The career theme can be any of the sixteen in the national career clusters taxonomy or variations on them, such as "green" industries, health sciences, or media arts. These academies have proliferated in recent years and by some counts, as many as 7,000 exist nationwide, incorporating variations on the original model.

A well-known evaluation of the Career Academy using random assignment methods found very strong positive and lasting effects. The earnings of young men, especially those considered at risk, increased by nearly 20 percent. The evaluation also found positive but smaller effects for young women. Participation in a Career Academy was also associated with higher marriage rates. Initially researchers found lower rates of dropping out for the Career Academy enrollees, but eventually these differences disappeared.

19. Bozick and Dalton (2013).

The study found no negative effects of Career Academy participation on any higher education outcomes, putting to rest the concern that the academies might track low-income students away from college. Still, recent efforts by the Career Academy to improve the preparation for higher education has led some to call themselves "College and Career Academies," especially in California.[20] Career Academies have also been part of broader school reform models, such as the Talent Development program and Small Schools of Choice, which have demonstrated important positive impacts on academic achievement and high school completion by disadvantaged urban students.[21]

Another model of CTE whose impact on educational attainment has been carefully analyzed is Tech Prep, a model used around the country in the 1990s that began with students in high school and provided pathways through two years of community college to associate degrees. Cellini's (2006) evaluation of Tech Prep programs—the forerunners of more recent career pathways and programs of study—shows positive impacts on high school completion and enrollment in two-year colleges, but a modest negative impact on four-year college enrollments. Concerns over the latter issue ultimately proved fatal to continued federal funding of this approach.

Some other prominent models that overlap with Career Academies and Tech Prep and that incorporate many of the attributes of high-quality CTE have achieved scale and generate strong academic outcomes among high school students. These models include High Schools That Work, a whole-school reform model emphasizing strong

20. These schools are part of the College and Career Academy Support Network in California. We have no serious estimates to date of their impacts on higher education enrollment or attainment.

21. Small Schools of Choice is a program in New York City where large comprehensive high schools were replaced by smaller schools with themes into which students sorted themselves. At least a few of these schools were either Career Academies or others with strong career themes. Talent Development is a program that begins in the ninth grade with intensive student support in small communities; many of them then offer Career Academies to students, beginning in tenth grade. See Kemple, Herlihy, and Smith (2005) and Bloom and Unterman (2012).

academics integrated into project- and work-based learning models, that has been implemented in 1,200 schools in thirty states; Linked Learning, a districtwide model that has been implemented in nine California districts (and is expanding to sixty-three), stressing universal access to career clusters and related programs of study; and P-Tech, a model that originally began with a partnership between IBM and CUNY, covering students in grades nine through fourteen (i.e., through all of high school and two years of community college) with strong ties to an industry and careers, and which is now being implemented in over sixty high schools in New York and other states.[22] We regard these models as promising examples of high-quality CTE, though we reserve judgment on their success until rigorous evaluations of their impacts on academic or earnings outcomes have been performed.

In addition to models of CTE at the school and district levels, most states are implementing initiatives to better engage employers in curriculum design and to encourage more rigorous academic preparation. The federal Carl D. Perkins Act requires each state to establish programs of study with standards for academic quality and links to key industry sectors and clusters of jobs. States are free to do this in a variety of ways, and some have been quite innovative.

Among the states where progress has been particularly noteworthy is Illinois, where Learning Exchanges create partnerships between employers and schools in career clusters and industries, primarily in STEM fields. In Massachusetts, each school district offers CTE options on its own or as part of a regional network, and CTE students must meet the same rigorous academic requirements statewide as those preparing for college.

An example of broad state efforts at the postsecondary level is in Tennessee, where employers such as Volkswagen have generated partnerships with community colleges and Tennessee Technical

22. For more information on these models and some evidence on student outcomes for High Schools That Work, see their respective websites: Southern Regional Education Board at http://www.sreb.org/page/1078/high_schools _that_work.html; and Connected California at www.connectedcalifornia.org /linked_learning; and www.ptech.org.

University for programs of study closely related to major career clusters. In addition, the state of Minnesota has created twenty-six consortiums of school districts, colleges, and employers around the state through which all funding for career and technical education must pass, ensuring greater coordination of CTE across these institutions.[23]

In summary, the evidence on overall CTE impacts has generally indicated positive effects on employment and earnings, but less clear effects on educational attainment. In contrast, more recent studies using rigorous methods and focusing on more disadvantaged populations and more recent programmatic innovations find positive effects on both sets of outcomes. A good deal more research is needed for us to better understand the effectiveness of these recent innovations.

Work-Based Learning: Apprenticeship and Other Models

Work-based learning, sometimes called learning while earning, may be part of high school or community college CTE programs, or it may take other forms, such as apprenticeships. Apprenticeships have long been prominent in Germany and other European countries, and attracted renewed attention in the United States under the Obama administration.

Work-based learning can both facilitate the acquisition of skills and credentials with strong value in the labor market and help young people gain work experience. The integration of work and learning is one of the most important mechanisms for ensuring the relevance of skills acquired in the classroom to the world of work. It is also an important way for students to develop employability skills and to reduce the financial pressures involved in gaining additional education and training.

Registered apprenticeships, regulated by the U.S. Department of Labor and its state-level offices, combine on-the-job training with

23. These states are all part of the Pathways to Prosperity Network of ten states that is run by Jobs for the Future: http://www.jff.org/publications/pathways -prosperity-network-state-progress-report-2012-2014.

more formal related instruction, often at postsecondary institutions.[24] These programs frequently have age requirements and require a high school diploma or GED, but many states have established preapprenticeship programs to prepare high school students and low-achieving adults for entry into apprenticeships.

Apprenticeship partnerships link industry associations representing employers with secondary or postsecondary institutions. Apprenticeship Schools in several states are postsecondary institutions that usually grant associate degrees, but also provide instruction in a particular career cluster or for a particular industry—such as the one in Newport News, Virginia, that specializes in shipbuilding skills, and those in South Carolina that focus primarily on information technology careers.

Apprenticeships are more prevalent in European countries such as Germany and the Scandinavian nations than in the United States. The German "dual model" of apprenticeship, which combines classroom courses with on-the-job training, is the route most students take if they decide not to enter the university system. As noted earlier, apprenticeships in these countries entail much more tracking away from universities than would likely be acceptable in the United States. They also build on a much stronger role for organized labor in both workplaces and policy formation than exists in the United States, but our country can surely learn from these well-developed models.

Apprenticeships have many appealing characteristics. One is that employers and trainees know with certainty that the training is specific to the tasks required in the available jobs. Many employers keep apprentices on as regular employees after their training is complete, diminishing uncertainty about finding secure employment.

Another advantage is that students are paid while they learn—a very appealing arrangement for students, who may be more motivated to persist and complete the training when they are paid. A central problem in the financing of postsecondary education, particularly for older students—and especially those with family responsibilities—is the difficulty of simultaneously studying and earning a living. Pell Grants and other grant aid are rarely adequate to cover living expenses,

24. Lerman (2010).

and work-based learning models could provide an important avenue for avoiding excessive debt while earning credentials that lead to family-sustaining careers.

Employers are willing to pay their apprentices because wages are usually below the market level for other workers. But if the training is very general and apprentices could take their skills to a competing company in the area, employers might be less willing to participate.[25]

On the other hand, a shortcoming of training tied to a specific job is that the skills might not be applicable in another industry or occupation, or even to other employers in the field. This may make the employer more willing to invest in workers, but it leaves the workers without long-term security. Thus it is particularly important for apprentices to receive some type of credential from a college or other postsecondary provider, signaling to other employers exactly which skills they have mastered.

Evidence from Europe suggests that the returns to apprenticeship and other forms of CTE appear to last, even after the apprentices move on to other jobs or industries.[26] Although the empirical evidence in the United States is not rigorous, it suggests quite strong earnings returns from apprenticeships.[27]

Other forms of work-based learning, such as internships and co-op projects, have similar, if smaller, benefits to students.[28] The relationships with employers in most other models are weaker, with less likelihood of regular employment afterward, and the attainment of a formal credential is rarer. Nonetheless, other forms of work-based learning can still have positive effects for students.

If apprenticeships and other forms of work-based learning have advantages for both employers and students, and they are also effective as a skill-building mechanism in the labor market, why don't we see more of them in the United States? There are only about 400,000

25. Becker (1996).

26. Geel and Backes-Gellner (2011).

27. A study of apprentice programs that uses nonexperimental methods finds significant positive impacts of these programs on earnings as well (Reed and others 2012).

28. Neumark (2007).

registered U.S. apprenticeships at this writing—a very small percentage of workforce training.[29]

There are several possible answers to these questions. One possibility is that market failures reduce the availability of apprenticeships below the socially optimal level. These can include a lack of information among employers, especially small and medium-sized firms, on how to set up apprenticeships; wage rigidities that prevent employers from reducing apprentice wages below market levels; and coordination failures among smaller firms that prevent them from sharing the fixed costs of setting up these programs.

Alternatively, American employers might be accurately assessing the benefits and costs and correctly preferring not to provide many apprenticeships. Perhaps in a labor market where workers frequently change jobs and geographic location, it is not a worthwhile investment of time and effort, even when most pecuniary costs are borne by the workers. Alternatively, perhaps nonuniversity-bound students have weak analytical or employability skills, making firms hesitant to invest in them.[30]

It is also possible that employers prefer to minimize labor costs rather than maximize the output of the workers they hire. Employers following this strategy might prefer to outsource their entire human resource operations to contractors rather than invest in workers themselves.[31] In general, American employers are relatively more likely than their European counterparts to see their workers as generating only short-term variable costs, rather than as resources in whom it is worth investing.

Interestingly, thousands of German manufacturing companies have opened production facilities in the United States in the past few decades. These companies want to take advantage of our relatively lower energy costs, taxes, and regulations, as well as proximity to the

29. U.S. Department of Labor (N.D.)

30. Heckman's (2008) notion of "dynamic complementarity" between cognitive skills developed early in life and effectiveness of occupational skill development later is relevant here.

31. See Holzer (2015a, b) and Weil (2015); in contrast, Ross (2015) presents examples of firms making strong new investments in worker training.

large U.S. consumer market. But they are frequently disappointed by the lack of effective training for U.S. workers, especially at the sub-BA level, and they sometimes try to set up their own apprenticeship programs here to solve this problem.[32]

Rigor vs. Access: The Dilemma Remains

High-quality CTE has to be academically rigorous in order to avoid the stigma of being lower in quality than college prep and the problem of tracking the disadvantaged away from postsecondary options. Yet, a major argument for CTE is to create high-quality pathways for those whose previous academic achievement or other inclinations make them hesitant to pursue higher education, at least right after high school. Many of these students, like those who ultimately attend community colleges, have math and language skills that are likely to impede their mastering of technical material needed for some of the best career pathways or apprenticeships.

How can we give them opportunities while retaining high-quality academic programs? One answer involves contextualized learning, as discussed earlier, through which some students learn better in an applied context. Contextualizing remediation—as in the I-BEST developmental programs in Washington state and in the LaGuardia Bridge program for potential college students described in chapter 6—might help students compensate for their weak academic backgrounds. Contextualized math instruction, even outside of a remedial situation, has also shown promise as a way of improving outcomes among otherwise lower performers.

CTE must offer a range of pathways to students of differing academic abilities. Just as the students taking AP classes and aiming for selective four-year colleges and universities should not be turned away from CTE by an absence of academically rigorous material, lower performers should not be turned away by an absence of appropriate options for them.

32. Schneider (2013).

What, then, becomes of the notion that all students finishing high school CTE should be both college- and career-ready? An appropriate goal—perhaps aspirational early on but achievable later—is that all students should be prepared for some postsecondary options, though not all the same ones. High school CTE programs should aim to prepare all students for at least some community college programs, including certificate and associate degree programs, through which they can pursue a credential with labor market value. They could then continue along career pathways in a postsecondary setting if they chose to do so. Other students who choose four-year routes, even at more selective institutions, should also be able to find appropriate CTE options. The idea is that students would have options that challenge them, but in which they have a good chance of succeeding while exploring career opportunities.

Conclusions

The goal of CTE should be to increase the availability of high-quality offerings to students at different levels of academic ability in secondary school, and to give them a range of pathways into higher education and/or the job market. In addition, there should be greater opportunities for apprenticeships and other versions of work-based learning to improve the odds that students can gain the skills and certification, as well as the work experience, needed for long-term labor market success.

More partnerships and consortiums of high schools, colleges, and employers should help in achieving these goals. Employers can help shape curriculums to ensure their relevance to the job market. High schools and colleges should cooperate to ensure that pathways beginning in the former continue into the latter, with appropriate articulation agreements and opportunities for college courses taken in high school.

The federal government has fairly limited leverage over high school curriculums and programs. The most obvious tool is the Perkins Act, which distributes roughly $1 billion a year to high schools and colleges for CTE through formula funding. This constitutes less than 10 percent of total expenditures on CTE at the state and local levels, but it is large enough to generate concerns whenever there is talk of reforming it.

Both the George W. Bush and Obama administrations proposed reforms to Perkins that would make it more of a competitive grant, rewarding innovation and promoting greater accountability at the state and local levels. Political reactions to these proposals from national representatives of the CTE community have not been positive, and no major changes in the design of the program have been approved.[33]

There are, however, other ways for the federal government to generate guidelines and sponsor rigorous research in this area. For instance, previous reauthorizations of the Perkins Act—especially what is often known as Perkins IV in 2006—created the Career Clusters and Pathways framework that has apparently led to major improvements in the state and local implementation of CTE programs. The Obama administration also developed competitive grant programs, including Youth Career Connect, designed to encourage innovative CTE programs with strong links to industry, and American Apprenticeship Grants, designed to spur the creation of more apprenticeships. Rigorous evaluations of these programs should teach us a good deal more about what is cost-effective in these areas.

But it is at the state level that the most important innovations in CTE will take place. Illinois, Massachusetts, and Minnesota have taken some major steps to link secondary CTE programs to colleges and employers. States will also implement new forms of accountability and assessment of CTE, though often with major input from national organizations like NASDCTEC.

Some states have made explicit commitments to expand apprenticeships. For example, Georgia and Wisconsin fund coordinators at the high school level to work with local employers to create apprenticeships. The state of South Carolina grants employers a $1,000 tax credit for each new apprentice hired in the state and engages in strong marketing to individual employers.[34] In 2015 the state had 7,000 apprenticeships—a modest number relative to their total young workforce, but a very large increase over a short period of time.

33. See Resmovits (2012).
34. Holzer and Lerman (2014).

This type of experimentation should continue, and the federal government should encourage it, along with evaluation that will provide a clearer sense of whether the promise of high-quality CTE and work-based learning as alternative pathways to college and/or careers can actually be realized.

8

Conclusion and Policy Implications

This book lays out the central challenges facing disadvantaged students who enroll in college. Many of these students fail to complete any postsecondary credential. Many of the credentials they obtain lack significant labor market value. In addition, many students pay high tuition rates and go into debt, even when they fail to earn a credential with market value. These problems are more severe for students from disadvantaged backgrounds—primarily those from low-income or minority families and older students who return to college for additional education or training—than for other students.

This book lays out the scope of the problems and their causes, and then identifies promising solutions in policy and practice. In part I, we presented the facts and evidence relating to low credential completion and low labor market returns among disadvantaged students, and we discussed the reasons their outcomes are weaker than those for students from more privileged backgrounds. In chapter 2 we showed that low-income students bring a range of personal disadvantages to college programs and attend institutions with fewer resources and generally weaker outcomes. In chapter 3 we analyzed the labor market rewards to the different credentials that students earn at these institutions and how they differ by major. We reported substantial variation in market returns across types of credentials and fields of study, highlighting the problem that many students earn credentials such as generic associate degrees that have little value unless they lead to successful transfer to bachelor's degree programs. Because difficulty with student debt is one of the consequences of low completion rates and low labor market returns among students, especially when the price of attending college is high, chapter 4 then presented a summary of facts regarding college financing—including general trends in college prices and the various types of financial aid, as well as in student debt and default rates.

In part II we discussed a range of potential policy and programmatic solutions to the problems we identified earlier. Though the distinctions between them are not always perfectly clear, chapter 5 presented a set of policies designed to help individual *students*, while chapter 6 focused on strategies that could change how postsecondary *institutions* operate. Chapter 7 then discussed additional pathways that start in high school with career and technical education and lead in various ways to postsecondary institutions and/or directly to the labor market. Work-based learning models such as apprenticeship constitute an important segment of these options.

In this final chapter, we review and summarize what we know about disadvantaged students in college and in the labor market, and the kinds of policy and programmatic efforts that might improve their outcomes. We consider a range of policy and practice remedies at the federal, state, and local levels, and some of the legislative vehicles through which these policies could be implemented. We also step back from some of the policy details to consider broader themes and questions that emerge from our work.

We can summarize our major conclusions as follows:

First, we can improve the rates at which disadvantaged students complete higher education credentials with labor market value by *improving a range of supports and services for students at the nonselective institutions most will attend, especially community colleges, and by strengthening and reforming the institutions themselves.*

The strengthened supports and services should include personalized academic and career guidance—some of which should be delivered *before* students commit to a specific institution or program—in addition to reforms in remediation and financial aid and other efforts such as intensive tutoring and child care. The institutional reforms include building guided pathways with more structured curriculums and transfer procedures, as well as strengthening occupational training programs, especially through sector partnerships and career pathways.

But these goals will not be accomplished without providing more *resources* to community colleges—carefully targeted to the needs just outlined—as well as stronger *incentives* for the institutions to spend the resources effectively. Federal and state policies will have to support these goals.

Second, constructive change will also require a healthy dose of *realism*. Even if we improve transfer mechanisms, the vast majority of students beginning in community college will likely not complete a bachelor's degree—and they should be aware of the odds they face. Students should also know that some associate degrees, particularly associate of science (AS) and some occupational associate of arts (AA) degrees, open better job opportunities than others; even some certificate programs lead to higher earnings than an associate degree in general or liberal studies. In addition, since not every student will succeed in a "college-only" pathway, high school students should face a wider range of high-quality pathways from high school into postsecondary education and careers, including strong career and technical education and work-based learning.

The Problem and Its Causes

Students from low-income backgrounds and those who enroll in college as older adults have lower completion rates than other students, and when they do complete their programs the credentials they earn too frequently fail to pay off in the labor market.

There is not one simple explanation for this problem. Many disadvantaged students enter college with weak academic preparation and having had little opportunity to develop clear goals and identify the appropriate paths toward the outcomes they seek. They enroll disproportionately in community colleges, but also in nonselective public four-year and for-profit institutions. But even among disadvantaged students with relatively strong academic preparation and high achievement, large numbers enroll in nonselective institutions. Many students from low-income backgrounds have no access to information about their postsecondary options; they face challenges meeting the financial costs of attending, including both direct costs and living expenses; and they must often work while attending college, which prevents them from enrolling full time or studying as much as they need to.

All of these factors, combined with geographic constraints, lead many low-income students to attend institutions with fewer resources per student and weaker peer environments than they would under other circumstances. Their personal characteristics and circumstances, as well as those of the institutions they attend, contribute to their low completion rates of credentials with labor market value.

These forces play out in a variety of ways. For instance, many students with weak academic preparation are required to enroll in developmental (or remedial) math or English classes and pass exams indicating proficiency in these areas before they are allowed to take courses for credit. A large fraction of them never successfully complete these requirements. Others have difficulty passing gateway classes such as anatomy in health-related fields.

Financial realities also limit the outcomes of disadvantaged students. Seemingly small increases in out-of-pocket expenses can create insurmountable barriers for students with the most limited resources. Even when community college tuition is covered by grant aid, managing living costs without working full time creates significant strains for low-income students.

As for the institutions themselves, their constrained resources cause them to limit course offerings as well as the supports and services so many students need. In addition, weak incentives to spend their resources effectively may prevent some colleges from steering their students into programs facing strong demand in the labor market.

Limited resources and inadequate incentives to spend resources effectively affect outcomes in several ways. For one thing, technical programs in community colleges are much more expensive to offer than liberal arts programs; so successfully encouraging community colleges to shift operational resources from the liberal arts to occupational fields will require additional funding. Indeed, there is already excess demand for instruction in high-paying areas such as nursing and health technician fields. Community colleges usually receive subsidies from their states based on enrollments, regardless of whether students complete their credentials and whether those credentials pay off in the labor market. If better career counseling and other reforms raise student demand in remunerative areas, colleges will have to be both financially assisted and given incentives to meet this demand.

Most community colleges offer students too little academic and career guidance and often build too little structure into their course offerings and programs. Students can meander aimlessly through courses and fields without purpose or direction, and this can be very costly to students in two-year programs. Those in four-year colleges have time to explore their interests, and bachelor's degrees usually pay off well over time in the labor market, even if they are not associated with specific occupations. But community college students, particularly those with family responsibilities and other financial pressures and those who struggle in the classroom, do not have the luxury of taking years to explore their strengths and interests. Realistically, many will be much better off on a clear and direct path to a specific career.

The possibility of transferring to a four-year institution raises another set of concerns. The majority of community college students say they hope to eventually earn a bachelor's degree. But only about one-quarter of them successfully transfer to a four-year college, and only half of those earn a BA. In other words, only 12 percent of all community college students, and even fewer among the disadvantaged, will ultimately complete a bachelor's degree.

There is clear tension between encouraging students to take the academic curriculum most likely to transfer into credits toward a bachelor's degree and encouraging them to earn an associate degree that will help them get a good job even if they never earn a higher degree. While we should certainly diminish the barriers to transfer, students should recognize that most are not likely to succeed on this path.

A real advantage of community colleges is that they do not just provide the first two years of undergraduate education in the mode of four-year institutions. They also offer shorter-term credentials with less rigorous academic requirements and more immediate labor market application to students whose primary goal is to get a better job. Students should understand this and be guided toward programs that can stand on their own, in addition to providing a building block for future studies.

The core of the policy proposals we recommend would better position students to make the choices that will be most likely to improve their lives. They would strengthen pathways to college and to the workforce, improve the probability that students will succeed on their chosen paths, and provide the individualized guidance that can help them make ambitious but realistic choices.

Other problems for disadvantaged students have emerged because so many of them enroll in for-profit institutions. A relatively small but growing percentage of community college students borrow, mainly to cover their living expenses. But the many low-income students attending for-profit institutions pay high tuition, receive virtually no institutional grant aid, and accumulate large amounts of debt. Students attending for-profit programs account for a substantial portion of the student debt "crisis" and the disturbingly high default rate on student loans. The vast majority of these students come from disadvantaged backgrounds and lack both the information and guidance required to make optimal decisions about postsecondary study and the academic preparation that will allow them to succeed in college.

Rising student debt has contributed to the recent support for free community college for all, and even free four-year college for most students. Providing free community college without doing so for the first two years at four-year institutions would likely worsen many of the problems we describe, since many students who now attend four-year institutions would instead choose to begin their studies at two-year colleges, diminishing their chances of completing a bachelor's degree. It would also exacerbate the capacity constraints that now limit enrollments in key fields like nursing, and make it harder for disadvantaged students to reach their goals at a community college. And free four-year college for most students seems, both politically and fiscally, very unlikely.

Thus, while state and federal policies should strengthen financial aid for those who need it and limit debt burdens on low-income students, we should focus primarily on improving success rates for students attending underresourced institutions, rather than merely lowering the tuition price to zero.

Policies and Programs to Improve Success

No one reform has the potential to transform educational outcomes for low-income students. Rigorous evaluation of some promising strategies has yielded encouraging results in the form of a statistically significant improvement in credit accumulation, completion rates, and near-term employment outcomes. But it seems clear that a balanced and diverse set of reforms holds the most promise and that even the most successful strategies are likely to leave many students behind. In other words, we must plan in a coherent and comprehensive way, while ensuring that we develop better options even for those individuals who do not succeed in earning a postsecondary credential.

In order to make good choices, institutions need better evidence about the effectiveness of specific reforms and about their cost. Given the limited resources available, it is critical to know both that a specific change might increase the completion rate on campus and what the cost of that improvement is likely to be. Some changes might have a small impact, but be low cost and thus cost-effective. Other reforms that promise larger gains might end up being real resource drains.

Unfortunately, we are not able to put price tags on the proposed reforms. However, we urge a focus on the expected costs of success, not just the upfront costs of different strategies. Because of their effectiveness, comprehensive reforms along the lines of CUNY's ASAP program may have high upfront per-student costs, but relatively lower costs per positive outcome.

Our goals should include helping disadvantaged students enroll in the colleges that are best suited to their needs and circumstances, but most will continue to attend nonselective colleges. Therefore we must improve services and supports at these colleges and put in place reforms that raise success rates—changes that will surely depend on increased funding. We propose the following specific policies and practices to achieve these goals.

Helping Students Choose the Right College

We can improve the rates at which disadvantaged students complete higher education credentials with labor market value by reducing the number of students who enroll at institutions where they have little prospect of success. Strategies include:

- Provide better personalized guidance for students making decisions about whether, where, and in what programs to enroll.

- Set higher standards for institutions to participate in federal student aid programs.

- Improve access to selective colleges and universities for disadvantaged students with strong academic credentials through a combination of better information and modified recruiting, admission, and financial aid policies.

Support Systems for College Students After They Enroll

To raise student success rates at nonselective institutions, we should:

- Strengthen tutoring, academic and career counseling, and specific financial supports such as child care and emergency assistance for low-income community college students.

- Provide more personalized information and career guidance to students, helping them to understand the relatively weak labor market rewards to general associate degrees and certificates, and the higher returns to occupational training in technical fields such as medical technology and information technology (IT) and nontechnical fields such as business and retail management. Just making information available is not sufficient; students need more direct guidance to make these complex decisions about the best paths given their circumstances.

- Transform remedial education to improve the placement system, make the requirements more relevant to the courses of study students are pursuing, and integrate the work into postsecondary pathways.

- Reform the financial aid system so that it:

- provides both ample resources to students with financial need and incentives and support for successful academic progress;

- is simpler, more predictable, and more flexible so students can access the aid for which they are eligible without jumping through unnecessary bureaucratic hoops and know well in advance about the funds that will be available to them; and

- is flexible enough to accommodate noncredit and innovative programs without ignoring the lessons from the for-profit postsecondary sector, which grew up as a direct response to the availability of federal student aid and has generated considerable fraud and abuse at the expense of at-risk students, despite developing some successful models for occupational preparation.

- Build on the insights of the behavioral and cognitive sciences to develop low-cost "nudges" that encourage constructive student behaviors, recognizing that concrete changes in student circumstances clearly matter, but that their choices and behaviors also affect their educational outcomes. Considerable evidence from behavioral experiments indicates that text messages to remind students about pre-enrollment steps, about appropriate choices of classes and majors, and about assignments can lead to constructive actions on their part.

Institutional Structures and Funding

Community colleges provide many opportunities but little guidance to students for taking advantage of them. Some structural changes have the potential to significantly improve student outcomes at community colleges. We should:

- Build guided pathways with more structured curricula and improved transfer mechanisms, so that students are not faced with a dizzying array of choices they are ill-equipped to make. With these changes, far fewer students would likely drift along without understanding what they want out of college and how to get there; more students would be motivated and better able to achieve their goals, in either academic or occupational programs.

- Strengthen occupational training, especially through sector partnerships and career pathways, attempting to replicate and scale the best programs in ways that do not sacrifice their quality. This includes expanding teaching capacity in high-demand fields like health care, where instructional costs are often higher than elsewhere because of equipment and instructor costs.

- Improve public funding for community and broad-access four-year colleges. The dramatic decline in per-student funding in recent years makes the idea of transferring funds from one segment of public higher education to another unappealing. But it is clear that the institutions that educate the vast majority of disadvantaged students are the most underresourced under current funding models. Targeting any new resources for public higher education in the United States toward these institutions seems appropriate.

- Carefully and gradually strengthen the academic and performance incentives facing these institutions.

The issue of strengthening incentives requires a bit more discussion. Some changes *within* institutions can strengthen incentives for improving student outcomes. Financial practices and rules governing how scarce resources are distributed across departments can create very different incentives within departments and programs. Revenue models that reward departments for successful outcomes may encourage faculty to focus more on student success.

A similar principle applies to state funding rules *across* public institutions. More and more states are adopting outcomes-based funding models that distribute a portion of state appropriations in accord with student outcomes. To date, the outcomes most heavily rewarded are academic ones, like completion rates and credit attainment. Also incorporating students' subsequent employment outcomes—especially those of disadvantaged and minority students—into funding formulas should motivate institutions to guide more students into fields with strong labor market value and to expand teaching capacity in those fields when needed. Like other reforms, outcomes-based funding should be implemented gradually and informed by rigorous evidence of what works, not by raising the bar in community college admissions or reducing completion requirements to improve measured outcomes.

There should also be some limits to the scope of these incentive changes. The four-year institutions whose main function is to generate graduates in the liberal arts and teach students analytical, critical thinking, and communication skills should not be punished for successfully carrying out their missions. Some students from these institutions are not immediately rewarded by the labor market, and substantial fractions of them go on to earn graduate degrees. Applying accountability based on immediate employment to these institutions should be done flexibly, if at all, while the accountability they face for academic outcomes could be strong.

Widening the Range of High-Quality Pathways

Finally, too many students come to college without clear goals. They know that most well-paid jobs require some form of postsecondary education or training. But they are not certain of their own preferences and capacities or knowledgeable about the career doors specific programs could open for them. Largely because of a history of inequitable tracking of students, very few high school students have the opportunity to explore career options before they must decide what to do after they graduate. Strengthening career and technical education (CTE) in high schools, as well as work-based learning options like apprenticeship, could provide all students with a chance to learn more about themselves and their options. Those who have no interest in more formal schooling immediately after high school could instead choose to acquire new skills that prepare them for a good job.

Implementing the many changes in policy and practice that we support will not be easy and will require policymakers and practitioners at all levels—federal, state, and local—to play important roles.

State and Local Roles

Public higher education in the United States is managed by the states, which must design and implement many of the policy changes we have proposed. Individual institutions will have to implement programmatic and practice changes and reforms.

For instance, only local community college administrators can decide to offer disadvantaged students new supports and services, such as better academic and career counseling, tutoring, and financial assistance. They will also be the ones to implement curricular changes, such as expansions of occupational training, building more sector partnerships and career pathways, and building the guided pathways that should help students make critical choices and more successfully transfer across institutions.

But such changes are unlikely to occur to any significant extent unless the community colleges receive more resources, since they are already so constrained financially and have to juggle their many roles with much smaller subsidies per student than four-year institutions receive from the states. And, given the likely resistance to the curricular changes from faculty and other administrators, as well as the higher costs of career programs relative to liberal arts, they will also need strong incentives to induce them to bear these costs.

To make significant progress, state governments will have to provide more resources to community colleges and require that those resources be used to implement evidence-based reforms that promote student success. They will have to focus on the resources colleges have available to support students—not just on the prices students pay.

States could also make policy changes. They can dictate remediation requirements and improve alignment between programs in their two-year and four-year public institutions, facilitating guided pathways and transfers across these institutions. States can also fund more sector partnerships and career pathway models and encourage more employers to create apprenticeships by providing financial and/or technical support.

The Federal Role

The federal government can promote and evaluate these changes and give schools the incentives to make them. Federal funds will almost certainly have to supplement scarce state funds to make many of the needed changes feasible. Increasing accountability and using existing resources more effectively is vital, but is not likely to be sufficient to meet the nation's ambitious goals.

One might, for example, imagine a new version of the federal Race to the Top, which encouraged accountability in public K–12 education during the Obama years; it could be designed now to motivate and fund public colleges to implement the new policies and practices we describe here. Although analysts continue to debate whether Race to the Top generated meaningful improvements in K–12 education outcomes,[1] there seems little doubt that it substantially affected state behavior in this realm.

As before, the federal government would offer large grants to states through a competitive process. States would have to increase the accountability of public higher education institutions through stronger and better-designed outcomes-based funding, with appropriate measures to prevent unintended consequences. The additional funding could be targeted on expanding teaching capacity in high-demand fields and support services for disadvantaged students.

The impending reauthorization of the Higher Education Act provides an opportunity to reform the federal framework for higher education. Simplifying the federal financial aid system, eliminating the complex application process, and making federal aid more predictable is an obvious starting point that need not require significant additional resources. Ensuring that the Pell Grant program, the foundation of the federal student aid system, supports student success—in addition to just access—and meets the needs of very diverse students is critical. In particular, it must meet the needs of both recent high school graduates and older adults returning to school, as well as of students pursuing bachelor's degrees at residential colleges and of individuals seeking short-term occupational preparation.

The student loan system is also an important component of the federal infrastructure for educational opportunity. Allowing students to spread the cost of investing in their futures over a long period of time is both rational and necessary for access. But the system should do more to protect students from getting into unmanageable circumstances and to support them when their outcomes are disappointing.

1. See, for example, Shah (2013); Miller and Hanna (2014).

This involves imposing higher standards for institutions to participate in federal student aid programs and ensuring that while most borrowers repay their federal loans, they have reliable insurance against unexpected hardships.

Other federal legislative vehicles also support postsecondary students. Since Congress reauthorized federal workforce legislation in 2014 as the Workforce Innovation and Opportunity Act (WIOA),[2] its funding levels have remained quite modest, both relative to past levels and in light of the many functions it is expected to perform.[3] Among the positive changes from its previous incarnation, when it was known as the Workforce Investment Act (WIA), it requires more coordination between local and state workforce boards and community colleges. It calls for comprehensive state workforce plans that actively integrate higher education and workforce goals. And it requires states to use a consistent set of metrics for outcomes that include credential attainment and worker earnings.

The Perkins Act, which is also due for reauthorization, could be designed to encourage more innovation in CTE programs. Its funding is even more modest than WIOA's, at roughly $1 billion a year, but adding new funds or converting some or all of the funds into competitive grants for innovative efforts could spur constructive changes.

2. WIOA is the most recent incarnation of federal workforce legislation that began with the Comprehensive Employment and Training Act (CETA) in 1973. It was changed to the Job Training Partnership Act (JTPA) in 1982, and to the Workforce Investment Act (WIA) in 1998.

3. Current federal funding of the different titles of WIOA adds up to about $5 billion, a drastic reduction from funding levels for CETA, which peaked in real terms in 1980. The current funding pays for adult worker, dislocated worker, and youth services at Job Centers (formerly One-Stop Centers) around the country, plus very modest short-term training through vouchers known as Individual Training Accounts (ITAs). WIOA also funds adult learning, Job Corps centers for youth, and administration of the Job Centers. The federal government also supports workforce efforts in a range of other federal programs run by other federal agencies, such as Temporary Assistance for Needy Families (TANF), run by the U.S. Department of Health and Human Services; and the Supplemental Nutritional Assistance Program (SNAP), formerly known as Food Stamps, run by the Department of Agriculture.

In both the George W. Bush and Obama administrations, the Departments of Education and Labor spent several billion dollars on competitive grant programs to encourage sector-based training and career pathway formation. Earlier we described the largest and best-known of these efforts—the Trade Adjustment Assistance Community College and Career Training (TAACCCT) grant program, which awarded $2 billion to individual community colleges and consortiums of colleges and employers over four rounds of funding between 2010 and 2014. The evaluation offices of these agencies are now assessing the outcomes, and we hope that some important lessons will emerge. Following up on these efforts with another round of major competitive grants, especially designed to replicate and scale up programs and practices that succeeded in smaller studies, should be high on the federal policy agenda.

Tough Choices Remain

The changes in policy and practice that we describe here, even as components of comprehensive change, are not likely to solve all of the problems we have described. For example, the highly successful ASAP program almost doubled completion rates, increasing the percentage of students earning a credential within three years from 22 percent to 40 percent.[4] At the City Colleges of Chicago, systemic reform more than doubled the three-year graduation rate—to 17 percent in 2014–15.[5] In other words, even major successful reforms in community colleges are likely to leave many students behind.

Clearly, we must ask some fundamental questions and make some hard choices. Some of the choices might be uncomfortable. It is easy to argue that every pathway should be available to every student. But the low completion rates and poor labor market outcomes in some areas require us to reconsider some basic characteristics of our current higher education and labor market model.

4. Scrivener and others (2015).
5. City Colleges of Chicago, FY2015 5-Year Plan Scorecard, https://www.ccc.edu/news/Documents/DO_FY15_Scorecard.pdf.

What can we do for students who have very low probabilities of succeeding in college?

Many high school graduates with inadequate academic preparation enroll at community colleges. They rarely complete an associate degree—much less a bachelor's degree. For instance, according to the Florida data we discussed in chapter 3, about 55 percent of students in the bottom achievement quartile of high school completers enrolled in associate degree programs, but only about 16 percent completed them. Completion rates were even lower for those in the lowest 10 or 20 percent of the achievement distribution.

We are wasting enormous amounts of time and other resources, both public and private. It is not just taxpayers and institutions whose resources are at risk—but also the time, energy, and futures of students themselves.

We do not advocate reducing access to higher education. Instead, we should provide a broader range of high-quality alternatives, including career and technical education (CTE) in high schools and work-based learning, so that students have good alternatives to enrolling immediately in college. The range of pathways to the labor market should include, but not be limited to, community colleges and other postsecondary institutions.

Some certificate programs provide reasonably strong market returns, and completion rates for low-achieving students in these programs are higher than those in associate degree programs. Informing low achievers and older adults of their likelihood of success on different paths and pointing them toward the most productive options would almost certainly be better than pretending that all pathways remain viable at this stage of their lives.

Should we encourage more students to consider an AA, AS, or certificate program with greater labor market value as stand-alone credentials instead of an associate degree in liberal arts?

Very few community college students transfer to a four-year college and ultimately earn a BA, particularly among those who were low achievers in high school or delayed college and are seeking credential at older ages. And an associate degree in the liberal arts is of little value in the labor market. In light of these facts, we should perhaps encourage more of these students to enroll in associate of science (AS) programs, including those in allied health and other technical fields, and in higher-paying AA programs such as business.

One issue we cannot ignore is that some more technical programs, especially AS degrees, likely present weakly prepared students not drawn to math and science with additional academic challenges. Helping students choose productive pathways requires focusing both on potential labor market opportunities and on individual capacities and preferences. But there are also high-demand and financially rewarding AA programs in fields such as business and management that require less math, as well as certificate programs that the market rewards well. Also, career pathways can include stackable credentials. Earning a credential with labor market value does not preclude a student's pursuit of more education and training later.

Arguing for guiding more students into certificate and associate degree programs that have labor market value even without further credentials does not mean abandoning the liberal arts and transfer opportunities. More structure and guided pathways for the liberal arts students at community colleges might well improve their transfer rates. But it is critical to expose students to occupational fields while they take their general studies classes and to provide them an opportunity to shift in directions more likely to lead to strong workforce outcomes.

Students with weak academic preparation or family responsibilities that force them to attend college part time should also be informed about the low odds they face of earning a bachelor's degree when they start in an AA program. No one wants to dampen student ambitions and expectations, especially those of minority and low-income students. However, hiding the truth on this issue does not help students. They need the information that will enable them to make the most sensible choices. But information is not enough. They need clear guidance about their own personal prospects, with realistic perspectives on where different paths are likely to take them.

Can we improve labor market outcomes for the many students who do not complete their associate or bachelor's degree programs?

A key theme of this book is the reality that many students enroll in college planning to earn a degree or certificate, but never make it to that goal. Other students, particularly at community colleges, never intend to get a degree or certificate. They enroll with the intention of taking a course or two to gain a specific skill that will enable them to advance in the job market. This scenario applies more to older nontraditional students than to those attending college right after high school.

To date, we have little evidence that individual classes are valuable in the job market. But California and other states are attempting to improve labor market outcomes for these students, who are known as "skill builders." There is some evidence that these students can benefit from relatively small amounts of coursework and credits. We need more evidence to understand under what circumstances this is true, and with which kinds of classes for which students. This type of evidence could improve the guidance provided both to students who intend to complete credentials and to those who do not.

Given the strong correlation between full-time college attendance and completion rates, should we discourage part-time enrollment?

There is real tension between the evidence about the correlation between full-time enrollment and degree completion and the time constraints faced by many disadvantaged students—particularly those who are older and have family responsibilities. On one hand, students who consistently enroll part time have disturbingly low completion rates. On the other hand, many people simply do not have enough hours in the day to go to college full time while meeting their other responsibilities.

There is no doubt that developing viable postsecondary options for people with both time and financial constraints is critical. That said, it is important to be realistic about how circumstances limit options. For example, the fact that very few students who consistently enroll part time ever earn a bachelor's degree should give us pause about encouraging students to follow this path. Similarly, failing to direct community college students whose chances of earning an associate degree and transferring to a four-year college are slim away from degrees that lack labor market value is irresponsible. Pointing them in less ambitious but more promising directions is the best way to improve their prospects.

Summing Up

Our society faces an urgent challenge to increase opportunities for disadvantaged individuals. The current high levels of inequality and low levels of social mobility are both unjust and unsustainable. Providing better access to postsecondary education is a necessary component of addressing the problems, but it is not sufficient. Too many young people and older adults seeking to improve their lives enroll in college but leave without a credential, having devoted considerable time, energy, and money to the effort. Too many who do earn credentials find that their work does not lead to the labor force outcomes that motivated them.

As we work to strengthen the elementary and secondary education systems in this country and make them more equitable, we must recognize the challenges facing individuals with weak academic preparation, limited support systems, and immediate family responsibilities. In other words, just telling people to go to college and set their sights as high as possible, and working to diminish the financial barriers they face, is not a viable strategy. We must guide students into programs that are most likely to provide them with valuable credentials. For all, following a clearly defined path with concrete attainable goals is imperative.

Many questions remain about the most promising approaches, but we know enough to push forward with significant systemic reforms in the higher education system.

Appendix: Mapping CIP Categories with Chapter 2 Categories

CIP code[a]	CIP_name	Category names used in this book
1	Agriculture, agriculture operations, and related sciences	STEM
3	Natural resources and conservation	STEM
4	Architecture and related services	STEM
5	Area, ethnic, cultural, gender, and group studies	Humanities
9	Communication, journalism, and related programs	Occupational
10	Communication technologies/technicians and support services	Occupational
11	Computer and information sciences and support services	STEM
12	Personal and culinary services	Occupational
13	Education	Education
14	Engineering	STEM
15	Engineering technologies and engineering-related fields	STEM
16	Foreign languages, literatures, and linguistics	Humanities
19	Family and consumer sciences/human sciences	Other
22	Legal professions and studies	Occupational
23	English language and literature/letters	Humanities
24	Liberal arts and sciences, general studies and humanities	Humanities

CIP code[a]	CIP_name	Category names used in this book
25	Library science	Other
26	Biological and biomedical sciences	STEM
27	Mathematics and statistics	STEM
30	Multi/interdisciplinary studies	Humanities
31	Parks, recreation, leisure, and fitness studies	Other
32	Basic skills and developmental/ remedial education	Other
33	Citizenship activities	Other
34	Health-related knowledge and skills	Health
36	Leisure and recreational activities	Other
38	Philosophy and religious studies	Humanities
40	Physical sciences	STEM
41	Science technologies/technicians	STEM
42	Psychology	Social sciences
43	Homeland security, law enforcement, firefighting and related protective services	Occupational
44	Public administration and social service professions	Social sciences
45	Social sciences	Social sciences
46	Construction trades	Occupational
47	Mechanic and repair technologies/ technicians	Occupational
48	Precision production	Occupational
49	Transportation and materials moving	Occupational
50	Visual and performing arts	Humanities
51	Health professions and related programs	Occupational
52	Business, management, marketing, and related support services	Occupational
53	High school/secondary diplomas and certificates	Other
54	History	Social sciences

a. CIP stands for Classification of Instructional Programs.

References

ACT. 2015. "Using Dual Enrollment to Improve the Education Outcomes of High School Students." ACT Policy Brief, December (www.act.org/content /dam/act/unsecured/documents/UsingDualEnrollment_2015.pdf).

Advance CTE. N.D. *The Common Careers Technical Core*. CTE Advance (https://careertech.org/CCTC).

Akers, B., and A. Soliz. 2015. "Mapping the Market for Higher Education." Washington, D.C.: Brookings Institution (www.brookings.edu/re search /papers/2015/09/24-mapping-market-higher-education-akers-soliz).

Alliance for Quality Career Pathways. 2014. *Shared Vision, Strong System: The Alliance for Quality Career Pathways Framework Version 1.0* (www .clasp.org/resources-and-publications/files/aqcp-framework-version-1-0 /AQCP-Executive-Summary-FINAL-PRINT.pdf).

Alon, S. 2015. *Race, Class, and Affirmative Action*. New York: Russell Sage Foundation.

Altonji, J., E. Blom, and C. Meghir. 2012. "Heterogeneity in Human Capital Investments: High School Curriculum, College Major, and Careers." *Annual Review of Economics* 4 (1): 185–223. DOI: 10.3386/w17985.

Andersson, F., H. J. Holzer, and J. Lane. 2005. *Moving Up or Moving On: Who Gets Ahead in the Low-Wage Labor Market?* New York: Russell Sage Foundation.

Andrews, R. J., J. Li, and M. F. Lovenheim. 2012. "Heterogeneous Paths through College: Detailed Patterns and Relationships with Graduation and Earnings." *Economics of Education Review* 42(C): 93–108 (www .human.cornell.edu/pam/people/upload/College_Path-2.pdf).

Angrist, J., D. Autor, S. Hudson, and A. Pallais. 2015. "Leveling Up: Early Results from a Randomized Evaluation of Post-Secondary Aid." Working Paper 20800. Cambridge, Mass.: National Bureau of Economic Research (www.nber.org/papers/w20800.pdf).

Angrist, J., D. Lang, and P. Oreopoulos. 2009. "Incentives and Services for College Achievement: Evidence from a Randomized Trial." *American Economic Journal: Applied Economics* 1 (1): 136–63. DOI: 10.1257/app.1.1.136.

Antonovics, K., and B. Backes. 2012. "Were Minority Students Discouraged from Applying to University of California Campuses after the Affirmative Action Ban?" University of California, San Diego (http://econweb.ucsd.edu/~kantonov/antonovics_backes_manuscrip.pdf).

Arcidiacono, P., and M. Lovenheim. 2016. "Affirmative Action and the Quality-Fit Trade-Off." *Journal of Economic Literature* 54 (1): 3–51.

Arum, R., and J. Roksa. 2011. *Academically Adrift: Limited Learning on College Campuses.* University of Chicago Press. DOI: 10.1093/sf/sos016.

———. 2014. *Aspiring Adults Adrift: Tentative Transitions of College Graduates.* University of Chicago Press. DOI: 10.1080/00091383.2012.691857.

Aspen Institute. 2014. "A Resource Guide for College / Career Navigators." Washington, D.C. (http://www.aspenwsi.org/wordpress/wp-content/uploads/CareerNavigators.pdf).

Autor, D. 2010. *The Polarization of Job Opportunities in the U.S. Labor Market: Implications for Employment and Earnings.* Washington, D.C.: Center for American Progress and The Hamilton Project.

———. 2014. "Skills, Education, and the Rise of Earnings Inequality among the 'Other 99 Percent.'" *Science* 344 (6186): 843–51 (http://science.sciencemag.org/content/344/6186/843.full).

Autor, D., J. Donohue III, and S. J. Schwab. 2006. "The Costs of Wrongful-Discharge Laws." *Review of Economics and Statistics* 88 (2): 211–31. DOI: 10.1162/rest.88.2.211.

Autor, D. H., D. Dorn, and G. H. Hanson. 2014. "The China Syndrome: Local Labor Market Effects of Import Competition in the United States." *American Economic Review* 103 (6): 2121–68 (http://economics.mit.edu/files/6613).

Backes, B., H. J. Holzer, and E. D. Velez. 2015. "Is It Worth It? Postsecondary Education and Labor Market Outcomes for the Disadvantaged." Washington, D.C.: Postsecondary Education and Labor Market Program at the Center for the Analysis of Longitudinal Data in Education Research (CALDER) (www.caldercenter.org/sites/default/files/WP117.pdf).

Backes, B., and E. D. Velez. 2014. "Who Transfers and Where Do They Go? Community College Students in Florida." Center for Analysis of Longitudinal Data in Education Research (CALDER). American Institutes for Research, Washington, D.C. (www.aefpweb.org/sites/default/files/webform /39th/backes_velez_commcollege_aefp2014.pdf).

Bahr, P. R., S. Dynarski, B. Jacob, D. Kreisman, A. Sosa, and M. Wiederspan. 2015. "Labor Market Returns to Community College Awards: Evidence from Michigan." New York: Center for the Analysis of Postsecondary Education and Employment, Teachers College, Columbia University (http:// capseecenter.org/wp-content/uploads/2015/03/labor-market-returns -michigan.pdf).

Bailey, T., and C. R. Belfield. 2013. "Community College Occupational Degrees: Are They Worth It?" In *Preparing Today's Students for Tomorrow's Jobs in Metropolitan America: The Policy, Practice, and Research Issues*, ed. Laura Perna. University of Pennsylvania Press.

Bailey, T., S. Jaggars, and D. Jenkins. 2015. *Redesigning America's Community Colleges*. Harvard University Press.

Bailey, T., and D. Merritt. 1997. "School to Work for the College Bound." MDS-799. National Center for Research in Vocational Education (www.nrccte .org/sites/default/files/publication-files/stw_for_the_college_bound.pdf).

Barnett, E., and others. 2012. "Bridging the Gap: An Impact Study of Eight Developmental Summer Bridge Programs in Texas." National Center for Postsecondary Research (www.postsecondaryresearch.org/i/a/document /22731_NCPR_TexasDSB_FullReport.pdf).

Baum, S., and C. Kurose. 2013. "Community Colleges in Context: Exploring Financing of Two- and Four-Year Institutions." In *Bridging the Higher Education Divide: Strengthening Community Colleges and Restoring the American Dream*. Washington, D.C.: Century Foundation (www.tcf.org /assets/downloads/20130523-Bridging_the_Higher_Education_Divide -Baum_Kurose.pdf).

Baum, S., J. Ma, and K. Payea. 2013. *Education Pays 2013: The Benefits of Higher Education for Individuals and Society*. New York: College Board (www.rilin.state.ri.us/Special/ses15/commdocs/Education%20Pays,%20 The%20College%20Board.pdf).

Baum, S., J. Ma, M. Pender, and D. Bell. 2015. *Trends in Student Aid 2015*. New York: College Board.

Baum, S., J. Ma, M. Pender, and M. Welch. 2016. *Trends in Student Aid 2016*. New York: College Board.

Baum, S., M. McDemmond, and G. Jones. 2014. "Institutional Strategies for Increasing Affordability and Success for Low-Income Students in the

Regional Public Four-Year Sector: Tuition and Financial Aid. Maximizing Resources for Student Success." HCM Strategists (http://hcmstrategists .com/maximizingresources/images/Tuition_Paper.pdf).

Baum, S., and J. Scott-Clayton. 2013. *Redesigning the Pell Grant Program for the 21st Century.* The Hamilton Project, Brookings Institution (www .hamiltonproject.org/assets/legacy/files/downloads_and_links/THP _BaumDiscPaper_Final.pdf).

Baum. S., and others. 2012. *Beyond Need and Merit: Strengthening State Grant Programs.* State Grant Aid Study Group, Brown Center on Education Policy, Brookings Institution.

Beaudry, P., D. A. Green, and B. M. Sand. 2013. "The Great Reversal in the Demand for Skill and Cognitive Tasks." *Labor Markets in the Aftermath of the Great Recession,* ed. D. Card and A. Mas. *Journal of Labor Economics* 34 (S1): S199–S247. DOI: 10.3386/w18901.

Becker, G. S. 1964. *Human Capital.* University of Chicago Press.

———. 1967. "Human Capital and the Personal Distribution of Income: An Analytical Approach." Woytinsky Lecture. Ann Arbor, Mich.: Institute of Public Administration (http://unionstats.gsu.edu/9220/Becker(1975) _Human%20Capital_Woytinsky.pdf).

———. 1996. "Unemployment in Europe and the United States." *Journal des Economistes et des Etudes Humaines* 7 (1): 1–4.

Belasco, A., K. Rosinger, and J. Hearn. 2014. "The Test-Optional Movement at America's Selective Liberal Arts Colleges: A Boon for Equity or Something Else?" *Educational Evaluation and Policy Analysis* (June): 1–18.

Bettinger, E. 2004. "How Financial Aid Affects Persistence." In *College Choices: The Economics of Where to Go, When to Go, and How to Pay For It,* ed. C. Hoxby. University of Chicago Press (www.nber.org/papers /w10242.pdf).

Bettinger, E., and R. Baker. 2014. "The Effects of Student Coaching: An Evaluation of a Randomized Experiment in Student Advising." *Educational Evaluation and Policy Analysis* 36 (1): 3–19 (http://epa.sagepub .com/content/36/1/3.full.pdf+html).

Bettinger, E. P., A. Boatman, and B. T. Long. 2013. "Student Supports: Developmental Education and Other Academic Programs." *The Future of Children* 23 (1) (http://futureofchildren.org/publications/docs/23_01_05 .pdf).

Bettinger, E. P., B. T. Long, P. Oreopoulos, and K. Sanbonmatsu. 2012. "The Role of Application Assistance and Information in College Decisions: Results from the H&R Block Fafsa Experiment." *Quarterly Journal of Economics* 12 (3): 1205–42. DOI: 10.1093/qje/qjs017.

Black, S. E., J. A. Lincove, J. Cullinane, and R. Veron. 2014. *Can You Leave High School Behind?* Working Paper. Cambridge, Mass.: National Bureau of Economic Research (www.nber.org/papers/w19842).

Blank, R. M. 1997. *It Takes a Nation: A New Agenda for Fighting Poverty.* Princeton University Press. DOI: 10.1080/00380237.1999.10571138.

Bloom, H., and R. Unterman. 2012. "Sustained Positive Effects on Graduation Rates Produced by New York City's Public High Schools of Choice." New York: MDRC (http://www.mdrc.org/publication/sustained -positive-effects-graduation-rates-produced-new-york-city-s-small -public-high).

Blumenstyk, G. 2016. "After ITT's Demise, More Trouble Is Likely for For-Profit Colleges." *Chronicle of Higher Education,* September 13.

Boatman, A. 2012. "Evaluating Institutional Efforts to Streamline Postsecondary Remediation: The Causal Effects of the Tennessee Developmental Course Redesign Initiative on Early Student Academic Success." National Center for Postsecondary Research (www.postsecondaryresearch.org/i/a /document/22651_BoatmanTNFINAL.pdf).

Borjas, G. J. 2003. "The Labor Demand Curve Is Downward Sloping: Reexamining the Impact of Immigration on the Labor Market." *Quarterly Journal of Economics* 118 (4): 1335–74. DOI: 10.3386/w9755.

Bound, J., M. F. Lovenheim, and S. Turner. 2010. "Why Have College Completion Rates Declined? An Analysis of Changing Student Preparation and Collegiate Resources." *American Economic Journal* 2 (3): 129–57 (www.nber.org/papers/w15566.pdf).

Bowen, W. G., M. M. Chingos, and M. S. McPherson. 2009. *Crossing the Finish Line: Completing College at America's Public Universities.* Princeton University Press. DOI: 10.1080/13603101003780475.

Bowen, W. G., M. A. Kurzweil, and E. M. Tobin. 2005. *Equity and Excellence in American Higher Education.* University of Virginia Press. DOI: 10.1353/jhe.2007.0010.

Bozick, R., and B. Dalton. 2013. "Balancing Career and Technical Education with Academic Coursework: The Consequences for Mathematics Achievement over the Last Two Years of High School." *Educational Evaluation and Policy Analysis* 35: 123–38.

Brown, M., A. Haughwout, D. Lee, J. Scally, and W. van der Klaauw. 2015. *Looking at Student Loan Defaults through a Larger Window.* Liberty Street Economics. Federal Reserve Bank of New York.

Bruni, F. 2015. "An Admissions Surprise from the Ivy League." *New York Times,* October 18 (www.nytimes.com/2015/10/18/opinion/sunday/an -admissions-surprise-from-the-ivy-league.html).

Brynjolffson, E., and A. McAfee. 2014. *The Second Machine Age: Work, Progress, and Prosperity in a Time of Brilliant Technologies.* New York: W. W. Norton. DOI: 10.1080/08963568.2015.1044355.

Caliber Associates. 2003. *Cultural Barriers to Incurring Debt: An Exploration of Borrowing and Impact on Access to Postsecondary Education.* Oakdale, Minn.: ECMC Group Foundation.

California Chancellor's Community College Office. 2015. "Community Colleges Task Force on Workforce Education Recommends Important Changes to Increase California Competitiveness and Job Creation" (http://californiacommunitycolleges.cccco.edu/Portals/0/DocDownloads /PressReleases/AUG2015/PR-CTE-Task-Force-Recos-2015-08-17-2 .html).

California Department of Education. 2015. *Early Assessment Program* (www.cde.ca.gov/ci/gs/hs/eapindex.asp).

Card, D. 1999. "The Causal Effect of Education and Earnings." In *Handbook of Labor Economics*, vol. 3, part A. DOI: 10.1016/S1573-4463(99) 03011-4.

Card, D., and J. E. DiNardo. 2002. "Skill Biased Technological Change and Rising Wage Inequality: Some Problems and Puzzles." *Journal of Labor Economics* 20: 733–83 (www.nber.org/papers/w8769.pdf).

Card, D., and L. Giuliano. 2015. "Can Universal Screening Improve the Representation of Low-Income and Minority Students in Gifted and Talented Programs?" Working Paper. Cambridge, Mass.: National Bureau of Economic Research.

Carneiro, P., J. Heckman, and E. Vytacil. 2011. "Estimating Marginal Returns to Education." *American Economic Review* 101 (6): 275–81.

Carnevale, A. P., S. J. Rose, and A. R. Hanson. 2012. *Certificates: Gateway to Gainful Employment and College Degrees.* Center on Education and the Workforce, Georgetown University (www.insidehighered.com/sites /default/server_files/files/06_01_12%20Certificates%20Full%20 Report%20FINAL.pdf).

Carnevale, A. P., J. Strohl, and A. Gulish. 2015. "College Is Just the Beginning: Employers' Role in the $1.1 Trillion Postsecondary Education and Training System." Center on Education and the Workforce, Georgetown University (https://cew.georgetown.edu/wp-content/uploads/2015/02 /Trillion-Dollar-Training-System-.pdf).

Carnevale, A. P., J. Strohl, and M. Melton. 2011. *What's It Worth? The Economic Value of College Majors.* Washington, D.C.: Center on Education and the Workforce, Georgetown University (https://cew.georgetown.edu /wp-content/uploads/2014/11/whatsitworth-complete.pdf).

Castleman, B. 2015. "Prompts, Personalization, and Pay-Offs: Strategies to Improve the Design and Delivery of College and Financial Aid Information." In *Decision Making for Student Success: Behavioral Insights to Improve College Access and Persistence*, ed. B. Castleman, S. Schwartz, and S. Baum. New York: Routledge.

Castleman, B., and J. Goodman. 2014. "Intensive College Counseling and the College Enrollment Choices of Low-Income Students." HKS Working Paper RWP14-031. Harvard Kennedy School (http://papers.ssrn.com /sol3/papers.cfm?abstract_id=2493103).

Castleman, B., and L. C. Page. 2013. "Summer Nudging: Can Personalized Text Messages and Peer Mentor Outreach Increase College-Going among Low-Income High School Graduates? EdPolicyWorks Working Paper 9 (http://curry.virginia.edu/uploads/resourceLibrary/9_Castleman _SummerTextMessages.pdf).

Cellini, S. R. 2006. "Smoothing the Transition to College? The Effect of Tech-Prep Programs on Educational Attainment." *Economics of Education Review* 25: 394–411 (http://home.gwu.edu/~scellini/Index/Research _files/EER_Tech-Prep.pdf).

Cellini, S. R., and C. Goldin. 2014. "Does Federal Student Aid Raise Tuition? New Evidence on For-Profit Colleges." *American Economic Journal: Economic Policy* 6: 174–206 (http://scholar.harvard.edu/files/goldin /files/does_federal_student.pdf?m=1383677951).

Center for Analysis of Postsecondary Education and Employment (CAP-SEE). N.D. (www.capseecenter.org).

Chaudhary, L., and S. R. Cellini. 2012. "The Labor Market Returns to a For-Profit College Education." Social Science Research Network (http:// papers.ssrn.com/sol3/papers.cfm?abstract_id=2111598).

Chen, X. 2016. *Remedial Coursetaking at U.S. Public 2- and 4-Year Institutions: Scope, Experiences, and Outcomes*. Washington, D.C.: National Center for Education Statistics.

Chetty, R., J. N. Friedman, and J. E. Rockoff. 2013. "Measuring the Impacts of Teachers I: Evaluating Bias in Teacher Value-Added Estimates." *American Economic Review* 104 (9): 2593–2632. DOI: 10.3386/w19423.

———. 2014. "Measuring the Impacts of Teachers II: Teacher Value-Added and Student Outcomes in Adulthood." *American Economic Review* 104 (9): 2633–79.

City Colleges of Chicago. 2015. *FY2015 5-Year Plan Scorecard* (https:// www.ccc.edu/news/Documents/DO_FY15_Scorecard.pdf).

Clotfelter, C., S. Hemelt, and H. Ladd. 2015. "Assessing Chapel Hill's Carolina Covenant Aid Program." Presentation at the Annual CALDER meeting, February 20. Washington, D.C.: American Institutes for Research.

Clotfelter, C. T., H. F. Ladd, C. G. Muschkin, and J. L. Vigdor. 2013. "Developmental Education in North Carolina Community Colleges." CALDER Working Paper. Washington, D.C.: American Institutes for Research.

College Measures. 2015. *Earnings and Other Outcomes of Florida's Postsecondary Graduates and Completers.* Stony Brook, N.Y.: College Measures (www.collegemeasures.org/post/2016/01/Florida-ESM-2015.aspx).

Complete College America. 2011. *Time Is the Enemy* (www.completecollege .org/docs/Time_Is_the_Enemy_Summary.pdf.

———. 2015. *Corequisite Remediation: Spanning the Completion Divide* (http://completecollege.org/spanningthedivide/#home).

Conway, M., and R. P. Giloth. 2014. *Connecting People to Work: Workforce Intermediaries and Sector Strategies.* Washington, D.C.: Aspen Institute.

Dadgar, M., and M. J. Trimble. 2015. "Labor Market Returns to Sub-Baccalaureate Credentials: How Much Does a Community College Degree or Certificate Pay?" *Educational Evaluation and Policy Analysis* 37 (4): 399–418 (http://epa.sagepub.com/content/early/2014/10/21 /0162373714553814).

Dahl, M., T. DeLeire, and J. Schwabish. 2013. *A Lost Generation? The Impact of High Unemployment Rates at College Graduation on Long-Term Earnings.* Washington, D.C.: Congressional Budget Office.

Danziger, S., and C. Rouse, eds. 2007. *The Price of Independence: The Economics of Early Adulthood.* New York: Russell Sage Foundation.

Darolia, R., C. Koedel, P. Martorell, K. Wilson, and F. Perez-Arce. 2014. "Do Employers Prefer Workers Who Attend For-Profit Colleges? Evidence from a Field Experiment." National Center for Analysis of Longitudinal Data in Education Research (www.caldercenter.org/sites/default /files/WP-%20116.pdf).

Deming, D., and S. Dynarski. 2010. "College Aid." In *Targeting Investments in Children*, ed. P. Levine and D.Zimmerman. University of Chicago Press.

Deming, D., and D. Figlio. 2016. "Accountability in U.S. Education: Applying Lessons from K–12 Experience to Higher Education." *Journal of Economic Perspectives* 30 (3): 33–56.

Deming, D. J., C. Goldin, and L. F. Katz. 2012. "The For-Profit Postsecondary School Sector: Nimble Critters or Agile Predators?" *Journal of Economic Perspectives* 26 (1): 139–64 (pubs.aeaweb.org/doi/pdfplus/10.1257/ jep.26.1.139).

———. 2013. "For-Profit Colleges." *The Future of Children* 23 (1): 137–63.

Deming, D. J., N. Yuchtman, A. Abulafi, C. Goldin, and L. F. Katz. 2015. "The Value of Postsecondary Credentials in the Labor Market: An Experimental Study." *American Economic Review* 106 (3): 778–806 (http://scholar.harvard.edu/files/ddeming/files/dyagk_audit_final_aer.pdf?m=1453407140).

Dougherty, K., S. Jones, H. Lahr, R. Natow, R. Pheatt, and V. Reddy. 2016. "Looking inside the Black Box of Performance Funding for Higher Education: Policy Instruments, Organizational Obstacles, and Intended and Unintended Impacts." *Journal of the Social Sciences* 2 (1): 147–73.

Douglas-Gabriel, D. 2016. "At Purdue, Student Aid Based on Future Earnings Could Revolutionize College Debt." *Washington Post*, April 11.

Dube, A. 2014. "Designing Thoughtful Minimum Wage Policy at the State and Local Levels: Improving Safety Net and Work Support." The Hamilton Project, Brookings Institution (www.hamiltonproject.org/assets/legacy/files/downloads_and_links/state_local_minimum_wage_policy_dube.pdf).

Duckworth, A. 2016. *Grit: The Power and Passion of Perseverance.* New York: Scribner.

Duke-Benfield, A. E. 2015. "Bolstering Non-traditional Student Success: A Comprehensive Student Aid System Using Financial Aid, Public Benefits, and Refundable Tax Credits." Center for Postsecondary and Economic Success (www.clasp.org/resources-and-publications/publication-1/Bolstering-NonTraditional-Student-Success.pdf).

Dynarski, S. M. 2003. "Does Aid Matter? Measuring the Effect of Student Aid on College Attendance and Completion." *American Economic Review* 93 (1): 279–88 (www.nber.org/papers/w7422.pdf).

———. 2008. "Building the Stock of College-Educated Labor." *Journal of Human Resources* 43 (3): 576–610 (www.nber.org/papers/w11604).

EAB Student Success Collaborative. 2016. *How Late Is Too Late? Myths and Facts about the Consequences of Switching College Majors* (https://www.eab.com/technology/student-success-collaborative/members/white-papers/major-switching).

Ehrenberg, R. G. 2014. "What's the Future of Public Higher Education? A Review Essay on Gary C. Fethke and Andrew J. Policano's *Public No More: A New Path to Excellence for America's Public Universities.*" *Journal of Economic Literature* 52 (4): 1142–50. DOI: 10.1257/jel.52.4.1142.

Farber, H. S. 2005. "Union Membership in the United States: The Divergence between the Public and Private Sectors." Princeton University Industrial Relations Section (https://core.ac.uk/download/files/153/6894934.pdf).

Federal Student Aid. 2015. "Official National Default Rates." U.S. Department of Education (www.ifap.ed.gov/eannouncements/attachments/0930 15AttachOfficialFY20123YRCDRBriefing.pdf).

Fein, D. 2012. "Career Pathways as a Framework for Program Design and Evaluation: A Working Paper from the Pathways for Advancing Careers and Education (PACE) Project." Office of Policy Research and Evaluation, Administration for Children and Families, U.S. Department of Health and Human Services.

Fethke, G. C., and A. J. Policano. 2012. *Public No More: A New Path to Excellence for America's Public Universities*. Redwood City, Calif.: Stanford Business Books.

Freeman, R. B. 1971. *The Market for College-Trained Manpower*. Harvard University Press.

Fryer, R. G., Jr., and L. F. Katz. 2013. "Achieving Escape Velocity: Neighborhood and School Interventions to Reduce Persistent Inequality." In *American Economic Review: Papers and Proceedings* (http://scholar.harvard .edu/files/lkatz/files/aer.103.3_fryer_katz_pp_2013_all_0.pdf).

Furchtgott-Roth, D., L. Jacobson, and C. Mokher. 2009. *Strengthening Community College Influence on Economic Mobility*. Philadelphia: Pew Charitable Trusts (www.frbsf.org/economic-research/files/Jacobson .pdf).

Geckeler, Christian. 2008. "Helping Community College Students Cope with Financial Emergencies: Lessons from the Dreamkeepers and Angel Fund Emergency Financial Aid Programs." New York: MDRC (www.mdrc.org /publication/helping-community-college-students-cope-financial -emergencies).

Geel, R., and U. Backes-Gellner. 2011. "Occupational Mobility within and between Skill Cluster: An Empirical Analysis Based on the Skill-Weights Approach." *Empirical Research in Vocational Education and Training* 3 (1): 21–38 (http://papers.ssrn.com/sol3/papers.cfm?abstract _id=1808230).

Glaeser, E. 2013. "A Review of Enrico Moretti's *The New Geography of Jobs*." *Journal of Economic Literature* 51 (3): 825–37.

Goldhaber, D., and J. Cowan. 2014. "How Much of a 'Running Start' Do Dual Enrollment Programs Provide Students?" Center for Education Data and Research (www.cedr.us/papers/working/CEDR%20WP%202014-7 .pdf).

Goldin, C. D., and L. F. Katz. 2008. *The Race between Education and Technology*. Cambridge, Mass.: Belknap Press.

Goldrick-Rab, S. 2010. "Challenges and Opportunities for Improving Community College Student Success." *Review of Educational Research* 80 (3): 437–69 (www.jstor.org/stable/40927288?seq=1#page_scan_tab_contents).

Goldrick-Rab, S., K. Broton, and D. Eisenberg. 2015. *Hungry to Learn: Addressing Food and Housing Insecurity among Undergraduates*. Madison: Wisconsin HOPE Lab (http://wihopelab.com/publications/Wisconsin_hope_lab_hungry_to_learn.pdf).

Goodman, S. 2012. *Learning from the Test: Raising Selective College Enrollment by Providing Information*. Columbia University Press (www.columbia.edu/~sfg2111/sgoodman_jobmarketpaper.pdf).

———. 2013. "Raising Selective College Enrollment by Providing Information." Finance and Economics Discussion Series Division of Research & Statistics and Monetary Affairs. Washington, D.C.: Federal Reserve Board (www.federalreserve.gov/pubs/feds/2013/201369/201369pap.pdf).

Gordon, R. J. 2014. "The Demise of U.S. Economic Growth: Restatement, Rebuttal and Reflections." Working Paper. Cambridge, Mass.: National Bureau of Economic Research (www.nber.org/papers/w19895.pdf).

Gross, J., O. Cekic, D. Hossler, and N. Hillman. 2010. "What Matters in Student Loan Default: A Review of the Research Literature." *Journal of Student Financial Aid* 39 (1): 19–29 (http://publications.nasfaa.org/cgi/viewcontent.cgi?article=1032&context=jsfa).

Hamilton, J. 2011. "Obama Administration Announces New Step to Protect Students from Ineffective Career College Programs." U.S. Department of Education (www.ed.gov/news/press-releases/obama-administration-announces-new-steps-protect-students-ineffective-career-college-programs).

Hanks, A. 2015. "Making Pell Work: How America's $30 Billion Investment in Need-Based College Aid Can Be More Job-Driven." National Skills Coalition (www.nationalskillscoalition.org/resources/publications/file/2015-07-Making-Pell-Work-How-Americas-30-Billion-Investment-in-Need-Based-College-Aid-Can-Be-More-Job-Driven.pdf).

Hansen, W. L. 1983. "The Impact of Student Financial Aid on Access." In *Proceedings of the Academy of Political Science: The Crisis in Higher Education* 35 (2): 84–96 (www.jstor.org/stable/3700892?seq=1#page_scan_tab_contents).

Hansen, W. L., and B. A. Weisbrod. 1969. "The Distribution of Costs and Direct Benefits of Public Higher Education: The Case of California."

Journal of Human Resources 4 (2): 176–91 (www.jstor.org/stable/144718 ?seq=1#page_scan_tab_contents).

Hanushek, E., and S. Rivkin. 2009. "Harming the Best: How Schools Affect the Black-White Achievement Gap." *Journal of Policy Analysis and Management* 28 (3): 366–93.

Harris, B. 2013. "Five Reasons College Has Become Unaffordable for the Masses." *Student Caring* (http://studentcaring.com/5-reasons-college -become-unaffordable-masses/).

Haynes, Michael. 2008. "The Impact of Financial Aid on Postsecondary Persistence: A Review of the Literature." *Journal of Student Financial Aid* 37 (3): 30–35.

HCM Strategists. 2012. "Context for Success" (www.hcmstrategists.com /contextforsuccess/).

Heckman, J. J. 2008. "Schools, Skills, and Synapses." *Economic Inquiry* 46 (3): 289–324. DOI: 10.1111/j.1465-7295.2008.00163.x.

Heckman, J. J., and T. Kautz. 2013. "Fostering and Measuring Skills: Interventions That Improve Character and Cognition." Working Paper. Cambridge, Mass.: National Bureau of Economic Research (www.nber.org /papers/w19656).

Heller, D. 1997. "Student Price Response in Higher Education: An Update to Leslie and Brinkman." *Journal of Higher Education* 68 (6): 624–59. DOI: 10.2307/2959966.

———. 2001. *The Effects of Tuition Prices and Financial Aid on Enrollment in Higher Education: California and the Nation.* Ed Fund (http:// docplayer.net/1011343-The-effects-of-tuition-prices-and-financial-aid -on-enrollment-in-higher-education.html).

Henderson, W. D., and R. M. Zahorsky. 2011. "Paradigm Shift." *ABA Journal* 40 (97) (http://heinonline.org/HOL/LandingPage?handle=hein.journals /abaj97&div=101&id=&page=).

Hendra, R., and others. 2016. "Encouraging Evidence on a Sector-Focus Advancement Strategy." New York: MDRC.

Hershbein, B. 2016. "A College Degree Is Worth Less if You Are Raised Poor" (blog). Brookings Institution, February 19.

Hillman, N. W., D. A. Tandberg, and A. H. Fryar. 2014. "Evaluating the Impacts of 'New' Performance Funding in Higher Education." *Educational Evaluation and Policy Analysis* 20 (10): 1–19 (https://news.education.wisc .edu/docs/WebDispenser/news-connections-pdf/performance-funding -eepa-study.pdf?sfvrsn=4).

Hinrichs, P. 2010. "The Effects of Affirmative Action Bans on College Enrollment, Educational Attainment, and the Demographic Composition of

Universities." *MIT Press Journal* 94 (3): 712–22 (www.mitpressjournals
.org/doi/pdf/10.1162/REST_a_00170).

Hirsch, B. 2008. "Sluggish Institutions in a Dynamic World: Can Unions
and Industrial Competition Coexist?" *Journal of Economic Perspectives* 22 (1): 153–76 (http://pubs.aeaweb.org/doi/pdfplus/10.1257/jep
.22.1.153).

Hoffman, N. 2011. *Schooling in the Workplace: How Six of the World's Best
Vocational Education Systems Prepare Young People for Job and Life.*
Cambridge, Mass.: Harvard Education Press.

Hoffman, N., J. Vargas, and J. Santos. 2009. "New Directions for Dual Enrollment: Creating Stronger Pathways from High School through College." *New
Directions for Community Colleges* (Spring): 43–58 (http://onlinelibrary
.wiley.com/advanced/search/results).

Holzer, H. J. 2010. "Is the Middle of the U.S. Job Market Really Disappearing? A Comment on the 'Polarization' Hypothesis." Washington,
D.C.: Center for American Progress (https://cdn.americanprogress.org
/wp-content/uploads/issues/2010/05/pdf/Holzer_memo.pdf).

———. 2015a. "Creating Skilled Workers and Higher-Wage Jobs." Brookings
Institution (www.brookings.edu/research/opinions/2015/04/10-skilled
-workers-higher-wage-jobs-holzer).

———. 2015b. "Job Market Polarization and U.S. Worker Skills: A Tale of
Two Middles." Brookings Institution (www.brookings.edu/research/papers/2015/04/job-market-polarization-worker-skills-holzer).

———. 2015c. "Should There Be a No Child Left Behind for U.S. Universities?"
Brookings Institution (www.brookings.edu/research/opinions/2015/04/13
-worker-training-universities-holzer).

Holzer, H. J., and E. Dunlop. 2013. "Just the Facts, Ma'am: Postsecondary
Education and Labor Market Outcomes in the U.S." IZA Discussion Paper
7319. Bonn: Institute for the Study of Labor (http://ssrn.com/abstract
=2250297).

Holzer, H., and R. Lerman. 2009. *The Future of Middle Skill Jobs.* Brookings Institution.

Holzer, H. J., and R. I. Lerman. 2014. *Work-Based Learning to Expand Jobs
and Occupational Qualifications for Youth.* Washington, D.C.: Center on
Budget and Policy Priorities (www.pathtofullemployment.org/wp-content
/uploads/2014/04/holzerlerman.pdf).

Holzer, H. J., D. Linn, and W. Monthey. 2013. *The Promise of High-Quality
Career and Technical Education: Improving Outcomes for Students,
Firms and the Economy.* College Board (http://www.sdlcillinois.org
/constitution/georgetown.pdf).

Hoxby, C., and C. Avery. 2013. "The Missing 'One-Offs': The Hidden Supply of High-Achieving, Low-Income Students." *Brookings Papers on Economic Activity* 46 (1): 1–65 (www.brookings.edu/~/media/projects /bpea/spring-2013/2013a_hoxby.pdf).

Hoxby, C., and S. Turner. 2013. "Expanding College Opportunities for High-Achieving, Low Income Students." SIEPR Discussion Paper 12-014. Stanford Institute for Economic Policy Research (www8.gsb.columbia .edu/programs/sites/programs/files/finance/Applied%20Microeconomics /Caroline%20Hoxby.pdf).

Hurwitz, M., and J. Smith. 2016. "Student Responsiveness to Earnings Data in the College Scorecard" (http://ssrn.com/abstract=2768157).

Hurwitz, M., J. Smith, S. Niu, and J. Howell. 2015. "The Maine Question: How Is 4-Year College Enrollment Affected by Mandatory College Entrance Exams?" *Educational Evaluation and Policy Analysis* 37 (1): 138–59.

Illinois State University. 2016. *Grapevine*. College of Education (https:// education.illinoisstate.edu/grapevine/).

Institute for College Access and Success. 2014. "At What Cost? How Community Colleges That Do Not Offer Federal Loans Put Students at Risk" (http://ticas.org/sites/default/files/pub_files/At_What_Cost.pdf).

Jacobson, L., and C. Mokher. 2009. *Pathways to Boosting the Earnings of Low-Income Students by Increasing Their Educational Attainments.* Washington, D.C.: Hudson Institute (http://files.eric.ed.gov/fulltext /ED504078.pdf).

Jaggars, S.S, and G. W. Stacey. 2014. "What We Know about Developmental Education Outcomes." Community College Research Center. Teachers College, Columbia University.

Jaimovich, N., and H. E. Siu. 2012. "The Trend Is the Cycle: Job Polarization and Jobless Recoveries." Working Paper 18334. Cambridge, Mass.: National Bureau of Economic Research (www.nber.org/papers/w18334.pdf).

Jenkins, D., and S. W. Cho. 2012. "Get with the Program: Accelerating Community College Students' Entry into and Completion of Programs of Study." Community College Research Center. Teachers College, Columbia University (http://ccrc.tc.columbia.edu/media/k2/attachments/accelerating -student-entry-completion.pdf).

Jenkins, D., and J. Fink. 2016. "Tracking Transfer: New Measures of Institutional and State Effectiveness in Helping Community College Students Attain Bachelor's Degrees." Aspen Institute and Community College Research Center, Columbia University.

Jepsen, C., K. Troske, and P. Coomes. 2014. "The Labor-Market Returns to Community College Degrees, Diplomas, and Certificates." *Journal of Labor Economics* 32 (1): 95–121. DOI: 10.1086/671809.

Jobs for the Future. 2014. "Pathways to Prosperity Network State Progress Report 2012–2014" (www.jff.org/publications/pathways-prosperity-network-state-progress-report-2012-2014).

Kahn, L. B. 2010. "The Long-Term Labor Market Consequences of Graduating from College in a Bad Economy." *Labor Economics* 17 (2): 303–16. DOI: 10.1016/j.labeco.2009.09.002.

Kane, T. J. 1995. "Rising Public College Tuition and College Entry: How Well Do Public Subsidies Promote Access to College?" Working Paper 5164. Cambridge, Mass.: National Bureau of Economic Research.

———. 1998. "Racial and Ethnic Preferences in College Admissions." *Ohio State Law Journal* 59 (3): 971–96 (https://kb.osu.edu/dspace/bitstream/handle/1811/64967/OSLJ_V59N3_0971.pdf).

———. 2007. "Evaluating the Impact of the D.C. Tuition Assistance Grant Program." *Journal of Human Resources* 42 (3): 555–82.

Kane, T. J., and C. E. Rouse. 1995. "Labor-Market Returns to Two- and Four-Year College." *American Economic Review* 85 (3): 600–14.

Kazis, R. 2016. "Case Study: Big Change on Campus." *Stanford Social Innovation Review* (Spring) (https://ssir.org/articles/entry/big_change_on_campus).

Kemple, J. J., C. M. Herlihy, and T. J. Smith. 2005. "Making Progress toward Graduation." New York: MDRC (www.mdrc.org/sites/default/files/full_432.pdf).

Kim, J., and K. Stange. 2016. "Pricing and University Autonomy: Tuition Deregulation in Texas." *Journal of the Social Sciences* 2 (1): 112–46.

Kingkade, T. 2014. "One Chart That Makes It Clear College Tuition Is Becoming Unaffordable." *Huffington Post* (www.huffingtonpost.com/2014/06/18/college-tuition-unaffordable-growth-median-income_n_5505653.html).

Kleiner, M. 2015. *Reforming Occupational Licensing Policies*. The Hamilton Project, Brookings Institution.

Klempin, S. 2014. *Redefining Full-Time in College: Evidence on 15-Credit Strategies*. Community College Research Center. Teachers College, Columbia University.

Krueger, A. B., E. A. Hanushek, and J. K. Rice. 2012. *The Class Size Debate*. Washington, D.C.: Economic Policy Institute (www.epi.org/publication/books_classsizedebate/).

Kurzweil, M., and D. Rossman. 2016. "Broad-Based and Targeted: Florida State University's Efforts to Retain Every Student" (www.sr.ithaka.org /publications/broad-based-and-targeted/?cid=eml_sr_casestudyApril).

Lavecchia, A. M., H. Liu, and P. Oreopoulos. 2014. "Behavioral Economics of Education: Progress and Possibilities." Cambridge, Mass.: National Bureau of Economic Research. DOI: 10.3386/w20609.

Leigh, D. E., and A. M. Gill. 2003. "Do Community Colleges Really Divert Students from Earning Bachelor's Degrees?" *Economics of Education Review* 22 (1): 23–30. DOI:10.1016/S0272-7757(01)00057-7.

Leonhardt, D. 2015. "College Access Index, 2015: The Details." *New York Times*, September 17 (www.nytimes.com/2015/09/17/upshot/college -access-index-2015-the-details.html?_r=0).

Lerman, R. 2010. "Apprenticeship in the United States: Patterns of Governance and Recent Developments." In *Rediscovering Apprenticeship: Research Findings of the International Network on Innovative Apprenticeship* (INAP), ed. E. Smith and F. Rauner. Berlin: Springer-Verlag.

Levy, F., and R. Murnane. 2013. *Dancing with Robots: Human Skills for Computerized Work*. Washington D.C.: The Third Way.

Lewin, T. 2008. "College May Become Unaffordable for Most in the U.S." *New York Times*, December 3 (www.nytimes.com/2008/12/03/education /03college.html?_r=0).

Light, A., and W. Strayer. 2000. "Determinants of College Completion: School Quality or Student Ability?" *Journal of Human Resources* 35 (2): 299–332 (www.jstor.org/stable/146327?seq=1#page_scan_tab_contents).

Long, B. T. 2014. "Addressing the Academic Barriers to Higher Education." The Hamilton Project, Brookings Institution (www.brookings.edu/~ /media/research/files/papers/2014/06/19_hamilton_policies_addressing _poverty/higher_education_remediation_long.pdf).

Looney, A., and C. Yannelis. 2015. "A Crisis in Student Loans? How Changes in the Characteristics of Borrowers and in the Institutions They Attended Contributed to Rising Loan Defaults." *Brookings Papers on Economic Activity* (Fall) (www.brookings.edu/~/media/projects/bpea/fall -2015_embargoed/conferencedraft_looneyyannelis_studentloandefaults .pdf).

Lovenheim, M. 2011. "The Effect of Liquid Housing Wealth on College Enrollment." *Journal of Labor Economics* 29 (4): 741–71.

Ma, J., S. Baum, M. Pender, and D. Bell. 2015. *Trends in College Pricing 2015*. New York: College Board.

Ma, J., S. Baum, M. Pender, and M. Welch. 2016. *Trends in College Pricing 2016*. New York: College Board.

Madrian, B., and D. Shea. 2001. "The Power of Suggestion: Inertia in 401(K) Participation and Savings Behavior." *Quarterly Journal of Economics* 16 (4): 1149–87 (www.retirementmadesimpler.org/Library/The%20Power %20of%20Suggestion-%20Inertia%20in%20401(k).pdf).

Magnuson, K., and J. Waldfogel. 2008. *Steady Gains and Stalled Progress: Inequality and the Black-White Test Score Gap.* New York: Russell Sage Foundation. DOI: 10.3386/w12988.

Maguire, S., J. Freely, C. Clymer, M. Conway, and D. Schwartz. 2010. *Tuning into Local Labor Markets.* Philadelphia: PPV (www2.oaklandnet .com/oakca/groups/ceda/documents/report/dowd021455.pdf).

Manufacturing Institute. 2015. *The Skills Gap in U.S. Manufacturing: 2015 and Beyond.* Manufacturing Institute and Deloitte (www.themanu facturinginstitute.org/~/media/827DBC76533942679A15EF7067A70 4CD.ashx).

Martin, V., and J. Broadus. 2013. "Enhancing GED Instruction to Prepare Students for College and Careers: Early Success in LaGuardia Community College's Bridge to Health and Business Program." Social Science Research Network (http://papers.ssrn.com/sol3/papers.cfm?abstract_id=2265891).

Matus-Grossman, L., and S. Gooden. 2002. "Opening Doors: Students' Perspectives on Juggling Work, Family, and College." New York: MDRC (www.mdrc.org/sites/default/files/full_466.pdf).

Mayer, A., R. Patel, T. Rudd, and A. Ratledge. 2015. "Designing Scholarships to Improve College Success: Final Report on the Performance-Based Scholarship Demonstration." New York: MDRC (www.mdrc.org /publication/designing-scholarships-improve-college-success).

McCarthy, M. A. 2014. "Beyond the Skills Gap: Making Education Work for Students, Employers, and Communities." Washington, D.C.: New America and Education Policy (www.luminafoundation.org/files/resources /beyond-the-skills-gap.pdf).

———. 2015. "Flipping the Paradigm." Washington, D.C.: New America (https://static.newamerica.org/attachments/11652-flipping-the-paradigm /Flipping-the-Paradigm.8ac8a0a5405d4f52a3a6657b62d0b3db.pdf).

McConnell, S., I. Perez-Johnson, and J. Berk. 2014. "Providing Disadvantaged Workers with Skills to Succeed in the Labor Market." The Hamilton Project, Brookings Institution (www.brookings.edu/~/media/research /files/papers/2014/06/19_hamilton_policies_addressing_poverty /disadvantaged_workers_skills_mcconnell_perez_johnson_berk.pdf).

McIntyre, F., and M. Simkovic. 2016. "Timing Law School." Research Paper 2015-4. HLS Center on the Legal Profession (http://papers.ssrn.com/sol3 /Papers.cfm?abstract_id=2574587).

McPherson, M., and L. Bacow. 2015. "On-Line Education: Beyond the Hype Cycle." *Journal of Economic Perspectives* 29 (4): 135–54. DOI: 10.1257/jep.29.4.135.

Michaelides, M., P. Mueser, and K. Mbwana. 2014. "Quasi-Experimental Impact Study of NFWS/SIF Workforce Partnership Programs: Evidence on the Effectiveness of Three Workforce Partnership Programs in Ohio." Boston, Mass.: IMPAQ International, LLC (www.impaqint.com/sites /default/files/files/NFWS%20Quasi-Experimental%20Impact%20 Study%20-%20March%202014%20-%20Release%20Copy-1.pdf).

Middaugh, M., R. Graham, and A. Shahid. 2003. *A Study of Higher Education Instructional Expenditures: The Delaware Study of Instructional Costs and Productivity.* NCES 2003-161. Washington, D.C.: U.S. Department of Education, Institute of Education Sciences (http://nces.ed.gov /pubs2003/2003161.pdf).

Miller, T., and R. Hanna. 2014. "Four Years Later, Are Race to the Top States On Track?" Washington, D.C.: Center for American Progress.

Miller-Adams, M. 2015. *Promise Nation: Transforming Communities through Place-Based Scholarships.* Kalamazoo, Mich.: W. E. Upjohn Institute for Employment Research (www.upjohn.org/sites/default/files/WEfocus /promise-nation.pdf).

Mincer, J. A. 1974. "Age and Experience Profiles of Earnings." In *Schooling, Experience and Earnings.* Cambridge, Mass.: National Bureau of Economic Research (www.nber.org/chapters/c1766.pdf).

Mishel, L., and J. Roy. 2006. "Accurately Assessing High School Graduation Rates." Bloomington, Ind.: Phi Delta Kappa. DOI: 10.1177 /003172170608800408.

Moretti, E. 2012. *The New Geography of Jobs.* Boston: Houghton Mifflin Harcourt.

Mosteller, F. 1995. "The Tennessee Study of Class Size in the Early School Grade." *The Future of Children* 5 (2) (www.princeton.edu/futureofchildren /publications/docs/05_02_08.pdf).

Mullainathan, S., and E. Shafir. 2013. *Scarcity: Why Having Too Little Means So Much.* New York: Times Books. DOI: 10.1080/10911359 .2014.1003732.

Mundel, D. 2008. "What Do We Know about the Impact of Grants to College Students?" In *The Effectiveness of Student Aid: What the Research Tells Us,* ed. S. Baum, M. McPherson, and P. Steele. New York: College Board (www.postsecondaryresearch.org/i/a/document/6963 _LongFinAid.pdf).

Murnane, R. J. 2013. "U.S. High School Graduation Rates: Patterns and Explanations." *Journal of Economic Literature*. DOI: 10.3386/w18701.

Murray, C. 2013. "For Most Students, College Is a Waste of Time." *Wall Street Journal* (www.wsj.com/articles/SB121858688764535107).

National Association of Student Financial Aid Administrators. 2013. *Reimagining Financial Aid to Improve Student Access and Outcomes*. Washington, D.C.: NASFAA.

National Center for Education Statistics (NCES). 2002. *Data Lab for Education Longitudinal Study*. U.S. Department of Education (https://nces.ed .gov/datalab/els/index.aspx).

———. 2009. *Data Lab for Beginning Postsecondary Longitudinal Study (BPS)*. Institute of Education Sciences, U.S. Department of Education (https://nces.ed.gov/surveys/bps/).

———. 2012. *Data Lab for National Postsecondary Student Aid Study*. U.S. Department of Education (http://nces.ed.gov/datalab/).

———. 2015a. *The Condition of Education 2015 (NCES 2015-144)*. Institute of Education Sciences, Department of Education (https://nces.ed.gov /fastfacts/display.asp?id=75).

———. 2015b. *Digest of Education Statistics 2014*. U.S. Department of Education (https://nces.ed.gov/programs/digest/2014menu_tables.asp).

———. 2016. *Digest of Education Statistics 2015*. U.S. Department of Education (https://nces.ed.gov/programs/digest/2015menu_tables.asp).

National Conference of State Legislatures. 2015. *Performance-Based Funding for Higher Education* (http://www.ncsl.org/research/education /performance-funding.aspx).

National Governors Association. 2013. *State Sector Strategies Coming of Age: Implications for State Workforce Policymakers* (www.nga.org/files /live/sites/NGA/files/pdf/2013/1301NGASSSReport.pdf).

National Research Council. 2012. *Education for Life and Work: Developing Transferable Knowledge and Skills in the 21st Century*. Washington, D.C.: National Academies Press. DOI: 10.17226/13398.

National Student Clearinghouse. 2014. *Current Term Enrollment Estimates Spring 2014*. Pearson Foundation (http://nscresearchcenter.org/wp -content/uploads/CurrentTermEnrollment-Spring2014.pdf).

Nelson, B., M. Froehner, and B. Gault. 2013. *College Students with Children Are Common and Face Many Challenges in Completing Higher Education*. Washington, D.C.: Institute for Women's Policy Research (www.iwpr.org /initiatives/student-parent-success-initiative/resourcespublications/#lates %20publications).

Neumark, D., ed. 2007. *Improving School-to-Work Transitions*. New York: Russell Sage Foundation.

Neumark, D., J. M. Ian Salas, and W. Wascher. 2014. "More on Recent Evidence on the Effects of Minimum Wages in the United States." *IZA Journal of Labor Policy* 3 (1) (www.nber.org/papers/w20619.pdf).

Newman, K., and H. Winston. 2016. *Reskilling America: Learning to Labor in the 21st Century*. New York: Macmillan.

Oreopoulos, P., and U. Petronijevic. 2013. "Making College Worth It: A Review of the Returns to Higher Education." *The Future of Children* 23 (1): 41–65.

Ottaviano, G. I. P., and G. Peri. 2006. "Rethinking the Effects of Immigration on Wages." IPC IN FOCUS 5,8. American Immigration Law Foundation's Immigration Policy Center (http://wp.econ.ucdavis.edu/06-34.pdf).

Owen, S., and I. V. Sawhill. 2013. "Should Everyone Go to College?" Center on Children and Families, Brookings Institution (www.brookings.edu/%7E/media/research/files/papers/2013/05/07-should-everyone-go-to-college-owen-sawhill/08-should-everyone-go-to-college-owen-sawhill.pdf).

Page, L. C., B. Castleman, and G. Sahadewo. 2016. "More Than Dollars for Scholars: The Impact of the Dell Scholars Program on College Access, Persistence, and Degree Attainment." Social Science Research Network (http://papers.ssrn.com/sol3/papers.cfm?abstract_id=2726320).

Page, L., and J. Scott-Clayton. 2016. "Improving College Access in the United States: Barriers and Policy Responses." *Economics of Education Review* 51: 4–22.

Patel, R., L. Richburg-Hayes, E. de la Campa, and R. Rudd. 2013. "Performance-Based Scholarships: What Have We Learned?" New York: MDRC.

Patel, R., and T. Rudd. 2012. "Can Scholarships Alone Help Students Succeed? Lessons from Two New York City Community Colleges." New York: MDRC (www.mdrc.org/sites/default/files/Can%20Scholarships%20Alone%20Help%20Students%20Succeed%20Full%20Report_1_0.pdf).

Paulsen, M. B., and E. P. St. John. 2002. "Social Class and College Costs: Examining the Financial Nexus between College Choice and Persistence." *Journal of Higher Education* 73 (2): 189–236 (www.jstor.org/stable/1558410?seq=1#page_scan_tab_contents).

Perez, C. 2012. "California Proposition 209: Minority Enrollments Down in UC Schools Despite Diversity Efforts." *Huffington Post* (www.huffingtonpost.com/2012/02/24/proposition-209_n_1300122.html).

Person, A. 2015. "Best Practices in Competency-Based Education: Lessons from Three Colleges." Mathematica Policy Research (www.mathetica -mpr.com/our-publications-and-findings/publications/best-practices-in -competencybased-education-lessons-from-three-colleges).

Pope, J. 2012. "For-Profit College Enrollment Falling as Companies Close Locations." *Huffington Post*, October 19 (www.huffingtonpost.com/2012 /10/19/for-profit-college- enrollment_n_1988186.html).

PTech. "PTech 9–14 School Model Playbook" (www.ptech.org).

Putnam, R. 2000. *Bowling Alone.* New York: Simon and Schuster. DOI: 10.1353/jod.1995.0002/

Putnam, R., L. Feldstein, and D. Cohen. 2003. *Better Together: Restoring the American Community?* New York: Simon and Schuster.

Radwin, D., J. Wine, P. Siegel, and M. Bryan. 2013. "2011–12 National Postsecondary Student Aid Study Student Financial Aid Estimates for 2011–12." In *First Look.* National Center for Education Statistics, U.S. Department of Education.

Reamer, A. 2015. *Information Resources to Facilitate Middle Skills Workforce Development.* George Washington University Press (https://scholars pace.library.gwu.edu/downloads/tq57nr00k).

Reardon, S. 2011. "The Widening Academic Achievement Gap between the Rich and the Poor: New Evidence and Possible Explanations." New York: Russell Sage Foundation (https://cepa.stanford.edu/sites/default /files/reardon%20whither%20opportunity%20-%20chapter%205.pdf).

Reardon, S., and X. Portilla. 2016. "Recent Trends in Income, Racial and Ethnic School Readiness Gaps at Kindergarten Entry." *AERA Open* 2 (3): 1–18.

Reed, D., A. Y. Liu, R. Kleinman, A. Mastri, D. Reed, S. Sattar, and J. Ziegler. 2012. *An Effectiveness Assessment and Cost-Benefit Analysis of Registered Apprenticeship in 10 States.* Oakland, Calif.: Mathematica Policy Research.

Reich, R. B. 2015. "Affirmative Action in College Admissions for the Rich" (blog) (http://robertreich.org/post/114356426465).

Resmovits, J. 2012. "Career Education Plan from Obama Administration Unlikely to Bear Fruit for a Year or More." *Huffington Post*, April 30 (www.huffingtonpost.com/2012/04/20/obama-career-education -technical-vocational_n_1440700.html).

Resnick, L. B. 1987. "The 1987 Presidential Address: Learning in School and Out." *Educational Research* 16 (9): 13–20 and 54 (http://people.ucsc .edu/~gwells/Files/Courses_Folder/ED%20261%20Papers/Resnick%20 In%20%26%20Out%20School.pdf).

Rethinking Pell Grants Study Group. 2013. *Rethinking Pell Grants.* College Board Advocacy & Policy Center (http://media.collegeboard.com/digital Services/pdf/advocacy/policycenter/advocacy-rethinking-pell-grants -report.pdf).

Roder, A., and M. Elliott. 2012. "Sustained Gains: Year Up's Continued Impact on Young Adults' Earnings." Economic Mobility Corporation (http://economicmobilitycorp.org/uploads/sustained-gains-economic -mobility-corp.pdf).

Roderick, M., J. Nagaoka, V. Coca, and E. Moeller. 2008. "From High School to the Future: Potholes on the Road to College." Research Report. Chicago: Consortium on Chicago School Research (http://files.eric.ed .gov/fulltext/ED500519.pdf).

Romano, R. M., R. Losinger, and T. Millard. 2010. "Measuring the Cost of a College Degree: A Case Study of a SUNY Community College." Cornell University ILR School (http://digitalcommons.ilr.cornell.edu/cgi/viewcon tent.cgi?article=1144&context=workingpapers).

Rosenbaum, J. E. 2002. "Beyond Empty Promises: Policies to Improve Transitions into College and Jobs." Education Resources Information Center ED465094 (http://files.eric.ed.gov/fulltext/ED465094.pdf).

———. 2011. "The Complexities of College-for-All: Beyond Fairy-Tale Dreams." *Sociology of Education* 84 (2): 113–17 (www.asanet.org /images/journals/docs/pdf/soe/Apr11SOEFeature.pdf).

Rosenbaum, J. E., R. Deil-Amen, and A. Person. 2006. *After Admission: From College Access to College Success.* New York: Russell Sage Foundation.

Ross, M. 2015. "A Win-Win: Home Health Aide Training Program Creates Better Care for Patients, Better Jobs for Workers" (blog). Brookings Institution, November 10 (www.brookings.edu/blogs/health360/posts/2015 /11/10-home-health-aide-training-program-ross).

Rothwell, J. 2015. "Using Earnings Data to Rank Colleges: A Value-Added Approach Updated with Scorecard Data." Brookings Institution (www .brookings.edu/research/reports2/2015/10/29-earnings-data-college-sco recard-rothwell).

Rouse, C. E. 2007. "The Labor Market Consequences of an Inadequate Education." In *The Price We Pay: The Economic and Political Consequences of Inadequate Education,* ed. C. Belfield and H. M. Levin. Brookings Institution Press.

Rueben, K., S. Gault, and S. Baum. 2015. "Simplifying Federal Student Aid: An Overview of Eight Plans." Washington, D.C.: Urban Institute (www .urban.org/sites/default/files/alfresco/publication-pdfs/2000506 -Simplifying-Federal-Student-Aid-An-Overview-of-Eight-Plans.pdf).

Ryan, P. 2001. "The School-to-Work Transition: A Cross-National Perspective." *Journal of Economic Literature* 39 (1): 34–92 (www.econ.cam.ac .uk/dae/repec/cam/pdf/Wp0014.pdf).

Sanders, R., and S. Taylor Jr. 2012. *Mismatch: How Affirmative Action Hurts Students It's Intended to Help, and Why Universities Won't Admit It*. New York: Basic Books (www.mismatchthebook.com).

Schneider, H. 2013. "Recasting High School, German Firms Transplant Apprentice Model to U.S." *Washington Post,* November 27 (www.washing tonpost.com/business/economy/recasting-high-school-german-firms -transplant-apprentice-model-to-us/2013/11/27/6b242be8-4e42-11e3 -ac54-aa84301ced81_story.html).

Schultz, T. W. 1961. "Investment in Human Capital." *American Economic Review* 51 (1): 1–17 (www.ssc.wisc.edu/~walker/wp/wp-content/uploads /2012/04/schultz61.pdf).

Schumacher, R. 2013. "Prepping Colleges for Parents: Strategies for Supporting Student Parent Success in Postsecondary Education." Washington, D.C.: Institute for Women's Policy Research (www.iwpr.org/publications /pubs/prepping-colleges-for-parents-strategies-for-supporting-student -parent-success-in-postsecondary-education).

Scott-Clayton, J. 2011a. "On Money and Motivation: A Quasi-Experimental Analysis of Financial Incentives for College Achievement." *Journal of Human Resources* 46 (3): 614–46.

———. 2011b. "The Shapeless River: Does a Lack of Structure Inhibit Students' Progress at Community Colleges?" Community College Research Center Working Paper 25. Teachers College, Columbia University (http:// academiccommons.columbia.edu/catalog/ac:146662).

———. 2015. "The Role of Financial Aid in Promoting College Access and Success: Research Evidence and Proposals for Reform." *The Higher Education Act at 50*. Special Issue, *Journal of Student Financial Aid* 45 (3) (http:// publications.nasfaa.org/cgi/viewcontent.cgi?article=1586&context=jsfa).

Scott-Clayton, J., P. Crosta, and C. Belfield. 2014. "Improving the Targeting of Treatment: Evidence from College Remediation." Working Paper. Cambridge, Mass.: National Bureau of Economic Research (www.nber .org/papers/w18457.pdf).

Scrivener, S., and E. Coghlan. 2011. "Opening Doors to Student Success: A Synthesis of Findings from an Evaluation at Six Community Colleges." Social Science Research Network (http://papers.ssrn.com/sol3/papers.cfm ?abstract_id=2019762).

Scrivener, S., and A. Logue. 2016. "Building College Readiness before Matriculation: A Preview of a CUNY Start Evaluation." New York: MDRC.

Scrivener, S., M. J. Weiss, A. Ratledge, T. Rudd, C. Sommo, and H. Fresques. 2015. "Doubling Graduation Rates: Three-Year Effects of CUNY's Accelerated Study in Associate Programs (ASAP) for Developmental Education Students." New York: MDRC (www.mdrc.org/sites/default/files/doubling _graduation_rates_fr.pdf).

Seftor, N., and S. Turner. 2002. "Back to School: Federal Student Aid Policy and Adult College Enrollment." *Journal of Human Resources* 37 (2): 336–52 (www.jstor.org/stable/3069650?seq=1#page_scan_tab_contents).

Shah, N. 2013. "Report: 'Race to the Top' a Flop." *Politico.com*. September 12 (http://www.politico.com/story/2013/09/race-to-the-top-for-education-a -flop-report-finds-096709_

Shapiro, D., A. Dundar, P. K. Wakhungu, X. Yuan, and A. Harrell. 2015. *Transfer and Mobility: A National View of Student Movement in Postsecondary Institutions, Fall 2008 Cohort*. Signature Report 9. Herndon, Va.: National Student Clearinghouse Research Center (https://nscresearchcenter .org/signaturereport9/).

Shapiro, D., A. Dundar, P. K. Wakhungu, X. Yuan, A. Nathan, and Y. Hwang. 2016a. *Completing College: A National View of Student Attainment Rates—Fall 2010 Cohort*. Signature Report 12. Herndon, Va.: National Student Clearinghouse Research Center (https://nscresearchcenter.org/wp -content/uploads/SignatureReport12.pdf).

———. 2016b. *Time to Degree: A National View of the Time Enrolled and Elapsed for Associate and Bachelor's Degree Earners*. Signature Report 11. Herndon, Va: National Student Clearinghouse Research Center.

Shipler, D. 2004. *The Working Poor: Invisible in America*. New York: Knopf Doubleday. DOI: 10.1080/0739314042000217142.

Shonkoff, J. P. 2012. *Leveraging the Biology of Adversity to Address the Roots of Disparities in Health and Development*. Proceedings of the National Academy of Sciences (PNAS) (http://developingchild.harvard.edu /wp-content/uploads/2015/07/Shonkoff_PNAS_Leveraging-the-Biology _10-8-2012.pdf).

Simmons, S., and S. Turner. 2003. "Taking Classes and Taking Care of the Kids: Do Childcare Benefits Increase Collegiate Attainment?" College of Information Sciences and Technology (http://citeseerx.ist.psu.edu/viewdoc /download?doi=10.1.1.199.6868&rep=rep1&type=pdf).

Singer, A. 2015. "Opt-Out Campaign Must Continue." *Huffington Post*, December 24 (www.huffingtonpost.com/alan-singer/opt-out-campaign-must -con_b_8803482.html).

Single Stop. 2014. "Community Colleges" (http://singlestopusa.org/program /community-colleges/).

Smith, A. 2016. "More For-Profits in U.S. Crosshairs." *Inside Higher Ed* (www.insidehighered.com/news/2016/02/02/education-department -denies-federal-aid-two-profit-chains).

Smith, J., M. Pender, and J. Howell. 2013. "The Full Extent of Academic Under-Match." *Economics of Education Review* 32 (February): 247–61.

Snyder, M. 2015. "Driving Better Outcomes: Typology and Principles to Inform Outcomes-Based Funding Models." HCM Strategists (http:// hcmstrategists.com/drivingoutcomes/wp-content/themes/hcm/pdf /Driving%20Outcomes.pdf).

Southern Regional Education Board. N.D. "High Schools That Work" (www.sreb.org/page/1078/high_schools_that_work.html).

———. 2015. *Credentials for All: An Imperative for SREB States.* Atlanta, Ga.: SREB.

State Higher Education Executive Officers (SHEEO). 2016. *SHEF FY2015: State Higher Education Finance* (http://sheeo.org/sites/default/files/project -files/SHEEO_FY15_Report_051816.pdf).

Stern, D. 2015. *Pathways or Pipelines: Keeping High School Students' Future Options Open while Developing Technical Skills and Knowledge.* Washington, D.C.: National Academies Press (http://sites.nationalacademies .org/cs/groups/pgasite/documents/webpage/pga_167702.pdf).

Stevens, A., M. Kurlaender, and M. Grosz. 2015. "Career Technical Education and Labor Market Outcomes: Evidence from California Community Colleges." Working Paper 21137. Cambridge, Mass.: National Bureau of Economic Research (www.nber.org/papers/w21137.pdf).

Stevens, E. L. 2012. "Will Law School Students Have Jobs after They Graduate? *Washington Post* (www.washingtonpost.com/lifestyle/magazine/will -law-school-students-have-jobs-after-they-graduate/2012/10/31/f9916726 -0f30-11e2-bd1a-b868e65d57eb_story.html).

Stokes, P. 2015. *Higher Education and Employability: New Models for Integrating Study and Work.* Harvard Education Press.

Stratford, M. 2015. "Default Rates Drop." *Inside Higher Ed* (www.inside highered.com/news/2015/10/01/student-loan-defaults-drop-obama -admin-again-tweaks-rates).

Stull, W., and N. Sanders, eds. 2003. *The School-to-Work Movement: Origins and Destinations,* Westport, Conn.: Praeger.

Swanson, C. B. 2004. "Graduation Rates: Real Kids, Real Numbers." Research Report. Washington, D.C.: Urban Institute (www.urban.org /research/publication/graduation-rates).

Symonds, W. C., R. B. Schwartz, and R. Ferguson. 2011. *Pathways to Prosperity: Meeting the Challenge of Preparing Young Americans for the 21st*

Century. Pathways to Prosperity Project, Harvard Graduate School of Education (https://dash.harvard.edu/bitstream/handle/1/4740480/Pathways_to_Prosperity_Feb2011-1.pdf?sequence=1).

Tamanaha, B. Z. 2012. *Failing Law Schools.* University of Chicago Press.

Tennessee Student Assistance Corporation. Tennessee Promise Scholarship (http://tennesseepromise.gov/about.shtml).

Thaler, R., and C. Sunstein. 2008. *Nudge: Improving Decisions about Health, Wealth, and Happiness.* Yale University Press.

Tinto, V. 2013. "Isaac Newton and Student College Completion." *Journal of College Student Retention: Research, Theory & Practice* 15 (1): 1–7 (http://csr.sagepub.com/content/15/1/1.full.pdf+html).

Tough, P. 2013. *How Children Succeed: Grit, Curiosity, and the Hidden Power of Character.* New York: Mariner Books. DOI: 10.1080/15582 159.2013.759845.

Trilling, B., and C. Fadel. 2009. *21st Century Skills: Learning for Life in Our Times.* San Francisco: John Wiley.

Turner, S. 2004. "Going to College and Finishing College: Explaining Different Educational Outcomes." In *College Choices: The Economics of Where to Go, When to Go, and How to Pay for It,* ed. C. M. Hoxby. Cambridge, Mass.: National Bureau of Economic Research (www.nber.org/chapters/c10097.pdf).

University of North Florida. N.D. "Child Care Access Means Parents in School Program (CCAMPIS) Grant. University of North Florida" (www.unf.edu/cdrc/CCAMPIS_Grant.aspx).

U.S. Census Bureau. 2016a. *Historical Income Tables: Families* (www.census.gov/hhes/www/income/data/historical/families/).

———. 2016b. *Historical Income Data: People.* Educational Attainment (https://www.census.gov/data/tables/time-series/demo/income-poverty/historical-income-people.html).

U.S. Department of Education. 2004. *National Assessment of Vocational Education: Final Report to Congress.* Office of the Under Secretary, Policy and Program Studies Service.

———. 2014. *National Assessment of Career and Technical Education—Full Report to Congress* (www2.ed.gov/rschstat/eval/sectech/nacte/career-technical-education/final-report.pdf).

———. 2015. *Federal Pell Grant Program Annual Data Reports 2014–15 and 2009–10* (www2.ed.gov/finaid/prof/resources/data/pell-data.html).

U.S. Department of Labor. N.D. "Apprenticeship" (www.dol.gov/featured/apprenticeship).

Vedder, R., C. Denhar, and J. Robe. 2013. *Why Are Recent College Graduates Unemployed? University Enrollments and Labor-Market Realities.* Washington, D.C.: Center for College Affordability and Productivity (CCAP).

Visher, M. G., M. J. Weiss, W. Weissman, T. Rudd, and H. D. Wathington. 2012. "The Effects of Learning Communities for Students in Developmental Education: A Synthesis of Findings from Six Community Colleges." National Center for Postsecondary Research (www.mdrc.org/sites/default /files/LC%20A%20Synthesis%20of%20Findings%20FR.pdf).

Walton, G., and G. Coehn. 2007. "A Question of Belonging: Race, Social Fit, and Achievement." *Journal of Personality and Social Psychology* 92 (1): 82–96 (www.ncbi.nlm.nih.gov/pubmed/17201544).

Weil, D. 2014. *The Fissured Workplace: Why Work Became So Bad for So Many and What Can Be Done to Improve It.* Harvard University Press. DOI: 10.7202/1026766ar.

———. 2015. "Strategic Enforcement in the Fissured Workplace." John T. Dunlop Memorial Forum (www.law.harvard.edu/programs/lwp/dunlop _forum/2015_Weil.pdf).

Weinstein, P., Jr. 2014. "Give Our Kids a Break: How Three-Year Degrees Can Cut the Cost of College." Washington, D.C.: Progressive Policy Institute (www.progressivepolicy.org/wp-content/uploads/2014/09/2014.09 -Weinstein_Give-Our-Kids-A-Break_How-Three-Year-Degrees-Can-Cut -College-Cost.pdf).

Wyner, J., K. C. Deane, D. Jenkins, and J. Fink. 2015. "The Transfer Playbook: Essential Practices for Two-Year and Four-Year Colleges." Aspen Institute and Community College Research Center, Columbia University.

Xu, D., and S. S. Jaggars. 2013. "The Impact of Online Learning on Students' Course Outcomes: Evidence from a Large Community and Technical College System." *Economics of Education Review* 37 (December): 46–57.

———. 2014. "Performance Gaps between Online and Face-to-Face Courses: Differences across Types of Students and Academic Subject Areas." *Journal of Higher Education* 85 (5): 633–59 (www.sciencedirect.com/science /article/pii/S0272775713001039).

Xu, D., and M. Trimble. 2016. "What about Certificates? Evidence on the Labor Market Returns to Nondegree Community College Awards in Two States." *Educational Evaluation and Policy Analysis* (May): 272–92.

Zakaria, F. 2015. *In Defense of a Liberal Education.* New York: W. W. Norton.

Zeidenberg, M., S. W. Cho, and D. Jenkins. 2010. "Washington State's Integrated Basic Education and Skills Training Program (I-BEST): New

Evidence of Effectiveness." Community College Research Center (http://ccrc.tc.columbia.edu/media/k2/attachments/i-best-evidence-effectiveness.pdf).

Zimmerman, S. 2014. "The Returns to College Admission for Academically Marginal Students." *Journal of Labor Economics* 32 (4): 711–54.

Zinn, R., and A. Van Kleunen. 2014. *Making Workforce Data Work: How Improved Education and Workforce Data Systems Could Help the US Compete in the 21st Century Economy*. Washington, D.C.: Workforce Data Quality Campaign (www.workforcedqc.org/sites/default/files/Resource%20PDF/WDQC%20report.pdf).

Index

Figures and tables are indicated by f and t following the page number.